MOVIES

OVER 100 TOP 10 LISTS

D1073153

For Daisybelle & Stanley

Publisher: Samantha Warrington
Editorial & Design Manager: Emma Hill
Designer: Eoghan O'Brien
Senior Production Manager: Peter Hunt

First published in 2014 by Bounty Books,
a division of Octopus Publishing Group Ltd
Endeavour House,
189 Shaftesbury Avenue,
London WC2H 8JY
www.octopusbooks.co.uk

An Hachette UK Company
www.hachette.co.uk

ISBN: 978-0-753725-70-2

A CIP catalogue record for this book is
available from the British Library

Printed and bound in China

TOP
10
LISTS

MOVIES
OVER 100 TOP 10 LISTS

ROB HILL

BB**Bounty**
Books

CONTENTS

INTRODUCTION

As with many of my generation it was *Star Wars* that first made me aware of a thing called 'movies'. They were like TV shows but went on for longer. The best would often parade the words *Steven* and *Spielberg* on screen before starting, which eventually made two things apparent to me: movies are made by people, and some of those people are better at it than others. As is probably common for most movie-lovers it wasn't until later that I became aware of cinema's full scope; that the visceral thrill of watching Indiana Jones fleeing a tumbling boulder was just one of many pleasures movies could provide. No less magical than Indy escaping is Ingmar Bergman contemplating. Jack Nicholson emoting. Quentin Tarantino reinventing or Katharine Hepburn and Spencer Tracy fighting.

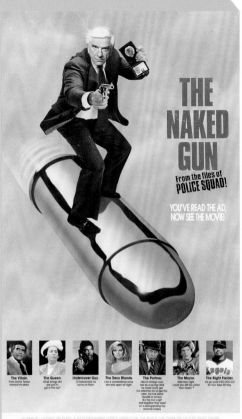

Cinema offers more opportunities for expression and creativity than any other medium. Some movies aim to make us laugh, others to make us think, marvel, cry or hide behind the sofa. To compare and rank such an assortment is not easy. If you judge a movie on how well it fulfills it's brief and satisfies it's audience, then perhaps Chuck Norris' *Delta Force* is the equal of Orson Welles' *Citizen Kane*. If it's about technique and pioneering artistry then probably it isn't. It sounds obvious but for a list to reflect cinema's diversity it needs to draw on the full spectrum of what it has to offer.

With the likes of Chuck Norris and Orson Welles potentially rubbing shoulders, the question of subjectivity is unavoidable. This book doesn't claim to be definitive. The lists of course reflect a personal perspective, but one that's

married to a practical consideration for the potential audience (which is why lists like 'Bruce Willis One-Liners' and 'Tea Drinking Scenes of Pre-War Japanese Cinema' are, you may be glad to hear, both omitted). The point is not to establish a definitive classification based on common themes. It's about using a flexible structure to showcase some of cinema's greatest moments, characters and concepts.

Some lists feature a tribute, which is a way of paying lip service to an entry so predictable its presence on lists like these is almost ubiquitous. There's no need to point out *The French Connection* features a great car chase or that Norman Bates was a psycho; we're not about to forget.

Hopefully this will help make most lists a little less obvious than my personal movie top 10:

10 *Spirited Away (2001)*
9 *Seven Samurai (1954)*
8 *The Awful Truth (1937)*
7 *Kind Hearts and Coronets (1949)*
6 *Evil Dead II (1987)*
5 *Tokyo Story (1953)*
4 *Brazil (1985)*
3 *The Good, the Bad and the Ugly (1966)*
2 *Star Wars: Episode IV - A New Hope (1976)*
1 *2001: A Space Odyssey (1968)*

The idea behind these lists is to prompt film fans to remember, discuss or perhaps discover something interesting. But as the legendary filmmaker John Huston said, 'I don't try and guess what a million people will like. It's hard enough to know what I like.'

TOP
10

The definition shifts as we redefine our ideas of heroism, but the antihero is always a figure at odds with the values of their society. They're seldom malicious and might inadvertently do good as they plough their narcissistic furrow. Han Solo tribute.

ANTIHEROES

10 CHARLIE CROKER
Fresh out of prison, nefarious cockney Charlie Croker organises a robbery of gold bullion to be carried out by British gangsters in the Italian city of Turin. This patriotic romp makes a big deal of encroaching on mafia territory, with the red, white and blue Minis used to escape being a final poke in the Cosa Nostra's eye.

9 THE BANDIT
After accepting a bet to haul a truck load of illicit beer from Texas to Georgia, Bo 'Bandit' Darville and his partner 'Snowman' (Jerry Reed) encounter a screwball Sheriff obsessed with stopping them.

8 JOHNNY STRABLER
On release *The Wild One* kicked up a storm, being banned in the UK and widely pilloried in the U.S.A. for

glamorising delinquents. With hindsight we can see it's a potent allegory, finely tuned to expose the chasm between the attitudes of Johnny's wayward generation and that which came before.

7 OH DAE-SU
This stylised tale of an unlikable businessman trying to learn why he was imprisoned and then released without explanation, grabbed the imagination of audiences worldwide.

6 FERRIS BUELLER
The enfant terrible of antiheroes, Ferris Bueller (aka 'The Sausage King of Chicago') is the sort of cocky wise guy you're either going to love or hate.

5 LUKE JACKSON
Sentenced to a Florida chain gang for a trivial crime, Luke Jackson refuses to accept the authority of corrupt guards or the established pecking order amongst the inmates. At first content to

win small victories against his tormentors, he eventually becomes determined to escape at all costs.

4 TRAVIS BICKLE

Clearly losing his grip on reality, Bickle drifts through a series of failed social encounters and bizarre confrontations until finding his purpose. When it comes, his explosion happens to be sparked by justifiable moral outrage and so is targeted positively, but we're left with the impression it could easily have been otherwise.

3 THE MAN WITH NO NAME

The first in director Sergio Leone's 'Dollars Trilogy' sees Eastwood's iconic gunslinger play both sides of a feuding village.

Although adept at handling the treachery and duplicity with which he's familiar, he's eventually caught out by an unexpected bout of compassion.

2 DRIVER

Not all antiheroes tend to be the quiet type, but it does seem a common attribute. Driver takes succinctness to the extreme in what seems to be *Taxi Driver* for a new generation.

1 SNAKE PLISSKIN

The archetypal antihero, Plisskin is a former bank robber, gun fighter, smuggler and all round degenerate reprobate. But there's something compulsively appealing about him, and when he's charged with being the good guy for once, it's impossible not to fall for his charms.

	CHARACTER	MOVIE	ACTOR
10	Charlie Croker	The Italian Job (1969)	Michael Caine
9	The Bandit	Smokey and the Bandit (1977)	Burt Reynolds
8	Johnny Strabler	The Wild One (1953)	Marlon Brando
7	Oh Dae-su	Oldboy (2003)	Choi Min-sik
6	Ferris Bueller	Ferris Bueller's Day Off (1986)	Matthew Broderick
5	Luke Jackson	Cool Hand Luke (1967)	Paul Newman
4	Travis Bickle	Taxi Driver (1976)	Robert De Niro
3	The Man With No Name	A Fistful of Dollars (1964)	Clint Eastwood
2	Driver	Drive (2011)	Ryan Gosling
1	Snake Plisskin	Escape From New York (1981)	Kurt Russell

TOP
10

Manic Pixie Dream Girls are identifiable by their likability, exuberant personality and girlish femininity. Their role in cinema is generally to show the male lead life is actually pretty good, which risks them seeming one dimensional when not played well.

MANIC PIXIE DREAM GIRLS

10 TONI SIMMONS
Straight laced dentist Dr. Julian Winston (Walter Matthau) and his free spirited neighbour Toni find themselves the common factor in various convoluted love lives.

9 MADISON
Unlucky in love grocer Allen Bauer (Tom Hanks) falls in love with Madison, a mermaid who twice saves his life. It's usual for the object of the MPDG's affection to be inspired to adopt aspects of her lifestyle, this extreme case has Allen abandoning life on land to live underwater with the mer-people.

8 SUGAR KANE
Beautiful singer Sugar Kane becomes the object of affection for two cross-dressing saxophone players on the run from the mob after witnessing the Valentines Day Massacre.

7 CLEMENTINE KRUCZYNSKI

This fascinating movie effectively deconstructs the romcom genre as a young couple discover they have been in a relationship before, but had their memories erased to remove the pain it caused both.

6 SAM

Sam, an eccentric pathological liar, shakes Andrew (Zach Braff) out of an anti-depressant induced metaphorical coma when he returns to his home town for his mother's funeral.

5 ANNIE HALL

The highbrow MPDG comes in the form of Annie Hall, outwardly intellectually confident but actually suffering many of the same insecurities as her lover Alvy Singer. Her positive outlook allows her to better manage her self-doubt and even attempt to tackle Alvy's emotionally stunted pretension.

4 CATHERINE

The capricious Catherine seduces two friends and has a lasting effect on both their lives.

3 SUSAN VANCE

Acerbic extrovert Susan hijacks levelheaded paleontologist Dr. David Huxley's (Cary Grant) life in a series of farcical escapades.

Having played with this sort of character before Hepburn nails it in *Bringing Up Baby*, in the process demonstrating just how long established an archetype the MPDG is.

2 CLAIRE COLBURN

The character that inspired film critic Nathan Rabin to coin the term Manic Pixie Dream Girl, Dunst excels as the impulsive flight attendant Claire in this movie about discovering what really matters in life.

1 HOLLY GOLIGHTLY

The ethereal Audrey Hepburn's signature role allows her unique blend of vulnerability and confidence to shine. Holly Golightly has

duality written into her core, appearing to be both worldweary call girl and wide-eyed ingenue depending on her mood. She somehow feels incomplete without the good man she so clearly deserves on her arm, but that good man needs her more than she him.

	CHARACTER	MOVIE	ACTOR
10	Toni Simmons	*Cactus Flower* (1969)	Goldie Hawn
9	Madison	*Splash (1984)*	Daryl Hannah
8	Sugar Kane	*Some Like it Hot* (1959)	Marilyn Monroe
7	Clementine Kruczynski	*Eternal Sunshine of the Spotless Mind (2004)*	Kate Winslet
6	Sam	*Garden State* (2004)	Natalie Portman
5	Annie Hall	*Annie Hall (1977)*	Diane Keaton
4	Catherine	*Jules and Jim* (1962)	Jeanne Moreau
3	Susan Vance	*Bringing Up Baby* (1938)	Katherine Hepburn
2	Claire Colburn	*Elizabethtown* (2005)	Kirsten Dunst
1	Holly Golightly	*Breakfast at Tiffany's (1961)*	Audrey Hepburn

TOP 10

Sport is one of the most indispensable tools at the moviemaker's disposal. The inherent conflict makes it an excellent dramatic device, it works perfectly as allegory and can manipulate emotion. The following touch on several ways in which the movies have used sport to make us cry, cheer or think.

SPORTING MOMENTS

10 IF YOU BUILD IT, HE WILL COME
Farmer Ray Kinsella (Kevin Costner) places his faith in a disembodied voice that commands him to build a baseball diamond. The emotional payoff when Ray is finally able to play catch with his long dead father hits like a wrecking ball.

9 CROSSING THE LINE
The improbable story of the Jamaican bobsled team's 1988 Winter Olympics was a big hit in 1993, largely thanks to this rousing finale. After their sled breaks, the team pick both it and themselves up off the ground, and march proudly across the finish line.

8 UNLIKELY CHAMP
Offered one last big fight as a favour, underdog Jim Braddock surprises everyone by winning. This true story tugs at the heart strings from the start, demanding considerable emotional investment that's eventually richly rewarded.

7 THE 'INCHES' SPEECH
If you need an actor to deliver a stirring motivational speech, you can do worse than Al Pacino. Here playing Tony D'Amato, coach of fictional team the Miami Sharks, Pacino based his performance on real life Dallas Cowboys coach Tom Landry.

6 DANIEL LARUSSO'S GOING TO FIGHT?
Daniel LaRusso (Ralph Macchio) is routinely bullied by students of the Cobra Kai karate dojo. When one of them injures Daniel with an illegal move in a tournament, he is initially ruled out, but soon finds the courage to return for the final fight.

5 EXPLODING GOLF COURSE
It's class warfare at the Bushwood Country Club. An obnoxious member challenges a caddy to a match, with wagers soon inflating its importance out of all proportion. The result is finally settled when a lunatic groundskeeper blows up half the course.

4 PLAYING THE LONG GAME
In a clash between the cocky upstart (Paul Newman's Fast Eddie) and the elder statesman

(Jackie Gleeson's Minnesota Fats), the younger man sprints into an early lead before realising, too late, he's competing in a marathon, not the 100 metres.

3 OVERCOMING TEAM EVIL

Using the secrets of Shaolin Kung Fu, Mighty Steel Leg Sing (Stephen Chow) and his soccer squad become almost unbeatable. But on reaching the finals of a prestigious Hong Kong tournament they must face Team Evil, a steroid-enhanced team of cheating malevolence.

2 ABRAHAMS WINS THE 100 METRES

Harold Abrahams (Ben Cross) sacrifices much as he trains for the 1924 Olympics. After being comprehensively beaten in the 200 metres, he unexpectedly triumphs in the 100, meaning he can retire from athletics and start to live a normal life.

1 GOING THE DISTANCE

As with Cool Runnings, what makes the final bout in Rocky so interesting is that we aren't inspired by how the winner wins, but by how the loser loses. As with the Jamaican bobsleigh team, merely making it to the end is a victory.

	MOMENT	MOVIE	SPORT
10	If you build it, he will come	*Field of Dreams (1989)*	Baseball
9	Crossing the line	*Cool Runnings (1993)*	Bobsled
8	Unlikely champ	*Cinderella Man (2005)*	Boxing
7	The 'inches' speech	*Any Given Sunday (1999)*	American Football
6	Daniel Larusso's going to fight?	*Karate Kid (1984)*	Karate
5	Exploding golf course	*Caddyshack (1980)*	Golf
4	Playing the long game	*The Hustler (1961)*	Pool
3	Overcoming team evil	*Shaolin Soccer (2001)*	Soccer
2	Abrahams wins the 100 metres	*Chariots of Fire (1981)*	Athletics
1	Going the distance	*Rocky (1976)*	Boxing

TOP 10

A quest can provide the perfect narrative structure for a movie. It keeps things moving, enables characters to encounter almost anything or anyone, can be manipulated to create easy suspense, pathos or humour and allows for a neatly tied up conclusion.

QUESTS

10 PAMELA ANDERSON The big screen outing for Sacha Baron Cohen's racist, sexist Kazakh journalist, Borat, is filmed in the style of a documentary. The format works well, with most of the comedy coming from Borat's interaction with Americans who tend to have very different values from his own.

9 THE 'ROOM' The Stalker guides clients through the physics-defying world of the Zone to a hidden room somewhere within. Anyone who enters this room will have their wish granted, but the journey is dangerous.

8 PIRATE BOOTY Their homes and community threatened with demolition, a bunch of kids set out on a journey to find long hidden pirate treasure. On the way they're pursued by a criminal family, menaced by local bullies and threatened by ancient booby traps.

7 THE GOLDEN FLEECE A staple of weekend television for decades, Jason and the Argonauts is arguably the definitive classical mythology adventure movie. Certainly it's the definitive Ray Harryhausen stop motion movie. The sword wielding marching skeletons are still mimicked today.

6 TREASURE After escaping from a chain gang with two other convicts, McGill leads a wild goose chase, supposedly to recover treasure before it's hiding place is flooded. Really he just wants to stop his ex-wife remarrying, a revelation that doesn't go down well with his fellow questers.

5 FIND THE DESTINATION OF A MYSTERIOUS SIGNAL A beacon is found on the moon and we follow a signal it emits to Jupiter, making this a quest where the objective is a mystery even to the participants. It turns out to be something quite important: alien intelligence and the next phase of mankind's evolution.

4 EL DORADO The first of their turbulent collaborations, Aguirre brought both star Klaus Kinski and director Werner Herzog to international attention. Kinski's performance as Aguirre is an electrifying descent through obsession into madness.

3 RETURN THE ONE RING TO MORDOR

The novel may have placed a little more emphasis on the quest to destroy the ring, but it's still central to Peter Jackson's triumphant trilogy. Wood is exceptional as Frodo, the reluctant hero, with the terrible toll taken by the ring evident in his voice and etched into his face.

2 THE ARK OF THE COVENANT

Some quests are for selfish reasons, others altruistic. Indy's first expedition lies somewhere between. Though, to be fair, with the Nazis also on the hunt for the ark, perhaps just leaving it where it was might not have been a good idea.

1 FIND A WAY HOME

Dorothy's attempt to get home from Oz (by way of some witch-killing and a social revolution) has inspired many subsequent movies. But this early colour classic is categorically the perfect specimen against which all pretenders must be judged.

	OBJECTIVE	MOVIE	QUEST LED BY	PLAYED BY
10	Pamela Anderson	*Borat: Cultural Learnings of America for Make Benefit Glorious Nation of Kazakhstan (2006)*	Kazakh journalist Borat Sagdiyev	Sacha Baron Cohen
9	The 'Room'	*Stalker (1979)*	The mysterious Stalker	Alexander Kaidanovsky
8	Pirate Booty	*The Goonies (1985)*	Adventurous Mikey Walsh	Sean Astin
7	The Golden Fleece	*Jason and the Argonauts (1963)*	Mythical Greek hero Jason	Todd Armstrong
6	Treasure	*O Brother Where Art Thou (2000)*	Escaped convict Everett McGill	George Clooney
5	Find the destination of a mysterious signal	*2001: A Space Odyssey (1968)*	Astronaut Dr. David Bowman	Keir Dullea
4	El Dorado	*Aguirre, Wrath of God (1972)*	Conquistador Don Lope de Aguirre Klaus Kinski	Klaus Kinski
3	Return the One Ring to Mordor	*The Lord of the Rings Series (2001-2003)*	Hobbit Frodo Baggins	Elijah Wood
2	The Ark of the Covenant	*Raiders of the Lost Ark (1981)*	Archaeologist Dr. Indiana Jones	Harrison Ford
1	Find a Way Home	*The Wizard of Oz (1939)*	Dorothy Gale	Judy Garland

TOP 10

Potentially the most charismatic of all non-cognisant movie characters, cars have been central to cinema's history and culture since their near simultaneous rise to popularity. To avoid half the list being Lotuses and Aston Martin's, this is a tribute to James Bond.

CARS

10 DODGE CHALLENGER R/T
Not just a car but an anti-authoritarian symbol of freedom. Kowalski must deliver the Challenger to its rightful owner on the other side of the country, but on the way this almost hypnotic movie reveals it's far more interested in abstract social concepts than it is plot.

9 HERBIE (VW BEETLE)
One of the biggest selling and most beloved cars in history was originally designed and manufactured by Ferdinand Porsche. However the Beetle's sporty credentials probably don't match up to those of its illustrious creator.

8 BATMOBILE (CUSTOMISED LINCOLN FUTURA)
Of the many Batmobile designs to feature on the big screen this fish-tailing, overly-sculpted boat on wheels has to be the best. Originally a Lincoln concept car built in Italy, the Batmobile was customised by legendary designer George Barris.

7 DODGE CHARGER R/T
Perhaps 'The General Lee' is the better known Dodge Charger, but Dominic Toretto's produces 900hp and does the quarter mile in nine seconds flat. It's also apparently indestructible, having been crushed, burnt and mangled several times in the Fast and Furious movies.

6 THE BLUESMOBILE (DODGE MONACO)
This 1974 sedan was chosen by car nut Dan Aykroyd for its reputation as the fastest vehicle in the Illinois police fleet of the 1970's. Aykroyd's character Elwood uses much the same reasoning to justify the purchase to his unconvinced brother.

5 ECTO-1 (CADILLAC MILLER-METEOR AMBULANCE)
Fabricator Steve Dane converted this dilapidated dual-purpose hearse/ambulance into the striking quick response vehicle we know from Ghost Busters. In 1984 it allegedly caused a string of accidents whilst being driven around New York to promote the movie.

4 THE MACH 5
A rare case where the car is almost certainly more popular than the movie. Bulletproof and equipped with a homing robot bird, rotary saws, tyre shields and all sorts of other gadgets, the Mach 5 is designed to compete in futuristic combative races.

3 LINCOLN CONTINENTAL MKIII
Probably less well known than most entries on this list, The Car is the undoubted star

hat behind the wheel when they see a black Trans Am. The movie that made Burt Reynolds a megastar did at least as much for this iconic muscle car.

1 DELOREAN

The story of John DeLorean's doomed attempt to revolutionise the sports car industry is worthy of its own movie. Until then, and probably even after, his infamous car will remain best known as the time machine in which Marty McFly travels back to 1955.

of the movie in which it appears. Allusions to Satanic influences don't fully explain how it works without a driver, but might reveal why it's so intent on running people down.

2 PONTIAC TRANS AM

Even today it seems likely most people of a certain age picture an enormous cowboy

	CAR	MOVIE	DRIVER	PLAYED BY
10	Dodge Challenger R/T	*Vanishing Point (1971)*	Kowalski	Barry Newman
9	Herbie (VW Beetle)	*The Love Bug (1968)*	Jim Douglas	Dean Jones
8	Batmobile (customised Lincoln Futura)	*Batman (1966)*	Batman	Adam West
7	Dodge Charger R/T	*The Fast and the Furious (2001-2011)*	Dominic Toretto	Vin Diesel
6	The Bluesmobile (Dodge Monaco)	*The Blues Brothers (1980)*	Elwood Blues	Dan Aykroyd
5	Ecto-1 (Cadillac Miller-Meteor ambulance)	*Ghost Busters (1984)*	The Ghost Busters	Various
4	The Mach 5	*Speed Racer (2008)*	Speed	Emile Hirsch
3	Lincoln Continental MKIII	*The Car (1977)*	A Satanic spirit	Nobody
2	Pontiac Trans Am	*Smokey and the Bandit (1977)*	The Bandit	Burt Reynolds
1	DeLorean	*Back to the Future (1985)*	Marty McFly	Michael J. Fox

TOP **10**

The haunted house has been a movie staple around the world since cinema's inception. Cheap to produce, universal in appeal, endlessly variable; potentially scary, funny, dramatic, gruesome... it's no surprise so many have been produced. Tribute to *The Shining*.

HAUNTED HOUSES

10 THE LEGEND OF HELL HOUSE (1973)
Sceptical physicist Professor Lionel Barrett leads a company of mediums and other believers in a search for evidence of life after death. They focus on Belasco House, the 'Mount Everest' of haunted houses.

9 POLTERGEIST (1982)
Tobe Hooper (director of the original *The Texas Chain Saw Massacre*) and Steven Spielberg are perhaps not the most obvious of collaborators. But their apparently opposing sensibilities each contribute something crucial to this chilling tale of a haunted house built on an Indian burial ground.

8 THE GHOST AND MRS. MUIR (1947)
The beautiful Gull cottage on the British coast is haunted by its former owner, Captain Daniel Gregg (Rex Harrison)

The arrival of recently widowed Lucy (Gene Tierney) does nothing to encourage his departure.

7 13 GHOSTS (1960)
Cyrus Zorba (Donald Woods) can't believe his luck when he inherits a rundown mansion from his eccentric, occultist uncle. After moving his family in, they start to experience strange goings on but remain determined to figure out what's what.

6 THE ORPHANAGE (2007)
A remote Spanish orphanage is the setting for this genuinely scary tale of a family who may, or may not, have lost their son to some sort of evil spirit that may, or may not, occupy the ancient building.

5 THE OTHERS (2001)
An inventive premise which sees the protagonists' children rendered allergic

to light (necessitating their rambling mansion be kept in constant darkness) does wonders for the creepy atmosphere of this psychological horror.

4 JU-ON: THE GRUDGE (2002)
A standout in the cycle of Japanese horror movies that made waves around the turn of the millennium, *The Grudge* is formed from a series of vignettes revolving around a family home, the central tenet being that sometimes a death is so awful or unjust that it can leave behind a terrible curse.

3 THE INNOCENTS (1961)
Miss Giddens (Deborah Kerr), governess to two orphaned children living at Bly, their uncle's estate, begins to suspect the spirits of a pair of former employees are inhabiting the children.

2 THE CONJURING (2013)

The Conjuring is, in some ways, a throwback to the 60's and 70's heyday of the haunted house movie. This contrast with the contemporary execution (excellent camerawork, naturalistic acting, perfectly polished screenplay etc.) leaves us unsure of what to expect and at the mercy of the filmmakers twisted imagination.

1 THE HAUNTING (1963)

According to renowned filmmaker Martin Scorsese, *The Haunting* is the most terrifying movie ever made. Few who have seen it seem likely to disagree, with the decrepit mansion's supernatural physicality and foreboding atmosphere enough to have audiences cowering with terror on its 1963 release.

	BUILDING	MOVIE	LOCATION
10	Mansion	*The Legend of Hell House (1973)*	Unspecified, England
9	Suburban house	*Poltergeist (1982)*	California, U.S.A.
8	Cottage	*The Ghost and Mrs. Muir (1947)*	Southern English coast
7	Suburban house	*13 Ghosts (1960)*	Unspecified, U.S.A.
6	Rural Orphanage	*The Orphanage (2007)*	Unspecified, Spain
5	Rural Mansion	*The Others (2001)*	Jersey, Channel Islands
4	Suburban house	*Ju-on: The Grudge (2002)*	Tokyo, Japan
3	Rural Mansion	*The Innocents (1961)*	Unspecified, England
2	Farm House	*The Conjuring (2013)*	Rhode Island, U.S.A.
1	Rural Mansion	*The Haunting (1963)*	New England, U.S.A.

TOP 10

The peculiarly American High School movie genre has long been an effective means of tracking the shifting social concerns and trends of the nation. As an allegory for the wider US, the high school is unbeatable, regardless of whether you're saying something serious or silly.

HIGH SCHOOL MOVIES

10 AMERICAN PIE (1999)
The burgeoning gross out comedy subgenre collided head on with the high school movie in this unexpected hit. Social schadenfreude is taken to new levels as a group of teen boys try all the tricks in the book to lose their virginity before graduation.

9 MEAN GIRLS (2004)
The perilous world of the modern school clique is exposed in this sharp comedy adapted by *Saturday Night Live*'s Tina Fey.

8 CLUELESS (1995)
Jane Austen's novel *Emma* is the unlikely source material for this look at superficial rich girls finding their places in life.

7 10 THINGS I HATE ABOUT YOU (1999)
Convoluted love lives at Padua High School are the subject of this teen romantic comedy based on Shakespeare's *The Taming of the Shrew*. Only by convincing someone to take out the dorky younger sister of class beauty Bianca (Larisa Oleynik) can Cameron (Joseph Gordon-Levitt) get a date with her.

6 GREASE (1978)
As the senior term at Rydell High School starts, Danny (John Travolta) recounts the story of his summer romance with Sandy (Olivia Newton-John), believing her to have returned home to Australia. Sandy, however, has just enrolled at the same school, but Danny's enforced bravado in front of his friends is not what she's used to.

5 BLACKBOARD JUNGLE (1955)
A new teacher encounters obnoxious students in a 1950's high school. The movie is credited with introducing a mainstream audience to rock and roll when it used Bill Haley's then unknown B-side *Rock Around the Clock* over the titles. Some theatres refused to show it for that reason alone, others saw nightly rioting from overexcited Teddy Boys.

4 HEATHERS (1988)
A high school in-crowd meets its match when school bad boy J.D. (Christian Slater) decides they've done enough harm.

3 ELECTION (1999)
A disillusioned teacher becomes obsessed with preventing a precocious student from winning the class election.

2 RUSHMORE (1998)
Max Fischer (Jason Schwartzman), a dedicated but far from gifted student at the Rushmore Academy private school, forms a friendship

with industrialist Herman Blume (Bill Murray). Both fall in love with teacher Mrs Cross (Olivia Williams) and engage in a petty war of attrition to win her heart.

1 THE BREAKFAST CLUB (1985)

Five students, each conforming to one traditional stereotype or another (jock, nerd, princess...) report for school detention on a sunny Saturday morning in a Chicago suburb. Over the course of the day they bond over a common hatred for the principal, each gradually lowering the barriers school life has forced them to erect. They learn they have more in common than the clichés they choose to present to the world suggest.

	MOVIE	DIRECTOR
10	American Pie (1999)	Paul Weitz
9	Mean Girls (2004)	Mark Waters
8	Clueless (1995)	Amy Heckerling
7	10 Things I Hate About You (1999)	Gil Junger
6	Grease (1978)	Randal Kleiser
5	Blackboard Jungle (1955)	Richard Brooks
4	Heathers (1988)	Michael Lehmann
3	Election (1999)	Alexander Payne
2	Rushmore (1998)	Wes Anderson
1	The Breakfast Club (1985)	John Hughes

TOP 10

Since at least 1915's *Der Golem*, monsters have been integral to the movie landscape. With so many to choose from (many of which are rather obvious), some rules have been introduced to exclude common standards such as ghosts, zombies, vampires and aliens.

MONSTERS

10 THE KRAKEN
The Kraken stems from Norse mythology but in the movie exists in a world governed by the Greek Gods. What degree of control Zeus has over the Kraken is unclear, although it appears to do his bidding it must be kept locked up.

9 GRABOIDS
Part comedy, part western and part horror movie, Tremors features gigantic, wormlike creatures terrorising a small Nevada settlement. Unfortunately for the locals, their apparent saviours and would-be heroes are halfwitted buffoons.

8 GREMLINS
With just two golden rules to abide by, Billy Peltzer (Zach Galligan) soon makes a hash of caring for his Mogwai. First he gets it wet, causing it to multiply. Then he feeds the resulting cuties after midnight, which as we all know turns them into little monsters.

7 THE CRAWLING EYE
In a remote Swiss mountain resort a strange force concealed in a radioactive cloud decapitates or possesses various hardy types. Although this sci-fi/horror B-movie seems fairly typical of the genre it has a campy watchability that's second-to-none.

6 CLOVER AKA LSA
An unusual 'found footage' approach lends Cloverfield some unique qualities. We see the beast only fleetingly and never learn what it wants or where it came from. Somehow this adds to the genuinely scary presence the movie possesses.

5 GIANT TROLLS
Students investigating bear killings in rural Norway stumble upon Hans (Otto Jespersen), a hunter employed by the government to track down several unfeasibly massive monsters that have escaped into the countryside.

4 KONG
The monster without which this list might not even be possible. Willis O'Brien's stop motion giant ape is legendary, inspiring an endless stream of budding make-up artists, animators and model makers.

3 BRUNDLEFLY
The Brundlefly (named, curiously, after a British racing driver) must be one of the most alarming and execrable creatures in the movies – the result of the genetic melding of man and insect. Anyone expecting the camp frolics of the 50's original is in for a shock.

2 GODZILLA
Today Godzilla brings to mind a Japanese stuntman in a comedy rubber suit. But in the original Gojira a lizard mutated into a huge raging monster by radioactive fallout, is an intriguing comment on mankind's dangerous pursuit of nuclear power.

1 THE MONSTER
The most important movie of Universal's 30's and 40's horror cycle still stands out as one of the best creature features ever made. The extent to which the design of the monster has become woven into the fabric of popular culture says it all.

	MONSTER	MOVIE	MONSTER PLAYED BY AND/OR CREATED USING
10	The Kraken	Clash of the Titans (1981)	Stop Motion
9	Graboids	Tremors (1990)	Mainly physical effects
8	Gremlins	Gremlins (1984)	Physical effects
7	The Crawling Eye	The Trollenberg Terror (1958)	Physical effects
6	Clover aka LSA	Cloverfield (2008)	CGI
5	Giant trolls	Troll Hunter (2010)	Mainly CGI
4	Kong	King Kong (1933)	Stop Motion
3	Brundlefly	The Fly (1986)	Jeff Goldblum and physical effects
2	Godzilla	Godzilla (Gojira) (1954)	Katsumi Tezuka and trick photography
1	The Monster	Frankenstein (1931)	Boris Karloff

TOP
10

The traditional cinematic stereotype of the family unit might leave some of us feeling our own clan is imperfect. But as cinema has evolved so has its depiction of the family, and we might be reassured to see more defective tribes than we used to on screen.

FAMILIES

10 THE BANKS
The harassed parents of newly in love Kay (a young Elizabeth Taylor) deal with the trials and tribulations of organising her expensive nuptials.

9 THE TENENBAUMS
Director Wes Anderson hit the big time with this brilliantly stylish movie about a dysfunctional family of high achievers. Though there's a plot of sorts involving Gene Hackman's estranged father Royal conning the family into believing he's dying, the movie is less about narrative than just hanging out with the kooky clan.

8 THE SAWYERS
Definitely not a family to invite round for Christmas, this tribe of cannibalistic abattoir workers would be more interested in carving up the host than the turkey.

7 THE BREWSTERS
With just Mortimer (Cary Grant) in possession of all his marbles, the Brewsters make for an interesting family. Teddy (John Alexander) thinks he's Theodore Roosevelt, Jonathan (Raymond Massey) is an escaped convict and elderly aunts Abby (Josephine Hull) and Martha (Jean Adair) have taken to poisoning anyone they feel sorry for and burying them in the basement.

6 THE HOOVERS
The Hoovers are certainly a diverse bunch with a suicidal Proust scholar, a teen who has undertaken a vow of silence and a heroin using grandfather amongst their number. Together they embark on a road trip to take youngest child Olive (Abigail Breslin) to the Little Miss Sunshine beauty pageant.

5 THE ADDAMS
Starting life as the subject of a New Yorker comic strip, the Addams family then became a hit TV show and cartoon serial before finally landing in movie theatres.

4 NAME UNIDENTIFIED
The everyday challenges of a working class North London family are documented in this beautifully subtle film from acclaimed director Mike Leigh.

3 THE SIMPSONS
The first family of television have so far only made one big screen outing, but that's enough to qualify for a top ten list.

2 THE CORLEONES
It's hard to say whether this is a family you'd want to be involved with or not. On one hand they clearly have a strong bond, (on the whole) taking care of one another at any cost. On the other... most of them are murderous gangsters.

1 THE GRISWOLDS
Determined to make the long drive to theme park Wally World in order to enjoy a family vacation, Griswald patriarch Clark (Chevy Chase) must overcome an endless slew of unreasonable challenges. One of the most popular comedies of the 80's provides the perfect vehicle for Chase's sporadic comedy genius. It also lead to a series of sequels of distinctly variable quality.

	FAMILY	MOVIE	EMMINENT MEMBERS
10	The Banks	*Father of the Bride (1950)*	Stanley (Spencer Tracy) and Kay (Elizabeth Taylor)
9	The Tenenbaums	*The Royal Tenenbaums (2001)*	Royal (Gene Hackman) and Etheline (Anjelica Huston)
8	The Sawyers	*The Texas Chain Saw Massacre (1974)*	Jed aka Leatherface (Gunnar Hansen)
7	The Brewsters	*Arsenic and Old Lace (1944)*	Mortimer (Cary Grant)
6	The Hoovers	*Little Miss Sunshine (2006)*	Olive (Abigail Breslin) and Richard (Greg Kinnear)
5	The Addams	*The Addams Family Series (1991-1998)*	Morticia (Angelica Huston) and Gomez (Raul Julia)
4	Name Unidentified	*Life is Sweet (1990)*	Andy (Jim Broadbent) and Wendy (Alison Steadman)
3	The Simpsons	*The Simpsons Movie (2007)*	Homer (Dan Castellanata) and Marge (Julie Kavner)
2	The Corleones	*The Godfather Series (1972-1990)*	Vito (Marlon Brando) and Michael (Al Pacino)
1	The Griswolds	*National Lampoons Vacation series (1983-1997)*	Clark (Chevy Chase) and Ellen (Beverly D'Angelo)

TOP 10

Similarly to a quest or road movie, revenge movies come with a ready-made plot structure, should anybody fancy having a go at making one. For a long time the preserve of westerns, then exploitation cinema, revenge movies are mainstream fare these days.

AVENGERS

10 MAXIMUS DECIMUS MERIDIUS

By favouring the popular General Maximus over his own psychopathic son Commodus (Joaquin Phoenix), Emperor Marcus Aurelius unwittingly signs both his own death warrant and that of Maximus' family. But Maximus will have his revenge, in this life or the next.

9 JENNIFER HILLS
A beautiful writer takes a house in rural Connecticut to finish her latest manuscript, but is attacked and sexually assaulted by a group of local hicks. She survives the ordeal and plans an uncompromising, bloody revenge.

8 BATMAN/BRUCE WAYNE
After his wealthy parents are killed in a botched mugging, young heir Bruce Wayne grows up to fight crime on the rotten streets of his native

Gotham. When The Joker (Jack Nicholson) takes over the organised crime racket and hatches a plot to poison the city's water supply, Batman recognises him as the street thug who killed his parents.

7 MAJOR CHARLES RANE
Returning home both physically and mentally scarred from years of captivity in a Vietnamese POW camp, Major Charles Rane sees his family murdered by petty thieves and vows vengeance.

6 COFFY
With her sister's life ruined and best friend crippled by drug dealers, a surprisingly tough nurse goes on the rampage, killing, maiming and otherwise battering anyone she can find who is involved in the drugs trade.

5 CHEN ZHEN
Master Huo Yuanjia of

the Jingwu kung fu school appears to have died of natural causes, but has actually been murdered by members of a Japanese dojo. Star pupil Chen

Zhen discovers the conspiracy and repeatedly raises the stakes in a bloody war between the two schools.

4 MATTIE ROSS

Although this John Wayne western is an undoubted classic, it's possible the Coen Brothers' 2010 remake is even better. But Kim Darby's portrayal of teenage tomboy Mattie Ross in the 1969 version is just a little more engaging than the 2010 equivalent.

3 GEUM-JA LEE

Framed and jailed for the murder of a child, the once naive Geum-ja Lee gains early release and is determined to do two things: find her daughter, now adopted by an Australian family, and kill anyone involved in the original crime.

2 PAUL KERSEY

When the wife of pacifist architect Paul Kersey is murdered and his daughter raped, he takes it upon himself to clean up the streets of his native New York.

1 THE BRIDE

Betrayed by Bill (David Carradine) and the rest of the assassination squad they are both part of, The Bride is left comatose in a hospital bed. Upon waking there is just one thing on her mind.

	AVENGER	MOVIE	ACTOR	AVENGING
10	Maximus Decimus Meridius	*Gladiator (2000)*	Russell Crowe	Murder of his family
9	Jennifer Hills	*I Spit On Your Grave (1978)*	Camille Keaton	Sexual assault
8	Batman/Bruce Wayne	*Batman (1989)*	Michael Keaton	Murder of his parents
7	Major Charles Rane	*Rolling Thunder (1977)*	William Devane	Murder of his family
6	Coffy	*Coffy (1973)*	Pam Grier	Death of her sister
5	Chen Zhen	*Fist of Fury (1972)*	Bruce Lee	Murder of his teacher
4	Mattie Ross	*True Grit (1969)*	Kim Darby	Murder of her father
3	Geum-ja Lee	*Lady Vengeance (2005)*	Yeong-ae Lee	Being framed for murder
2	Paul Kersey	*Death Wish (1974)*	Charles Bronson	Murder of his wife
1	The Bride	*Kill Bill: Vol. 1 & 2 (2003 & 2004)*	Uma Thurman	Betrayal by friends

TOP 10

Time to put pen to paper and create your own top 10 list of revenge movies...

10

9

8

7

6

5

4

3

2

1

TOP
10

Audiences clearly derive satisfaction from watching charming men form and execute complicated plans, to the extent that we don't really care that they're inherently unlawful. If anything we tend not to want them to get caught. Tribute to *Reservoir Dogs*.

HEISTS

10 CASH ON DEMAND (1962)
This brilliantly played but often overlooked British take on the heist movie is a uniquely civilised and low key affair. The crook is impeccably polite and the bank manager unquestioningly cooperative, which somehow leads to incredible tension.

9 SNATCH (2000)
Although the diamond heist sequence in *Snatch* is essentially just there to set up later plot points, Ritchie still executes it with a bewilderingly stylish explosion of energy. The only entry on this list in which the ultimate prize ends up inside a dog.

8 RUN LOLA RUN (1998)
The least well planned and most frenetic of bank robberies, Lola must find money for her low level gangster boyfriend or he will be killed by his boss. We see the plot work out three times in three different ways before a satisfactory conclusion is reached.

7 INSIDE MAN (2006)
This underrated thriller from Spike Lee utilises one of the most original escape plans imaginable to keep Russell one step ahead of both police and audience. Features excellent support from Denzel Washington and a Spike Lee at the top of his game.

6 THE KILLING (1956)
An early example of how non-linear narrative can raise the tension, Stanley Kubrick's breakout film is both a tightly plotted thriller and an examination of how human weakness and simple bad luck can scupper even the most perfectly conceived plan.

5 THE LAVENDER HILL MOB (1951)
Charged with supervising gold bullion deliveries, Henry Holland seems to be an unambitious bank clerk, exceptional only in his profound professionalism. In reality he has spent 20 years developing the perfect cover and planning the perfect crime.

4 OCEAN'S ELEVEN (2001)
Not content with robbing one Las Vegas casino, Danny Ocean and his cohorts plan to rob three at the same time, all of which belong to the same man. The elaborate scheme may or may not stand up to real world scrutiny, but it's definitely a cinematic winner.

3 DOG DAY AFTERNOON (1975)
Based on the true story of John Wojtowicz and Sal Naturale's attempt to rob a Brooklyn bank, *Dog Day Afternoon* presents us with a bank robbery instigated

in order to pay for the sexual reassignment surgery of one of the participant's girlfriends.

2 RIFIFI (1955)

Very cool men plan and carry out a very cool diamond heist. Not much else needs to be said about this exceptionally classy French masterpiece, though it's worth noting the (silent) burglary at its centre is one of the most tense scenes in cinema.

1 THE ITALIAN JOB (1969)

A band of professional thieves are brought together by a charismatic crime boss to conduct a near-impossible robbery on the home soil, and right under the noses, of the Italian mafia. For reasons too convoluted to go into, they must do it in Minis.

	MOVIE	DIRECTOR	TARGET	MASTERMIND
10	Cash on Demand (1962)	Quentin Lawrence	Cash from a bank	Colonel Gore Hepburn (André Morrell)
9	Snatch (2000)	Guy Ritchie	Diamonds from a wholesaler	Franky Four Fingers (Benecio Del Toro)
8	Run Lola Run (1998)	Tom Tykwer	Cash from a bank	Lola (Franka Potente)
7	Inside Man (2006)	Spike Lee	Cash from a bank	Dalton Russell (Clive Owen)
6	The Killing (1956)	Stanley Kubrick	Cash from a racetrack	Johnny Clay (Sterling Hayden)
5	The Lavender Hill Mob (1951)	Charles Crichton	Shipment of gold bullion	Henry "Dutch" Holland (Alec Guinness)
4	Ocean's Eleven (2001)	Steven Soderbergh	Cash from casinos	Danny Ocean (George Clooney)
3	Dog Day Afternoon (1975)	Sidney Lumet	Cash from a bank	Sonny Wortzik (Al Pacino)
2	Rififi (1955)	Jules Dassin	Jewels from a jewellery store	Tony (Jean Sarvis)
1	The Italian Job (1969)	Peter Collinson	Shipment of gold bullion	Charlie Croker (Michael Caine)

TOP 10

In the days of the studio system it was common for stars to play just one character type. Although that's less the case nowadays, a tendency to typecast actors persists, and their inevitable attempts to escape those pigeonholes can result in fascinating performances.

PERFORMANCES AGAINST TYPE

here left audiences shocked.

7 ROBIN WILLIAMS
Usually: the guy who brings the funny. Here: killer psychopath. In the early 2000's Robin Williams made a couple of successful attempts to break into more mature roles. Here he plays a photo lab worker who becomes obsessed with a local family.

10 DEBORAH KERR
Usually: prim and proper English rose. Here: beach-romping adulteress. Kerr would continue to dabble with her chaste school ma'am type characters, but she caused quite a stir with this successful attempt to escape typecasting.

9 CHARLIZE THERON
Usually: Hollywood Princess. Here: serial killing prostitute. If there was surprise when screen beauty

Theron won the role of dowdy serial killer Aileen Wuornos, there was amazement when she appeared in character having discarded her ego along with her makeup and gained 40 pounds.

8 HYE-JA KIM
Usually: loving mother. Here: sociopathic mother. Although unknown in the west, Hye-Ja Kim is renowned in her native South Korea as TV's favourite cuddly maternal type. The crazed matriarch we see

6 JENNIFER ANISTON
Usually: ditzy love interest. Here: nymphomaniac bully. Director Seth Gordon has a lot of fun casting against type in this great black comedy about a group of friends who are bullied, in one way or another, by their bosses.

5 DENZIL WASHINGTON
Usually: charming man of honour. Here: profoundly corrupt cop. Washington is one of those actors who seem to exude moral responsibility, so it was a shock to see him

playing a crooked and unscrupulous cop on the take.

4 HENRY FONDA

Usually: seeker of truth. Here: ruthless gunslinger. Fonda was known for two things in Hollywood, his liberal views and being the nicest guy in town. Director Sergio Leone must have been deliberately challenging audience expectations when he has Frank kill children in cold blood within the first few minutes of the movie.

3 ALBERT BROOKS

Usually: cuddly neurotic. Here: brutal criminal kingpin. Brooks is clearly having as much fun playing this unflinchingly evil crime boss as the audience has watching him.

2 ANGELA LANSBURY

Usually: everyone's favourite Aunt. Here: mother from hell. Given Lansbury's later TV career playing top sleuth Jessica Fletcher, the definitive cuddly aunty, it's even more striking to go back and watch her play pure evil in John Frankenheimer's cold war classic.

1 PATRICK SWAYZE

Usually: cooler than cool ladies man. Here: child pornographer. One of the best examples of an actor's public image being played with by filmmakers, Swayze is superb as the hideous hypocrite Jim Cunningham.

	ACTOR	CHARACTER	MOVIE
10	Deborah Kerr	Karen Holmes	*From Here to Eternity (1953)*
9	Charlize Theron	Aileen Wuornos	*Monster (2003)*
8	Hye-ja Kim	Mother	*Mother (Madeo) (2009)*
7	Robin Williams	Seymour Parrish	*One Hour Photo (2002)*
6	Jennifer Anniston	Dr. Julia Harris	*Horrible Bosses (2011)*
5	Denzil Washington	Det. Alonzo Harris	*Training Day (2001)*
4	Henry Fonda	Frank	*Once Upon a Time in the West (1968)*
3	Albert Brooks	Bernie Rose	*Drive (2011)*
2	Angela Lansbury	Mrs. Eleanor Shaw Iselin	*The Manchurian Candidate (1962)*
1	Patrick Swayze	Jim Cunningham	*Donnie Darko (2001)*

Essentially film noir describes American films of the 40's and 50's that marry a stark, expressionistic visual style to the themes, plots and characters of hardboiled crime fiction. Although the genre moved beyond post WWII Hollywood, there's no doubting that is its home.

FILM NOIR

10 THE BIG CLOCK (1948)

Less well known than many of it's contemporaries, though no less good for it, *The Big Clock* sees successful magazine editor George Stroud (Ray Milland) framed for murder by publishing tycoon Earl Janoth (Charles Laughton).

9 THE POSTMAN ALWAYS RINGS TWICE (1946)

Drifter Frank Chambers (John Garfield) is working at a roadside burger bar in the California desert when he falls in love with Cora (Lana Turner), the wife of friendly proprietor Nick (Cecil Kellaway). Together they hatch a plan to bump off Nick and live happily ever after, but paranoia and guilt start to compromise what begins as the perfect crime.

8 THIEVES HIGHWAY (1949)

Nick Garcos (Richard Conte) returns home from war a hero only to find his father has been crippled by a corrupt market dealer and his truck stolen by a competitor. Nick quickly decides to get even and becomes embroiled in the surprisingly dangerous world of fruit truck delivery drivers.

7 BLOOD SIMPLE. (1984)

Although film noir is closely associated with the post war period, they have continued to be made in small numbers ever since. The Coen brothers' debut feature sees rich Texas club owner Julian Marty (Dan Hedaya) hire private detective Loren Visser (M. Emmet Walsh) to kill his wife Abby (Frances McDormand).

6 GILDA (1946)

Small time crook Johnny Farrell (Glenn Ford) becomes the right-hand man of crime boss Ballin Mundson (George Macready). But when Mundson returns to his Argentinian fiefdom after a long trip, he brings with him the beautiful Gilda (Rita

Hayworth), who has history with Johnny.

5 THE ASPHALT JUNGLE (1950)
The fallout from a successful major jewellery heist threatens to swallow up all concerned as double crosses and bad luck scupper a perfect plan.

4 THE BIG SLEEP (1946)
The convoluted plot (that even author Raymond Chandler famously can't explain) is secondary to Lauren Bacall's smouldering performance and the incredible chemistry she shares with Humphrey Bogart's private eye Philip Marlowe.

3 ODD MAN OUT (1947)
Needing to raise funds for the Irish Nationalist group of which he is part, Johnny (James Mason) takes too many risks and the hold up is a disaster. Badly wounded, he's relentlessly pursued through Belfast's back streets by the police.

2 LAURA (1944)
A Detective (Dana Andrews) investigating the murder of a beautiful woman (Gene Tierney) gradually falls in love with her while interviewing the people she knew.

1 DOUBLE INDEMNITY (1944)
Insurance agent Walter Neff (Fred MacMurray) is convinced by unhappily married Phyllis Dietrichson (Barbara Stanwyck) to murder her husband as part of a life insurance scam. The definitive film noir: crime, betrayal, infatuation and the model femme fatale.

	MOVIE	DIRECTOR
10	The Big Clock (1948)	John Farrow
9	The Postman Always Rings Twice (1946)	Tay Garnett
8	Thieves Highway (1949)	Jules Dassin
7	Blood Simple. (1984)	Joel Coen
6	Gilda (1946)	Charles Vidor
5	The Asphalt Jungle (1950)	John Huston
4	The Big Sleep (1946)	Howard Hawks
3	Odd Man Out (1947)	Carol Reed
2	Laura (1944)	Otto Preminger
1	Double Indemnity (1944)	Billy Wilder

TOP
10

Passion for the subject is essential for a documentary maker dealing with art & entertainment. It follows that if you're passionate enough to want to make movies you'll be passionate about movies, and that shows in the plethora of exceptional documentaries on the subject.

DOCUMENTARIES ABOUT CINEMA

10 A.K. (1985)
Chris Marker, the French writer, photographer and documentarian, was fascinated by Japanese culture, so it's no surprise he should have chosen to make a film about Akira Kurosawa, the most revered of all Japanese directors. It's an in-depth study – insightful and personal. Essential viewing for fans of the great man.

9 MY BEST FIEND (1999)
Herzog's wry reminiscence on his explosive relationship with actor Klaus Kinski makes for a compelling watch. Whether or not Herzog ever needed to direct Kinski at gunpoint remains a contentious point.

8 LOST IN LA MANCHA (2002)
The calamitous shoot for Terry Gilliam's aborted Don Quixote adaptation is documented in harrowing detail.

7 THE CELLULOID CLOSET (1995)
Based on Vito Russo's book of the same name, *The Celluloid Closet* examines how cinema has represented members of the LGBT community.

6 VISIONS OF LIGHT (1992)
A quarter of a century on *Visions of Light* is still indispensable for anyone interested in the visual aesthetic of film.

5 MAN WITH A MOVIE CAMERA (1929)
Although ostensibly a documentary on urban life, *Man With a Movie Camera* becomes an analysis of filmmaking itself when it references the technical processes used.

4 THE PERVERT'S GUIDE TO CINEMA (2006)
Celebrated Russian philosopher and cultural

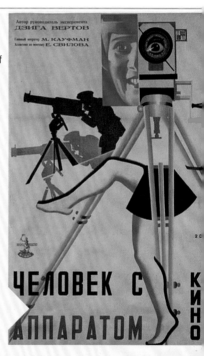

critic Slavoj Zizek examinesa series of films from a psychoanalytical perspective.

3 A PERSONAL JOURNEY WITH MARTIN SCORSESE THROUGH AMERICAN MOVIES (1995)
Martin Scorsese himself could

lay claim to producing the most important body of work of any American filmmaker. But he eschews comment on his own output, as he does that of his contemporaries, instead focusing on the quality American movies that have inspired him since childhood.

2 HEARTS OF DARKNESS: A FILMMAKER'S APOCALYPSE (1991)

It's a common opinion that this documentary, filmed on the troubled set of Francis Ford Coppola's *Apocalypse Now*, is a better film than its subject.

1 THE STORY OF FILM (2011)

This staggering 15 hour monument to cinema is a fantastic achievement by Cousins. He demonstrates unexpected but highly compelling links between seemingly disparate elements.

Gaps in the conventional history of film are filled and light is shone on the most vibrant and underexposed cinematic movements throughout history, and the world.

	MOVIE	DIRECTOR(S)	SUBJECT
10	*A.K. (1985)*	Chris Marker	Filmmaker Akira Kurosawa
9	*My Best Fiend (1999)*	Werner Herzog	Actor Klaus Kinski
8	*Lost in La Mancha (2002)*	Keith Fulton and Louis Pepe	Terry Gilliam's Don Quixote
7	*The Celluloid Closet (1995)*	Rob Epstein and Jeffrey Friedman	Homosexuality on screen
6	*Visions of Light (1992)*	Arnold Glassman and Todd McCarthy and Stuart Samuels	Cinematography
5	*Man With a Movie Camera (1929)*	Dziga Vertov	The process
4	*The Pervert's Guide to Cinema (2006)*	Sophie Fiennes	Psychoanalysis of film
3	*A Personal Journey with Martin Scorsese Through American Movies (1995)*	Martin Scorsese and Michael Henry Wilson	American cinema
2	*Hearts of Darkness: A Filmmaker's Apocalypse (1991)*	Eleanor Coppola, Fax Bahr and George Hickenlooper	Apocalypse Now
1	*The Story of Film (2011)*	Mark Cousins	Film

TOP
10

Cinematic androids have been grabbing our imagination since at least 1896's *The Future Eve*, and as they become a reality our fascination isn't letting up. The term android is here used very loosely to define any vaguely anthropomorphic android, cyborg or robot.

ANDROIDS

10 GIGOLO JOE
Jude Law is well cast as a lovebot, a robot designed to do nothing but pleasure women, in Steven Spielberg's Pinocchio themed sci-fi drama.

9 JOHNNY 5
The caterpillar-tracked Johnny 5 started life as a military robot before gaining a self aware human intelligence when struck by lightning.

8 THE IRON GIANT
Possibly the last masterpiece of American animation not to be dominated by CGI (though it is used subtly), *The Iron Giant* is a sadly under seen throwback, both to the 1950's sci-fi it references and a time when animated characters brimmed with simple charm.

7 MARIA
In a future dystopia society has split in two. The wealthy live amongst the clouds atop giant structures, the rest toil underground to keep the lights on upstairs. Freder (Gustav Fröhlich), the son of Metropolis' ruler, falls in love with Maria, a lowly worker. Their plan to bring equality to Metropolis results in a robot Maria being manufactured in order to create havoc amongst the now restless workers.

6 ROBBY THE ROBOT
Although originally intended for Forbidden Planet only, Robby's popularity was such that he developed a healthier career than many of his co-stars, featuring in dozens of movies, TV shows and commercials.

5 THE GUNSLINGER
As anyone who has seen Westworld may have guessed, Yul Brynner's dead-eyed, unstoppable killer was a key inspiration for the Terminator character made famous by Arnold Schwarzenegger.

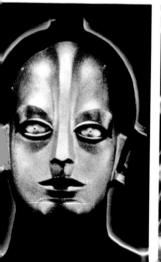

4 MOTOKO KUSANAGI

Mamoru Oshii's movie, based on Masamune Shirow's cyberpunk manga, presents a future in which androids are commonplace and even humans are augmented, to one degree or another, with cybernetic technology. Kusanagi, an operative for Public Security Section 9, is charged with battling cyber terrorism and capturing a hacker known as the Puppet Master.

3 C-3PO

Protocol droid C-3PO was likely to have been the first experience of androids for at least one generation. The stroke of genius that brings Threepio (as he's known to his friends) to life was the decision by Anthony Daniels to play him as a priggishly fussy English butler.

2 DATA

Over seven seasons of TV and four movies, Data's desire to become more human and his effort to understand our idiosyncrasies, have exposed the nature of humanity to an extent non-fans might find surprising.

1 WALL-E

The physical resemblance to Johnny 5 is clear, but beating inside Pixar's eponymous caretaker is a unique heart. Technically he doesn't look like an android. But it's arguably all human characteristics, including personality, that distinguish an android from a robot, and he's got more personality than some actors.

	ANDROID	MOVIE	PLAYED BY
10	Gigolo Joe	A.I. Artificial Intelligence (2001)	Jude Law
9	Johnny 5	Short Circuit (1986)	Tim Blaney
8	The Iron Giant	The Iron Giant (1999)	Vin Diesel
7	Maria	Metropolis (1927)	Brigitte Helm
6	Robby the Robot	Forbidden Planet (1956)	Frankie Darro
5	The Gunslinger	Westworld (1973)	Yul Brynner
4	Motoko Kusanagi	Ghost in the Shell (1995)	Atsuko Tanaka
3	C-3PO	Star Wars series (1977-ongoing)	Anthony Daniels
2	Data	Star Trek series (1994-2002)	Brent Spiner
1	Wall-E	Wall-E (2008)	Ben Burtt

TOP 10

Whether sounding board, tale-gunner, whipping boy or hero in waiting, there have been some great movie sidekicks over the years. The list is a tribute to Star Wars' Chewbacca, without whom Han Solo would clearly be lost.

SIDEKICKS

10 PEDRO SÁNCHEZ
Near mute Mexican exchange student Pedro bonds with local crackpot Napoleon Dynamite (Jon Heder), largely because nobody else wants to be friends with either.

9 HAROLD 'MITCH' MITCHELL
Karl Malden spent a good deal of his career being Marlon Brando's sidekick, often adopting the role of the great man's moral conscience. Here in Streetcar Malden plays Mitch, best friend and apologist to Brando's vile Stanley; though he does eventually see through the facade to the contemptible brute beneath.

8 WANG CHI
Loudmouth truck driver Jack Burton (Kurt Russell) and his restaurant owning buddy Wang Chi become embroiled in an ancient Chinese curse when Wang's girlfriend is kidnapped by a sorcerer.

7 CAL NAUGHTON JR.
Put upon Cal Naughton plays wingman to Will Ferrell's Ricky Bobby, NASCAR's star driver. But when Bobby cracks under the pressure, Naughton is only too happy to step out of his shadow... not to mention marry his wife and move into his house.

6 SAMWISE GAMGEE
There could be no more faithful sidekick than Sam, gardener and best friend to ring bearer Frodo Baggins (Elijah Wood). Sam demonstrates extraordinary devotion to his 'master', proving himself time and again to be worthy of the trust Frodo must place in him in the quest to destroy the ring.

5 GARTH ALGAR
With *Saturday Night Live* skits stretching back to 1988, affable Wayne (Mike Myers) and nervous sidekick Garth have been part of the cultural furniture for a long time. While Myers went on to other successes, Carvey has never topped his magnificent metalhead Garth.

4 DUDE
Drunken former sheriff's deputy Dude is penniless and desperate when old friend John Chance (John Wayne) finds him on the floor of a saloon. Chance gives him

the tough love he needs and a place to sleep, in return Dude comes though for his saviour when the bullets start flying.

3 DR. JOHN WATSON

Thrown together by fate when the two men move into shared rooms together, Watson soon becomes personally, if not professionally, essential to Holmes. There have been many interpretations of the character, but Nigel Bruce's (in the successful film series opposite Basil Rathbone's Holmes) has to be the most fun.

2 R.M. RENFIELD

Dracula's (Gary Oldman) brainwashed, bug eating vassal is brought to life with a deranged intensity by Waits in Francis Ford Coppola's epic adaptation.

1 SHORT ROUND

It's never explained how orphaned taxicab driver Short Round came to be in the service of Indiana Jones (Harrison Ford). But the fan favourite is instrumental in saving both Indy and the child slaves of Mola Ram (Amrish Puri). As he say's himself, 'you listen to me, you live longer'.

	CHARACTER	SIDEKICK TO	MOVIE	ACTOR
10	Pedro Sánchez	Napoleon Dynamite	Napoleon Dynamite (2004)	Efren Ramirez
9	Harold 'Mitch' Mitchell	Stanley	A Streetcar Named Desire (1951)	Karl Malden
8	Wang Chi	Jack Burton	Big Trouble in Little China (1986)	Dennis Dun
7	Cal Naughton Jr.	Ricky Bobby	Talladega Nights: The Ballad of Ricky Bobby (2006)	John C. Reilly
6	Samwise Gamgee	Frodo Baggins	The Lord of the Rings series (2001-2003)	Sean Astin
5	Garth Algar	Wayne Campbell	Wayne's World series (1992 and 1993)	Dana Carvey
4	Dude	Sheriff John T. Chance	Rio Bravo (1959)	Dean Martin
3	Dr. John Watson	Sherlock Holmes	Various (1939-1946)	Nigel Bruce
2	R.M. Renfield	Count Dracula	Dracula (1992)	Tom Waits
1	Short Round	Indiana Jones	Indiana Jones and the Temple of Doom (1984)	Jonathan Ke Quan

TOP
10

The movies have presented us with many an extravagant and excessive festivity, but interesting on screen parties come in many forms. Whether the sort of in-crowd blowout we'd love to be invited to, or the cultist rituals we'd rather avoid, they're all covered here.

PARTIES

10 MASQUE OF THE RED DEATH (1964)
The evil Prince Prospero hosts a lengthy ball as a means of keeping he and his guests safe from the plague raging outside his castle walls. In addition to leaving the townspeople to die he plans to sacrifice a beautiful young girl and summon up Satan.

9 SOCIETY (1992)
This bizarre black comedy sees Bill (Billy Warlock) return home one day to find his parents unexpectedly hosting a party for friends. All seems well until everyone strips to their underwear and starts eating a young kidnap victim. Bill doesn't fancy staying.

8 OLD SCHOOL (2003)
Central to this broad comedy is a fraternity house party as excessive as any on film. It effectively made Will Ferrell's big screen career with his performance as Frank 'The Tank' (a once legendary drinker who explodes out of retirement) becoming an instant classic.

7 BOOGIE NIGHTS (1997)
Pretty much what you might expect a social event at the Playboy mansion circa mid 70's to look like. The infamous party in PT Anderson's breakout hit features the most stylish and refined of cinematic techniques, the same can't be said of the guests.

6 THE PARTY (1968)
Hollywood often wasn't sure what to do with Peter Sellers' extraordinary comedy talent. In this overlooked Blake Edwards movie things are kept simple as Sellers, a buffoon mistakenly invited to a Hollywood gathering, performs a string of hilarious set pieces.

5 EYES WIDE SHUT (1999)
Apparently an exceptionally restrained and tasteful affair, unlike the masked ball and orgy featured later in the film, Bill and Alice Harford (Tom Cruise and Nicole Kidman) each lap up the attention of sophisticated admirers amid the exquisitely luxurious decor.

4 THIS IS THE END (2013)

Outside, the apocalypse rages and the worthy ascend to heaven. Inside, Hollywood's comedy elite have barricaded the doors and decided to keep the party going as long as they can. The base nature of the guests means nobody has been whisked skyward anyway.

3 LA DOLCE VITA (1960)

Leave it to Fellini to use a party to examine the existential issues of his protagonists. The unbearably cool Marcello (Marcello Mastroianni) leads a drunken band of Rome's most elite revellers as they break into a beach house and indulge in debauched mayhem.

2 WEIRD SCIENCE (1985)

When two teenage boys create their dream woman from a computer programme, she decides to organise a party at one of their homes in an attempt to make them popular. The fun is complicated by the arrival of a gang of mutant bikers and a ballistic missile.

1 ANIMAL HOUSE (1978)

The Delta Tau Chi fraternity has the lowest academic scores on campus, a reputation for belligerence and drunkenness, and is facing exclusion after one prank too many. Spirits are low, and there's only one thing that can be done about it: Toga! Toga! Toga!

	MOVIE	HOST	LOCATION	DIRECTOR(S)
10	Masque of the Red Death (1964)	Prince Prospero (Vincent Price)	Medieval castle	Roger Corman
9	Society (1992)	The Whitney's (Connie Danese and Charles Lucia)	Suburban home	Brian Yuzna
8	Old School (2003)	Students	Frat house	Todd Phillips
7	Boogie Nights (1997)	Jack Horner (Burt Reynolds)	A pornographer's mansion	Paul Thomas Anderson
6	The Party (1968)	General Clutterbuck (J. Edward McKinley)	Hollywood mansion	Blake Edwards
5	Eyes Wide Shut (1999)	Victor Ziegler (Sydney Pollack)	New York mansion	Stanley Kubrick
4	This Is the End (2013)	James Franco (James Franco)	Hollywood mansion	Evan Goldberg and Seth Rogen
3	La Dolce Vita (1960)	Nobody, the owner is absent	A beach house in Lazio, Italy	Federico Fellini
2	Weird Science (1985)	Lisa (Kelly LeBrock)	Suburban home	John Hughes
1	Animal House (1978)	The Delta Tau Chi fraternity	Frat house	John Landis

TOP 10

This is not a list of female characters who can deal with adversity or have the tenacity to achieve the impossible (hence no Ripley from Alien etc.). This is a list of female characters who are born to kick serious ass, and in some cases do nothing but.

TOUGH GIRLS

10 THE BRIDE
Former member of the Deadly Viper Assassination Squad, expert in the tiger and crane kung fu styles, trained by legendary master Pai Mei (Gordon Liu) and one of few practitioners of the Five Point Exploding Heart Technique. You don't mess with The Bride.

9 CHINA O'BRIEN
With the explosion in popularity of martial arts movies in the 1980s, a number of western performers picked up the baton from the Asian film industries. Although few were women, Rothrock was unquestionably the best of them, with China O'Brien her signature character.

8 RED SONJA
Based on the exploits of the Marvel comic heroine (who in turn was based on a character from an R.E. Howard short story), Red Sonja is a Hyborian era sword-wielding avenger who can give even Arnold Schwarzenegger a run for his money.

7 NEYTIRI
Any 10-foot tall bright blue alien can be intimidating. When they're defending their home from violent aggressors they can be outright terrifying.

6 SARAH CONNOR
Having spent years honing her body and mind to become the perfect fighting machine, Connor is as ready as she can be for the mech revolution only she knows is coming.

5 MAGGIE FITZGERALD
Tragic Maggie is a promising boxer who rises to the top of her profession only to have success cruelly snatched away and replaced with devastation.

4 MAY DAY
Grace Jones' unforgettable May Day is the bodyguard, assassin and all round henchwoman of crazed industrialist Max Zorin (Christopher Walken). She demonstrates superhuman strength and martial arts skills during her spats with James Bond (Roger Moore)

3 XIAO MEI
With the Tang Dynasty collapsing, rebel groups have sprung up across the region, leaving the authorities battling

a tide of freedom fighters. One of them is Mei, an exceptional martial artist embroiled in a complicated web of deceit that leaves the principal characters baffled as to who's who and which side they're on.

2 SELENE

Selene is a vampire, specifically a Death Dealer, descended from an ancient race of warriors who have done battle through the ages with the Lycans, a fierce species of werewolf. As proficient with weapons as she is in hand to hand combat, Selene faces a variety of challenges throughout the series.

1 ALICE

Based on the computer games that follow an evil corporation which has created a zombiefying virus, the central figure in the Resident Evil mythology is Alice. She awakens suffering from amnesia, but soon finds she's more than capable of handling the horde of zombies with whom she discovers she shares the underground facility in which she's trapped.

	CHARACTER	MOVIE	ACTOR
10	The Bride	*Kill Bill: Vol. 1 & 2 (2003 & 2004)*	Uma Thurman
9	China O'Brien	*China O'Brien (1990)*	Cynthia Rothrock
8	Red Sonja	*Red Sonja (1985)*	Brigitte Nielsen
7	Neytiri	*Avatar (2009)*	Zoe Saldana
6	Sarah Connor	*Terminator 2: Judgement Day (1991)*	Linda Hamilton
5	Maggie Fitzgerald	*Million Dollar Baby (2004)*	Hilary Swank
4	May Day	*A View to a Kill (1985)*	Grace Jones
3	Xiao Mei	*The House of Flying Daggers (2004)*	Ziyi Zhang
2	Selene	*Underworld series (2003-2012)*	Kate Beckinsale
1	Alice	*Resident Evil series (2002-2012)*	Milla Jovovich

TOP 10

Often assumed to be a hasty rehash designed to cash in on success, the sequel doesn't have a great image. But the best of them develop characters and ideas that were already strong, perhaps the perfect example being this list's tribute movie: *The Godfather Part II*.

SEQUELS AS GOOD AS THE ORIGINALS

10 INFERNAL AFFAIRS II (2003)
This prequel to the great Hong Kong thriller that inspired Martin Scorsese's *The Departed* focuses on the early careers of the first film's protagonists Yue and Chen.

9 28 WEEKS LATER (2007)
Danny Boyle's original *28 Days Later* was a breath of fresh air when it hit screens in 2002. Although less experimental, the sequel captures all the same qualities.

8 HELLBOY II: THE GOLDEN ARMY (2008)
This pet project of Guillermo del Toro flies strangely under the radar for a big budget comic book series. Having established the characters and relationships in the first film, del Toro sits back and lets them do their thing in this better balanced and bigger

hearted sequel.

7 DAWN OF THE DEAD (1978)
Having flirted with social commentary in predecessor *Night of the Living Dead*, Romero ramps up the allegory in this sequel. Consumerism is the target, as a small band of survivors find themselves holed up in that most commercial of American institutions: the shopping mall.

6 THE BOURNE SUPREMACY (2004)
Critics and moviegoers were pleasantly surprised by the *Bourne Identity* when it was released in 2002. News of a sequel may have pleased some but many were unconvinced it would match up, so imagine the surprise when incoming director Paul Greengrass produced one of the most impressive action thrillers of the era.

5 MAD MAX 2 (1981)
While the first film toyed with the idea of a shattered society terrorised with impunity by feral gangs, the sequel throws itself wholeheartedly into an apocalyptic nightmare.

4 ONCE UPON A TIME IN CHINA II (1992)
More martial arts antics for Jet Li's heroic kung fu legend Wong Fei Hung. This time he must defeat the White Lotus Society, a dangerous cult who have targeted any Chinese who demonstrates an affinity for western culture.

3 MANON DES SOURCES (1986)
The inevitable sequel to Jean de Florette (both films are based on a two volume novel by French author Marcel Pagnol) details the attempts of Manon (Emmanuelle Béart) to avenge the death of her father.

2 TOY STORY II (1999)
Originally planned as a budget, straight to video release, *Toy Story II* arguably had a more profound effect on moviegoers (not to mention Pixar, the studio behind it) than the original. Toy Story showed us CGI movies can work, the sequel demonstrates they can be special.

1 BRIDE OF FRANKENSTEIN (1935)
With *Frankenstein*, director James Whale kicked off a craze for gothic horror that would bankroll studio Universal for years. Returning to further explore the genre must have seemed an unnecessary risk to many, but if anything Whale surpasses the near perfection of that first film, further developing the monster whilst introducing a fascinating new mad scientist in the form of Dr Pretorius (Ernest Thesiger).

	MOVIE	DIRECTOR(S)
10	*Infernal Affairs II (2003)*	Wai-keung Lau and Alan Mak
9	*28 Weeks Later (2007)*	Juan Carlos Fresnadillo
8	*Hellboy II: The Golden Army (2008)*	Guillermo del Toro
7	*Dawn of the Dead (1978)*	George A. Romero
6	*The Bourne Supremacy (2004)*	Paul Greengrass
5	*Mad Max 2 (1981)*	George Miller
4	*Once Upon a Time in China II (1992)*	Hark Tsui
3	*Manon des Sources (1986)*	Claude Berri
2	*Toy Story II (1999)*	John Lassiter
1	*Bride of Frankenstein (1935)*	James Whale

TOP 10

Whilst few of us would want to visit Sin City, and less still Mordor or the Death Star, the movies have given us a plethora of fanciful locations it would be a pleasure to look in on. Some are impossibly quaint, some are incredibly good fun, sadly all are fictional.

FICTIONAL MOVIE PLACES IT WOULD BE GREAT TO VISIT

10 THE CAPITOL, PANEM

In the totalitarian world of the *Hunger Games* movies, the Capitol is the base of power from which Panem (essentially the North American continent) is ruled. When compared to the rest of the country, the wealth and comfort enjoyed by the elite residents of the Capitol is staggering.

9 SEAHAVEN

A town so perfect it can't be real... and, sure enough, it isn't.

8 THE HUNDRED ACRE WOOD

Who wouldn't like to stroll through Hundred Acre Wood, perhaps visiting the bridge for a game of Pooh Sticks with Piglet before stopping for lunch at A Nice Place for Picnics? Based on the Five Hundred Acre Wood of Ashdown Forest, close to the home of author A A Milne, in which the real life Christopher Robin would often play.

7 SHANGRI-LA

The plane of British diplomat Robert Conway (Ronal Colman) and his party crash lands in a remote part of the Himalayas. They are rescued and taken to Shangri-La, a mythical nirvana that doesn't conform to any of Earth's natural laws. Shangri-La has the power to heal wounds, cure disease and offers practical immortality for those who choose to stay.

6 THE NEXUS

A bit like a pepped up Shangri-La, The Nexus is located through a rift in space-time and has the power to provide anything the heart desires, if you can make it there alive.

5 NARNIA

You would need to carefully time your visit to Narnia, the magical realm located behind a wardrobe. Avoid the period ruled over by Jadis, the White Witch (circa 900-1000), and instead head for the Golden Age that followed her downfall.

4 HOGSMEADE

The only town in Britain to be inhabited solely by magical folk, Hogsmeade sits adjacent to Hogwarts School of Witchcraft and Wizardry in the Scottish Highlands. Attractions include The Three Broomsticks, where the renouned Butterbeer is tipple of choice, and the Shrieking

Shack, believed to be the most haunted place in Britain.

3 NEVERLAND
Populated by mermaids, fairies, gnomes and pirates, as well as a collection of ageless children, Neverland is the enchanted world created by author J M Barrie for his Peter Pan series.

2 WONDERLAND
Perhaps a little menacing for some travellers of the imagination, the surreal world of Wonderland must nevertheless be amongst the most desirable of hallucinatory holiday hot spots.

1 TOONTOWN
Just when we think we've seen everything the bizarre alternative universe of Roger Rabbit has to offer, we're taken to Toontown. In this entirely cartoon world everything is 'alive', with cars, trees and even buildings given personality.

	LOCATION	MOVIE
10	The Capitol, Panem	The Hunger Games series (2012-)
9	Seahaven	The Truman Show (1998)
8	The Hundred Acre Wood	The Many Adventures of Winnie the Pooh (1977)
7	Shangri-La	Lost Horizon (1937)
6	The Nexus	Star Trek: Generations (1994)
5	Narnia	The Chronicles of Narnia series (2005-ongoing)
4	Hogsmeade	Harry Potter series (2001-2011)
3	Neverland	Peter Pan (1953)
2	Wonderland	Alice in Wonderland (1951)
1	Toontown	Who Framed Roger Rabbit (1988)

TOP 10

Although no legitimate devotee would consider religious affiliation (or lack of it) a reason to victimise others or a means to exploit or control, the movies have given us numerous less worthy, misguided, deranged or plain phoney believers.

MISGUIDED BELIEVERS

10 SISTER JEAN
In love with local priest Urbain Grandier, the head of a 17th century convent slips into madness when she realises he has secretly wed. After a series of false accusations and vile assaults, her venom results in Grandier being burned alive as a witch.

9 ABIN COOPER
Apparently inspired by the infamous Fred Phelps of the Westboro Baptist Church (an American extremist Christian sect), Cooper is a snake-like figure of pure evil.

8 MOLA RAM
Thuggee high priest Mola Ram is responsible for enslaving hundreds of children, can rip the beating heart from his victims with his bare hands, and is trying to summon up Kali, the lord of darkness, to reign over a new era of terror. So he's not the most amiable chap.

7 CARDINAL ROARK
Occasional cannibal and full time evil mastermind, Cardinal Roark and his corrupt family pulls the strings in Basin City. It's Roark who has the prostitute Goldie murdered, which kick-starts the movie's central plot.

6 FREDDIE QUELL
Another fictional cult to be at least partially inspired by a real one. This time it's Scientology and it's founder L. Ron Hubbard that seems to be in the firing line. Joaquin Phoenix's Freddie Quell is a war veteran struggling to find meaning in his life when he's taken in by Lancaster Dodd (Philip Seymour Hoffman), the charismatic leader of 'The Cause'.

5 SIMON THE HOLY MAN
Without doubt the most benign entry on the list, Simon the holy man is no less misguided than the others. After taking a vow of silence he spends 18 years sitting in a hole, until Brian turns up and stands on his foot.

4 JIMMY LEE FARNSWORTH
This TV evangelist isn't the most dishonest character in the movie, but he comes pretty close.

3 LORD SUMMERISLE
Lee gives one of his greatest performances as the patriarch of a Hebridean island community. He and his pagan followers lure Christian Police

Sergeant Howie from the mainland in order to sacrifice him to the Gods, whom they believe keep the ground fertile.

2 REVEREND HARRY POWELL
Believing he is doing God's work, this self appointed preacher roams America marrying and killing women for their money. Pure evil has seldom been better personified than in the Reverend Harry Powell, and his entrance is one of the most memorable moments in cinema.

1 BARRY
Barry, a white, British fundamentalist Muslim, is an aspiring suicide bomber in this hilarious satire from the comedy genius Chris Morris. Barry, like the film, might at first sound like a crass, tasteless stereotype. But, again like the film, closer inspection reveals a subtly drawn ribbing of the human flaws that can scupper law enforcement officer and terrorist alike.

	CHARACTER	MOVIE	ACTOR
10	Sister Jean	*The Devils (1971)*	Vanessa Redgrave
9	Abin Cooper	*Red State (2011)*	Michael Parks
8	Mola Ram	*Indiana Jones and the Temple of Doom (1984)*	Amrish Puri
7	Cardinal Roark	*Sin City (2005)*	Rutger Hauer
6	Freddie Quell	*The Master (2012)*	Joaquin Phoenix
5	Simon the Holy Man	*The Life of Brian (1979)*	Terry Jones
4	Jimmy Lee Farnsworth	*Fletch Lives (1989)*	R. Lee Ermey
3	Lord Summerisle	*The Wicker Man (1973)*	Christopher Lee
2	Reverend Harry Powell	*Night of the Hunter (1955)*	Robert Mitchum
1	Barry	*Four Lions (2010)*	Nigel Lindsay

TOP
10

Even though it's arguably cinema's defining character archetype, what makes a hero is extremely subjective. For this list it's been kept very simple: a hero is the kind of person who will sacrifice everything for what's right, and for those who need help.

HEROES

10 INDIANA JONES
Whilst many of Indy's adventures benefit few outside the niche group that is enthusiastic museum-goers, the second film in the series (*Temple of Doom*) sees him spurn safe passage home in favour of risking his life attempting to free hundreds of child slaves.

9 SHOSANNA DREYFUSS
In occupied France during WWII, a cinema owner learns she will be forced to host a premiere attended by the upper echelons of the Nazi party. Once she realises she must burn it to the ground her resolve doesn't waver for a moment, even though it means certain death.

8 WILL KANE
The marshal of a New Mexico town receives word that a murderer he once brought in is returning on the noon train and intent on revenge. In spite of the locals urging him to run and refusing to help, Kane knows what he must do.

7 ATTICUS FINCH
Voted the greatest hero of the 20th century by the AFI, Atticus Finch is a respected lawyer tasked with defending an African American accused of rape in 1930s Alabama. Regardless of his popularity the townspeople react violently to his perceived betrayal.

6 ERIN BROKOVICH
Residents of a small town suffer an abnormally high rate of cancer and a struggling mother turned legal assistant vows to help them. After suffering intimidation and threats she wins the case and a substantial payout from a corporation operating a nearby factory.

5 JEFFERSON SMITH
Hard as it is to imagine now, there was a time when politicians could be presented as heroes and the audience

would go along with it. Naive young Senator Jefferson Smith arrives in Washington and, finding it less than wholesome, resolves to tackle the corruption.

4 JOHN T. CHANCE

The brother of a powerful rancher is arrested for murder in a Texas town. The Sheriff and a ragtag band of allies hole up in the jailhouse and for several days must hold off a gang of hired guns until a United States Marshal arrives to collect the prisoner.

3 REE DOLLY

Teenager Ree is the soul carer for her younger siblings and mentally ill mother in an impoverished Ozark community. When it transpires her absent father put up their

ramshackle family home as a bail bond before absconding, she must do what she can to find him.

2 ROBIN HOOD

There has been much discussion as to whether Robin Hood was a real figure and, if so, whether he was quite as altruistic as the legend portrays him. What we can be sure of is that the movie character is a hero of the first order, robbing the rich to give to the poor.

1 SPARTACUS

Surely the definition of a hero. Thracian gladiator Spartacus leads an uprising against the Roman Republic in the first century BC. His heroism during the Third Servile War famously inspired hundreds of slaves to give their lives in a doomed attempt to save him.

	CHARACTER	MOVIE	ACTOR
10	Indiana Jones	Indiana Jones series (1981-2008)	Harrison Ford
9	Shosanna Dreyfuss	Inglourious Basterds (2009)	Mélanie Laurent
8	Will Kane	High Noon (1952)	Gary Cooper
7	Atticus Finch	To Kill a Mocking-bird (1962)	Gregory Peck
6	Erin Brokovich	Erin Brokovich (2000)	Julia Roberts
5	Jefferson Smith	Mr. Smith Goes to Washington (1939)	James Stewart
4	John T. Chance	Rio Bravo (1959)	John Wayne
3	Ree Dolly	Winter's Bone (2010)	Jennifer Lawrence
2	Robin Hood	The Adventures of Robin Hood (1938)	Errol Flynn
1	Spartacus	Spartacus (1960)	Kirk Douglas

TOP
10

The Hollywood studio system apparently failed to identify the potential of the buddy movie dynamic. Although there were examples of a sort it wasn't really until the American new wave that the archetype was clearly established, and from there it's never looked back.

BUDDY MOVIES

10 STIR CRAZY (1980)
Failing writer Skip and equally unsuccessful actor Harry are framed for a bank robbery and sentenced to 125 years in prison. It's debatable whether there are funnier Wilder/Pryor collaborations amongst their successes, but this is easily their best 'buddy' movie.

9 MIDNIGHT COWBOY (1969)
On the face of it Midnight Cowboy is a depressing movie about seedy people. But, if there is anything uplifting to be found amongst the detritus of shattered dreams on offer, it's the strength of the friendship between Ratso and Joe.

8 UP IN SMOKE (1978)
Cheech and Chong's debut feature is by far their best, assuming you enjoy this sort of thing. After getting

stuck on the wrong side of the U.S./Mexico border, the pair must drive home in a van made from marijuana, but they're unaware the police are on their tail.

7 THE DEFIANT ONES (1958)

After escaping from a crashed prison truck, two convicts (crucially one white and one black), chained together and full of mutual hatred, must learn to work together, eventually coming to like and respect one another.

6 BUTCH CASSIDY AND THE SUNDANCE KID (1969)

The chemistry between Paul Newman and Robert Redford made them the perfect choice to play these celebrated outlaws. Just how historically accurate the movie might be is up for debate, but what isn't is the magic these two bring to the screen.

5 WHEELS ON MEALS (1984)

Jackie Chan's Hong Kong movies still have something of a niche appeal in the west. But

Wheels on Meals is pleasingly slick and accessible, making it a good place to start for anyone wanting to dip their toe in the water of classic kung fu cinema.

4 DUMB AND DUMBER (1994)

The film that cemented Jim Carrey's reputation as the leading comedy actor of his generation has surprisingly touching overtones. Lloyd and Harry have nothing in the world but each other, and you feel they're quite happy about it.

3 HEAVENLY CREATURES (1994)

Psychotics needs buddies too. Peter Jackson's film about murderous teens completely changed the way we perceived the Kiwi director, and gave us one of the most powerful friendships cinema has so far produced.

2 LETHAL WEAPON (1987)

Lethal Weapon arguably defines what the action oriented buddy movie would be from the 1980s onwards. Learning a trick from *The Odd Couple*, it first throws two characters with diametrically opposed personalties together, then injects stress.

1 MIDNIGHT RUN (1988)

Catching De Niro between the sort of serious method roles in which he made his name, and the generic comedy roles that would later make his fortune, *Midnight Run* has the best of both worlds. Endlessly quotable, re-watchable, satisfying fun.

	MOVIE	DIRECTOR	BUDDIES
10	*Stir Crazy (1980)*	Sidney Poitier	Skip and Harry (Gene Wilder and Richard Pryor)
9	*Midnight Cowboy (1969)*	John Schlesinger	Ratso and Joe (Dustin Hoffman and Jon Voight)
8	*Up In Smoke (1978)*	Lou Adler	Pedro and Anthony (Cheech Marin and Tommy Chong)
7	*The Defiant Ones (1958)*	Stanley Kramer	Joker and Noah (Tony Curtis and Sidney Poitier)
6	*Butch Cassidy and the Sundance Kid (1969)*	George Roy Hill	Butch and Sundance (Paul Newman and Robert Redford)
5	*Wheels On Meals (1984)*	Sammo Hung Kam-Bo	Thomas and David (Jackie Chan and Yuen Biao)
4	*Dumb and Dumber (1994)*	Peter Farrelly	Lloyd and Harry (Jim Carrey and Jeff Daniels)
3	*Heavenly Creatures (1994)*	Peter Jackson	Pauline and Juliet (Melanie Lynskey and Kate Winslet)
2	*Lethal Weapon (1987)*	Richard Donner	Riggs and Murtaugh (Mel Gibson and Danny Glover)
1	*Midnight Run (1988)*	Martin Brest	Jack and Jonathan (Robert De Niro and Charles Grodin)

TOP 10

Doctors are amongst the most prolific characters in the movies, perhaps because drama, pathos and even comedy are inherent at the point life and death meet. However it's unfortunate to note how few women have had the chance to play memorable doctors, and, as such, none make this list.

MEDICAL DOCTORS

10 DR. MONTGOMERY
The gloomy Dr. Montgomery has a small but unforgettable part in this quiet movie about a WWII deserter attempting to save his marriage.

9 DR. MALCOLM SAYER
Decades after an encephalitis epidemic consigns a number of patients to comas, Dr. Malcolm Sayer develops an experimental treatment that produces astounding results.

8 DR. CHRISTIAN SZELL
Marathon Man sees history student Babe (Dustin Hoffman) embroiled in a plot by a former leading Nazi to acquire a fortune in stolen diamonds. Szell, the Nazi in question, uses his dentistry skills in an attempt to force information from Babe in one of the most memorable and gruelling scenes of torture in mainstream cinema.

7 DR. STEPHEN MATURIN
The Charles Darwin inspired Dr. Maturin acts as conscience, sounding board and physician to Captain Jack Aubrey (Russell Crowe), in this first of several proposed movies based on Patrick O'Brian's 'Aubrey-Maturin' series of novels.

6 PROFESSOR MILLAR
The crazed modern day Frankenstein of Lindsay Anderson's acerbic satire is as vivid and enjoyable a character as any to appear in the films of the great director. It takes character to unveil a talking brain to the Queen Mother.

5 DR. NIKOLAS VEN HELSING
Taking part in an illegal cross country street race, JJ McClure (Burt Reynolds) and Victor Prinzim (Dom DeLuise) field a suped up ambulance in order to avoid police attention. But they need a doctor to add

authenticity (and latterly keep their 'patient' unconscious), unfortunately Victor can only find Van Helsing, a physician who would look more at home receiving treatment than administering it.

4 DR. BLOCK
Block could be Van Helsing's son in some terrifying parallel universe. He shares the same propensity for administering mysterious injections and even shares a passing resemblance. But where Van Helsing was merely incompetent, Block is malevolent.

3 DR. NICHOLAS GARRIGAN
After graduating medical school in his native Scotland, Nicholas Garrigan travels to Uganda to work in a missionary clinic. A chance encounter with Idi Amin leaves the dictator impressed, and Garrigan becomes his personal

doctor, confidant and advisor.

2 DR. HAWKEYE PIERCE

Hawkeye's caustic wit and self deprecating sense of humour have endeared him to more than one generation. Although played brilliantly here by Donald Sutherland, his TV incarnation in the hands of Alan Alda is every bit as good.

1 DR. YURI ZHIVAGO

Amidst the Russian revolution and WWI, the romantically inclined doctor Yuri Zhivago, invariably stationed in front line field hospitals, falls helplessly in love with Lara (Julie Christie), a beautiful nurse.

	CHARACTER	MOVIE	ACTOR
10	Dr. Montgomery	*Waterloo Road (1945)*	Alastair Sim
9	Dr. Malcolm Sayer	*Awakenings (1990)*	Robin Williams
8	Dr. Christian Szell	*Marathon Man (1976)*	Laurence Olivier
7	Dr. Stephen Maturin	*Master and Commander: The Far Side of the World (2003)*	Paul Bettany
6	Professor Millar	*Britannia Hospital (1982)*	Graham Crowden
5	Dr. Nikolas Ven Helsing	*Cannonball Run (1981)*	Jack Elam
4	Dr. Block	*Planet Terror (2007)*	Josh Brolin
3	Dr. Nicholas Garrigan	*The Last King of Scotland (2006)*	James McAvoy
2	Dr. Hawkeye Pierce	*MASH (1969)*	Donald Sutherland
1	Dr. Yuri Zhivago	*Doctor Zhivago (1965)*	Omar Sharif

TOP 10

An underrated masterpiece is usually relatively well known. It's not about being an undiscovered gem or obscure arthouse classic. It's about being misinterpreted or misunderstood, perhaps it wasn't what the audience were expecting or was ahead of its time.

UNDERRATED MASTERPIECES

10 TRANSFORMERS: THE MOVIE (1986)

The extent to which a movie is underrated depends on the margin between the perception and reality of its quality. The original animated *Transformers* movie is a masterclass in screenplay construction and fully deserves a spot on this list. Seriously.

9 THE GAME (1997)

After the success of *Se7en*, Fincher continued to mine the darker reaches of the human psyche in this highly original thriller. A significantly less populist narrative and more ambiguous characters probably *contributed to The Game*'s relative commercial failure.

8 DREAMS (1990)

Although well respected, *Dreams* is seldom compared favourably with Kurosawa's better known earlier masterpieces. But

it's a bravura flourish from a genius nearing the end of his career, albeit one that diverts significantly from his signature style.

7 LONE STAR (1996)

Lone Star deals with how men cope living in the shadow of a legend, and how they react when those legends prove to be fraudulent. In a genre more used to creating mythology than shattering it, this Western failed to find an audience that reflected its quality.

6 NOSFERATU THE VAMPYRE (1979)

This atmospheric remake of the 1922 original is frequently overlooked in the discussion on vampire cinema. It makes few concessions to the audience and (as with the original) is centred around an extremely unsettling lead performance, this time from Klaus Kinski.

5 THE CABLE GUY (1996)

Starring Jim Carrey, directed by Ben Stiller and Produced by Judd Apatow, *Cable Guy* would surely be a smash if released today. But in 1996 the public expected something much sunnier from the triptych, if they knew their names at all. Dark, thought-provoking and hilarious.

4 NAKED LUNCH (1991)

Naked Lunch has a peculiar relationship with both cinemagoers and fans of author William S. Burroughs. Some revel in the surreal mashup of Burroughs (real) life and most famous (fictional) work, while others struggle with the onslaught of crazy.

3 SATURDAY NIGHT FEVER (1977)

Can one of the most popular movies of all time be underrated? When it's seen as some sort of kitsch time capsule and not appreciated as an uncompromising examination of the travails facing teenage America in fast changing times, yes, it can.

2 LADY VENGEANCE (2005)

The last instalment of Park's 'Vengeance Trilogy' suffered from following on the heels his hugely successful breakout hit *Oldboy*. While it has all *Oldboy*'s inventiveness and style, the lead is more interesting, the narrative more digestible and the movie is generally more textured.

1 EYES WIDE SHUT (1999)

Eyes Wide Shut was widely regarded as a disappointment on release, with critics citing un-

engaging themes and an incoherent message. But although it addresses more mundane issues than his earlier successes, Kubrick's swansong is every bit as impressive and rewarding.

	MOVIE	DIRECTOR
10	Transformers: The Movie (1986)	Nelson Shin
9	The Game (1997)	David Fincher
8	Dreams (1990)	Akira Kurosawa
7	Lone Star (1996)	John Sayles
6	Nosferatu the Vampyre (1979)	Werner Herzog
5	The Cable Guy (1996)	Ben Stiller
4	Naked Lunch (1991)	David Cronenberg
3	Saturday Night Fever (1977)	John Badham
2	Lady Vengeance (2005)	Chan-wook Park
1	Eyes Wide Shut (1999)	Stanley Kubrick

TOP
10

Time to put pen to paper and create your own top 10 list of Westerns...

10

9

8

7

6

5

4

3

2

1

BUTCH CASSIDY

TOP 10

Some say the 1980s saw the high water mark for big, dumb and shiny action movies. Others believe the popular subgenre was reduced to generic flag-waving spectacles that eschewed traditional acting talent in favour of muscle-bound grunters. But what's wrong with that?

80'S ACTION MOVIES

10 THE DELTA FORCE (1986)

A list like this would be incomplete without Chuck Norris, and *The Delta Force* is arguably his signature movie. With appropriately grim support from Lee Marvin, Chuck's Major McCoy is called on to overcome the Lebanese hijackers of a New York bound commercial jet.

9 THE RUNNING MAN (1987)

The Running Man is a deceptively cerebral adaptation of the Stephen King novel. In the future, ordinary people obsess over a TV reality game show and vie to become contestants. However the system is corrupt and only the executives can really win. Sound familiar?

8 RAMBO: FIRST BLOOD PART II (1985)

The second of four instalments (so far) in the Rambo franchise is, if not the best, the most '80's actionest'. Several prominent themes of the era are addressed, with Rambo returning to Vietnam to rescue POW's abandoned by a U.S. wanting to wash its hands of the war.

7 ROAD HOUSE (1989)

Pure 1980s hokum, *Road House* sees a super-tough bouncer move to a small town in the middle of nowhere and start working at a particularly rough trucker bar. Love, local corruption, cheesy music and bad hair must all be navigated safely.

6 ROBOCOP (1987)

In near future Detroit society is crumbling and a disillusioned police force is effectively privatised. Director Paul Verhoeven's ability to weave social commentary into apparently mindless blockbusters is demonstrated brilliantly.

5 BLOODSPORT (1988)

Based on the experiences of martial artist Frank Dux, *Bloodsport* marks the first significant role for action legend Jean-Claude van Damme. Doubts over the authenticity of Dux's story remain, but the movie itself is no less enjoyable as a result.

4 LETHAL WEAPON (1987)

Lethal Weapon's mix of blistering action, cartoon villains and acerbic one liners lifts much from James Bond. But it's packaged in such a way that it became a prototype to which all that followed owe a debt.

3 PREDATOR (1987)

Inspired by a joke suggesting Rocky would one day have to fight an alien if the sequels kept coming, *Predator* didn't have an auspicious start. But the tale of commandos hunted by a deadly predator ended up a huge hit.

2 ALIENS (1986)

Wisely deciding it was folly to try and outdo the tense scares of the first Alien movie, director James Cameron took the sequel in a different direction. Subtlety is left at the door as Cameron amps everything up, arming the whole cast with absurdly massive guns.

1 DIE HARD (1988)

It's hard to believe now but Bruce Willis wasn't offered the role that would define him until a succession of unlikely candidates had turned it down. Among them 80's icons like Schwarzenegger and Stallone, plus everyone from Burt Reynolds to Frank Sinatra.

	MOVIE	DIRECTOR
10	The Delta Force (1986)	Menaheim Golan
9	The Running Man (1987)	Paul Michael Glaser
8	Rambo: First Blood Part II (1985)	George P. Cosmatos
7	Road House (1989)	Rowdy Herrington
6	Robocop (1987)	Paul Verhoeven
5	Bloodsport (1988)	Newt Arnold
4	Lethal Weapon (1987)	Richard Donner
3	Predator (1987)	John McTiernan
2	Aliens (1986)	James Cameron
1	Die Hard (1988)	John McTiernan

TOP 10

Movies can clearly be very effective at tapping into our deepest emotions, so it's no surprise they can be very inspiring. Told well, a simple story of humanity triumphing over harsh indifference will speak to all of us, and maybe even making a difference to our lives.

INSPIRATIONAL MOVIES

10 THE SCHOOL OF ROCK (2003)

The story of a free-spirited teacher galvanising schoolchildren into passionate enthusiasm is not unique to *The School of Rock*. In fact it appears again later in this list. But what is unique is the brilliantly light touch and emotional honesty Linklater brings.

9 BILLY ELLIOT (2000)

In a tough Northern England mining community, 11 year old Billy Elliot discovers a love for ballet. At first his father is not willing to support Billy's passion, but after coming to understand its importance to him a change of heart leads to success.

8 THE PIANIST (2002)

Pianist Władysław Szpilman, a Polish Jew, is force into the Warsaw Ghetto when the Nazis invade Poland in 1939. His talent and determination to survive help him endure the aftermath of the Warsaw Uprising and the Treblinka concentration camp.

7 DEAD POETS SOCIETY (1989)

Encouraged by their English teacher to seize the day, two shy and awkward students start to come out of their shells. Some have found *Dead Poets Society* to be overly manipulative and sentimental, but that misses the point of this devastatingly effective movie.

6 LIFE IS BEAUTIFUL (1997)

Guido Orefice (Roberto Benigni), an eternally optimistic Italian, and his wife and child are consigned to a concentration camp during WWII. Determined to protect his son from the abundant horrors, he makes a game of their incarceration.

5 THE GRAPES OF WRATH (1940)

When the Joad clan lose the family ranch during the Great Depression, they head west for California in search of work. The injustices young Tom (Henry Fonda) witnesses on the journey encourage him to fight for social reform.

4 AMÉLIE (2001)

The very definition of charm (both the movie and the character), Amélie (Audrey Tautou) is a waitress to various eccentric customers at a Montmartre cafe. Though unlucky in love, her imagination is matched only by her kindness to others.

3 TO KILL A MOCKINGBIRD (1962)

In 1930s Alabama a community deals with the fallout from an accusation of rape. That it is made by a white woman against a black man only serves to amplify the tension in a town which is eventually forced to ask itself some difficult questions.

2 THE SHAWSHANK REDEMPTION (1994)
Wrongly jailed for the murder of his wife, Andy Dufresne (Tim Robbins) spends decades in a brutal prison. Determined to maintain hope and his integrity, Andy does what he can to improve conditions whilst hatching a daring plan to escape.

1 IT'S A WONDERFUL LIFE (1946)
Like *A Christmas Carol* in reverse, *It's a Wonderful Life* delves into a kind of magical realism to show suicidal family man George Bailey (James Stewart) just how much better off his community is thanks to his kindness.

	MOVIE	DIRECTOR(S)
10	The School of Rock (2003)	Richard Linklater
9	Billy Elliot (2000)	Stephen Daldry
8	The Pianist (2002)	Roman Polanski
7	Dead Poet's Society (1989)	Peter Weir
6	Life is Beautiful (1997)	Roberto Benigni and Rod Dean
5	The Grapes of Wrath (1940)	John Ford
4	Amélie (2001)	Jeanne-Pierre Jeunet
3	To Kill a Mockingbird (1962)	Robert Mulligan
2	The Shawshank Redemption (1994)	Frank Darabont
1	It's a Wonderful Life (1946)	Frank Capra

TOP 10

In one way an ambiguous ending is incompatible with a traditional narrative. As an audience we tend to find closure important, it's a key return on our emotional investment. But handled carefully it's a way of keeping the movie alive even after the credits roll.

AMBIGUOUS ENDINGS

10 LOCK, STOCK AND TWO SMOKING BARRELS (1998)
After a protracted series of cons, bluffs and misfortunes, a pair of shotguns are all that's left to show for some serious exertion by a bunch of good natured schemers. They discover the guns are worth a small fortune, but can they save them in time?

9 CAST AWAY (2000)
Stranded on an uninhabited island for four years, time-obsessed Fed Ex worker Chuck Noland (Tom Hanks) finally returns home. After realising he can't slot back into his old life, we leave him literally standing at a crossroads considering which way to go.

8 FIVE EASY PIECES (1970)
A troubled former piano prodigy leads a simple life working the California oil fields. After taking his gauche girlfriend to meet his family their difficult relationship worsens, and he eventually abandons her before hitching a ride on the first truck he sees.

7 PAN'S LABYRINTH (2006)
In Franco era Spain, Ofelia (Ivana Baquero) moves in with her brutal stepfather, soon retreating into what seems to be a fantasy world. It isn't clear what's real and what isn't, with this twisted fairytale ending on a vague note, the audience not even sure whether our heroine survives.

6 THE KING OF COMEDY (1983)
Jailed for kidnapping his TV host hero, struggling comedian Rupert Pupkin (Robert De Niro) seems to achieve fame for his crime and is released into the media spotlight he so craves. But the whole experience may just be another of Rupert's fantasies.

5 ANATOMY OF A MURDER (1959)
This superb courtroom drama presents us with an abhorrent conundrum. The setup is simple: a husband kills a man who his wife claims raped her. But was she really raped? Complicated motives are revealed, but doubts over the wife's honesty are never settled.

4 SHANE (1953)
Gunslinger Shane (Alan Ladd) wades into a dispute between an evil cattle baron and a hard toiling homesteader. After things come to a head in a saloon gunfight, Shane decides to move on, but inadvertently reveals he has been badly wounded and may die.

3 INCEPTION (2010)

Several viewings are required to even begin to understand the dream within a dream within a dream structure of Inception. Whether any amount of re-watching will illuminate us as to whether the final scene is 'real' is unclear.

2 THE THING (1982)

A shape-shifting alien invades an American Antarctic research station, picking off the scientists one by one. Eventually believing they've overcome the creature, two survivors sit at a camp fire awaiting rescue. But could one of them be the alien?

1 TAKE SHELTER (2011)

The patriarch of an Ohio family dreams of a terrible yellow storm and is compelled to build a shelter. When the storm doesn't come it seems he's suffering from mental illness. But in the final moments what looks like the storm of his nightmares appears to be gathering.

	MOVIE	DIRECTOR	AMBIGUITY
10	Lock, Stock and Two Smoking Barrels (1998)	Guy Ritchie	Are the priceless shotguns saved in time?
9	Cast Away (2000)	Robert Zemeckis	What's he going to do?
8	Five Easy Pieces (1970)	Bob Rafelson	What happens to Robert?
7	Pan's Labyrinth (2006)	Guillermo del Toro	Is Ofelia dead or safe in the underworld?
6	The King of Comedy (1983)	Martin Scorsese	Is Rupert a success or just crazy?
5	Anatomy of a Murder (1959)	Otto Preminger	Did Laura consent or not?
4	Shane (1953)	George Stevens	Does Shane live or die?
3	Inception (2010)	Christopher Nolan	Reality or dream?
2	The Thing (1982)	John Carpenter	Is Childs infected?
1	Take Shelter (2011)	Jeff Nichols	Is Curtis right, or mad?

TOP 10

This is not a list for villainous or murderous monsters, there are no serial killers or child abductors. This is a list for the sort of nasty, vindictive, manipulative types that enjoy making people miserable or would step over their own mother to get ahead.

MOVIE BITCHES

10 EVE HARRINGTON
Ambitious acting ingenue Eve ingratiates herself into the inner circle of established star Margo (Bette Davis). Then, like a persistence hunter, she stalks her prey until she finds weakness and strikes.

9 KATHARINE PARKER
After stealing her secretary Tess McGill's (Melanie Griffiths) plan for a client to diversify, Parker breaks her leg skiing and is forced off work for a spell. In her absence McGill decides to masquerade as the executive in order to get her own career moving.

8 CAPTAIN DOREEN LEWIS
After being conned into joining the army, Judy Benjamin (Goldie Hawn) finds herself under the thumb of Captain Lewis, a miserable, bullying old battle-axe with a vendetta against perky Judy.

7 NURSE RATCHED
Fletcher won an Academy Award for her portrayal of the sadistic nurse Ratched, who dominates the vulnerable patients of a mental institution. When her cruelty leads to the suicide of a popular resident, retribution very nearly costs her her life.

6 BABY JANE HUDSON
This time, Bette David dishes out rather than takes the abuse. She plays a former child star slowly losing her mind whilst tormenting her crippled sister Blanche (Joan Crawford).

5 REGINA GEORGE
The spiteful leader of high school in-crowd 'The Plastics', Regina gets a taste of her own medicine when new girl Cady Heron becomes Queen Bee. At least Regina learns her lesson... eventually.

4 MARGARET WHITE
Mother to the titular telekinetic teen, Maggie White

is a twisted religious fanatic who seems intent on battering the character out of her troubled daughter. But when the verbal abuse turns profoundly physical, Carries decides she's had enough.

3 LADY TREMAINE

The softly spoken stepmother to Cinderella, Lady Tremaine conceals a loathsome nature behind her demure demeanour. Cinderella is browbeaten into servitude, her life reduced to bowing to the every whim of her appalling stepsisters.

2 HEATHER CHANDLER

The ultimate teenage 'queen bee' persecutor must be Heather Chandler, the leader of the dominant clique (made up entirely

of girls called Heather) at her high school. After vowing to destroy Veronica Sawyer (Winona Ryder), who has embarrassed her, Sawyer and her boyfriend J.D. (Christian Slater) decide enough is enough and the terrible reign of 'The Heathers' must come to an end.

1 MRS. DANVERS

With an otherworldly calm and air of superiority that could intimidate the child of a Russian oligarch, the po-faced Danvers sets about destroying the confidence of her employers new wife (Joan Fontaine). She gives the impression of channeling the nameless bride's predecessor, who died in a boating accident the previous summer.... at least she probably died.

	CHARACTER	MOVIE	ACTOR
10	Eve Harrington	*All About Eve (1950)*	Anne Baxter
9	Katharine Parker	*Working Girl (1988)*	Sigourney Weaver
8	Captain Doreen Lewis	*Private Benjamin (1980)*	Eileen Brennan
7	Nurse Ratched	*One Flew Over the Cuckoo's Nest (1975)*	Louise Fletcher
6	Baby Jane Hudson	*What Ever Happened to Baby Jane? (1962)*	Bette Davis
5	Regina George	*Mean Girls (2004)*	Rachel McAdams
4	Margaret White	*Carrie (1976)*	Piper Laurie
3	Lady Tremaine	*Cinderella (1950)*	Eleanor Audley
2	Heather Chandler	*Heathers (1988)*	Kim Walker
1	Mrs. Danvers	*Rebecca (1940)*	Judith Anderson

TOP
10

Playing a real person generally recognised by the audience is considered to be amongst the greatest challengers an actor can take on. It's little wonder such roles have a reputation for attracting career-boosting acclaim, not to mention awards.

BIOPICS

10 YANKEE DODDLE DANDY (1942)

James Cagney is cast against type but excels as the vaudeville legend George M. Cohan, a role he'd wanted to play for years.

9 LA VIE EN ROSE (2007)

The extraordinary life of Édith Piaf (as the tagline ran) makes for an emotionally demanding but rewarding movie. The Little Sparrow, as she was known, inherited her mother's passion for singing and began plying her trade on the streets of Paris before finding international success.

8 LINCOLN (2012)

Spielberg's account of the 16th President of the United States features a bravura performance from Day-Lewis that perfectly matches the man's eminent historical standing.

7 THE SOCIAL NETWORK (2010)

The Social Network is a great demonstration of what makes a story work. On the face of it computer geeks setting up a website isn't the most intriguing of subjects. But Zuckerberg's mix of greed, competitiveness and passion ensure some of the oldest dramatic tropes are present and correct.

6 MALCOLM X (1992)

Spike Lee's heartfelt chronicle of the human rights activist and Muslim minister attracted controversy both before and after its release. It remains the rarest of things: a film of genuine social importance.

5 PERSEPOLIS (2007)
An unusual biopic in that it focuses on an unknown subject, *Persepolis* is the life story of a girl growing up in Iran after the defeat of the Shah in 1979. Her unwillingness to conform to the now strictly Islamic culture leads to many challenges.

4 24 HOUR PARTY PEOPLE (2002)
The highly charged music scene in Manchester, England in the 1980s is documented via this biopic of one of its leading lights. The brains behind both the infamous Hacienda nightclub and Factory Records label, Tony Wilson played a significant role in the 'Madchester' movement.

3 THE ELEPHANT MAN (1980)
The bleak tale of Joseph (aka John) Merrick, a severely deformed Victorian era sideshow curiosity who escaped a cycle of exploitation to live his final years in relative peace at The London Hospital.

2 TOPSY TURVY (1999)

Topsy Turvy at first appears to be something of a departure for Mike Leigh. But although the lush colour, focus on the upper class and brash performances appear out of character for the director, they neatly reflect Gilbert & Sullivan's style of opera. And as Leigh himself says, the film deals with character and narrative in the same way as his other work.

1 SCHINDLER'S LIST (1993)

Seldom has cinema presented us with such palpable visions of good and evil men. Schindler's altruism seems to know no bounds as he works to save Jews from the Nazi concentration camps of WWII. In contrast the unforgettable SS Officer Amon Goeth (a breathtaking Ralph Fiennes) is as loathsome a figure as any committed to film.

	MOVIE	SUBJECT	ACTOR(S)	DIRECTOR
10	*Yankee Doddle Dandy (1942)*	George M. Cohan	James Cagney	Michael Curtiz
9	*La Vie en Rose (2007)*	Édith Piaf	Marion Cotillard	Olivier Dahan
8	*Lincoln (2012)*	Abraham Lincoln	Daniel Day-Lewis	Steven Spielberg
7	*The Social Network (2010)*	Mark Zuckerberg	Jesse Eisenberg	David Fincher
6	*Malcolm X (1992)*	Malcolm X	Denzel Washington	Spike Lee
5	*Persepolis (2007)*	Marjene Satrapi	Chiara Mastroianni and Gabrielle Lopes Benites	Vincent Paronnaud and Marjane Satrapi
4	*24 Hour Party People (2002)*	Tony Wilson	Steve Coogan	Michael Winterbottom
3	*The Elephant Man (1980)*	Joseph Merrick	John Hurt	David Lynch
2	*Topsy Turvy (1999)*	Gilbert & Sullivan	Jim Broadbent and Allan Corduner	Mike Leigh
1	*Schindler's List (1993)*	Oskar Schindler	Liam Neeson	Steven Spielberg

TOP 10

Usually the term 'family movie' is a euphemism for 'kids movie', but not here. Unless they're a devout cynic each entry on this list should be just as entertaining for parents as kids, which is one of several reasons why *The Care Bears Movie* doesn't feature.

FAMILY MOVIES

10 WHERE THE WILD THINGS ARE (2009)

It's hard to imagine how such a slight book (just 338 words) could be adapted into a full length movie, but the extended narrative grows so naturally from the source text that you'd never guess it was so limited. Perhaps not one for very young children.

9 WALLACE & GROMIT IN THE WRONG TROUSERS (1993)

Arguably the highlight of Aardman Animation's popular *Wallace & Gromit* series. The Wrong Trousers sees the unlikely inventor and his faithful hound foiling a diamond robbery.

8 E.T. THE EXTRA-TERRESTRIAL (1982)

Little boy finds alien in his shed, movie history is made.

7 MY NEIGHBOUR TOTORO (1988)

A simple tale of two sisters who discover a forest spirit living near their new home. The 'Japanese Disney' Hayao Miyazaki found unprecedented success (eventually) with this gentle masterpiece.

6 THE WIZARD OF OZ (1939)

Recognised as the most watched movie in history, *The Wizard of Oz* is a curious mix of political allegory and musical fantasy. Literally something for all ages.

5 WILLY WONKA AND THE CHOCOLATE FACTORY (1971)

This first adaptation of Roald Dahl's children's book (titled *Charlie and the Chocolate Factory*) has all the charm and personality so lacking in the 2005 version. Gene Wilder was born to play the titular chocolatier, a mysterious, vaguely threatening figure we never really get a handle on.

4 THE PRINCESS BRIDE (1987)

Starting life as a bedtime story author and screenwriter William Goldman told his children, *The Princess Bride* is a throwback to the sort of wholesome fantasies that have long been out of fashion. With heroes, giants, villains and princesses it's comparable to a classic animated Disney movie but doesn't talk down to the children in the audience.

3 THE JUNGLE BOOK (1967)

And speaking of Disney, *The Jungle Book* must be amongst the most universally loved of all their movies. Light and frothy it may be, but there's more to appeal to the adult than the likes of *Snow White* or *The Little Mermaid* can offer.

2 TOY STORY (1995)

Pixar's debut movie is also the first fully CG feature, the first animated movie to be nominated for a best screenplay Academy Award, and the first to receive one for Special Achievement. But such accolades hardly matter when the brilliance of the storytelling and characterisation are so plain to see.

1 SPIRITED AWAY (2001)

Channeling *Alice In Wonderland*, Miyazaki's remarkable animé is a striking example of a great imagination let off the leash. He creates a stylish world of vivid colour, populating it with ambiguous creatures and bizarre architecture. If you can take the leap into a world of real fantasy, this is an unmissable experience.

	MOVIE	DIRECTOR	SEEN IT BUT WOULD LIKE SOMETHING SIMILAR?
10	Where the Wild Things Are (2009)	Spike Jonze	The Never Ending Story (1984)
9	Wallace & Gromit in The Wrong Trousers (1993)	Nick Park	Chicken Run (2000)
8	E.T. The Extra-Terrestrial (1982)	Steven Spielberg	Close Encounters of the Third Kind (1977)
7	My Neighbour Totoro (1988)	Hayao Miyazaki	Kiki's Delivery Service (1989)
6	The Wizard of Oz (1939)	Victor Fleming	Bedknobs and Broomsticks (1971)
5	Willy Wonka and the Chocolate Factory (1971)	Mel Stuart	Danny the Champion of the World (1989)
4	The Princess Bride (1987)	Rob Reiner	Stardust (2007)
3	The Jungle Book (1967)	Wolfgang Reitherman	Dumbo (1941)
2	Toy Story (1995)	John Lasseter	Shrek (2001)
1	Spirited Away (2001)	Hayao Miyazaki	Alice in Wonderland (1951)

TOP 10

Most creative mediums provide an outlet for artists compelled to criticise or highlight flaws in the world's pervasive authority systems. Cinema perhaps offers the most literal and universal opportunity, and as a result there are many movies that challenge the establishment in one way or another.

ANTI-ESTABLISHMENT MOVIES

10 PUNISHMENT PARK (1971)

In an alternate 1970, President Nixon decrees a state of emergency and sentences thousands of students, feminists and civil rights activists to Punishment Park. Essentially a desert full of trigger happy law enforcement trainees, the park is supposed to offer a chance of freedom to those who survive it for three days, but is actually corruptly controlled by the state.

9 FOOTLOOSE (1984)

The establishment can be the bigoted elders of a small town just as much as a dictatorial government. In his own way, Kevin Bacon's Ren McCormack is a revolutionary for the way he challenges the oppressive patriarchs of his small town.

8 THE LONELINESS OF THE LONG DISTANCE RUNNER (1962)

Part of the 'angry young men' creative strain (characterised by working class novelists and dramatists disillusioned with modern Britain), the movie focuses on a borstal boy who starts to question the privileged position he gains as a result of his sporting prowess.

7 REDS (1981)

An American journalist is caught up in the 1917 Russian Communist revolution and attempts to introduce some of its spirit to American shores.

6 NETWORK (1976)

One of the most prescient movies of the 1970s, *Network* is a satirical swipe at TV's quest for ratings.

5 PUTNEY SWOPE (1969)

Allegorical tale of an advertising firm which accidentally places it's only African American board member in charge. The radical, bizarre and hilarious changes he instigates lead to a unique working environment, and attract the unwelcome attentions of the US government.

4 THE NINTH CONFIGURATION (1980)

Set in an insane asylum for military personnel, what starts as a surreal farce soon becomes something far more serious as it begins to deal with the concepts of sanity, religion and suffering. Its examination of the American experience is hit and miss, some adore the movie, others hate it, but it's never less than fascinating.

3 ONE FLEW OVER THE CUCKOO'S NEST (1975)

R P McMurphy (Jack Nicholson), either mentally ill or feigning to avoid a prison sentence, fails to adapt to the authority of an unsympathetic and unyielding mental health institution.

2 EASY RIDER (1969)

A man went looking for America. And couldn't find it anywhere. Unquestionably one of the most important films ever made, *Easy Rider* is a searing strike at the values of an indifferent government and the corruption of the American dream.

1 IF... (1968)

The British class system is denounced for its inherent inequities in this brutally frank portrayal of life at an English boarding school.

After building to a surreal crescendo of violence the audience is left exhausted by a first class intellectual workout.

	MOVIE	DIRECTOR	THE ESTABLISHMENT IS REPRESENTED BY
10	*Punishment Park (1971)*	Peter Watkins	U.S. Government
9	*Footloose (1984)*	Herbert Ross	Bigoted town elders
8	*The Loneliness of the Long Distance Runner (1962)*	Tony Richardson	The British elite
7	*Reds (1981)*	Warren Beatty	U.S. Government
6	*Network (1976)*	Sidney Lumet	The media
5	*Putney Swope (1969)*	Robert Downey Sr.	The corporate system
4	*The Ninth Configuration (1980)*	William Peter Blatty	State, military and healthcare systems
3	*One Flew Over the Cuckoo's Nest (1975)*	Milos Forman	U.S. Government
2	*Easy Rider (1969)*	Dennis Hopper	Conventional America
1	*if... (1968)*	Lindsay Anderson	The British elite

TOP
10

A character paradigm that has lead to some of cinema's most memorable performances. Free from any responsibility to traditional behavioural codes, that their free will can be as intoxicating as their profligacy is disturbing. Tribute to Darth Vader.

VILLAINS

7 DR. SZELL
Anyone with a phobia of dentistry will remember Dr. Szell. The former Nazi, master criminal, double agent and torture enthusiast travels to America to sell jewels stolen from Jews in Auschwitz. So, all in all, not the most endearing of men.

6 SCAR
Disney's reputation for creating dazzlingly diabolical villains was further enhanced in 1994 with the release of *The Lion King*. Scar's betrayal of his family and attempt to seize control of their kingdom is Shakespearean in its malevolent skullduggery.

10 MR. POTTER
Henry F. Potter maintains an iron grip on Bedford Falls, the American town of which he is de facto boss. He exploits honest workers, intimidates anyone who challenges him and brings about the near suicide of his thoroughly decent rival.

9 SILVA
With so many great Bond villains over the years it's hard to single out just one. There may be more celebrated examples but Silva (Javier Bardem), the former agent turned megalomaniac, wins out through being so unique and enigmatic.

8 JANINE CODY
This brutal and utterly reprehensible matriarch of a Melbourne crime family has no compunction over doing what's necessary. When it comes to protecting her business, even killing her grandson doesn't require a second thought.

5 THE CHILD CATCHER
One sensation shared by almost everyone who saw *Chitty Chitty Bang Bang* as children is an almighty terror of the Child Catcher. His appearance, dressed all in black with bug-eyes and a

long, pointy nose, is enough to shiver the spine decades on.

4 NOAH CROSS

It was a stroke of genius to cast legendary director John Huston as the villain in this dark tale of greed and power. His physical presence suggests a man twisted by hate and bloated by avarice, his black soul all too apparent to anyone passing through his orbit.

3 COLONEL HANS LANDA

Flitting between friendly conversationist and brutal executioner in the blink of an eye, Nazi 'Jew hunter' Hans Landa is possibly the most memorable and certainly the most execrable of director Quentin Tarantino's

numerous villains.

2 KHAN NOONIEN SINGH

The superbly extravagant performance from Montalban is the most fun aspect to this popular entry in the Star Trek movie series. He's like a slightly mad, ageless matinee idol determined to do his own thing regardless of what's going on around him.

1 EDWIN EPPS

Fassbender's portrayal of a slave owner who believes he has a biblical right to beat, rape and murder who he chooses chills to the bone. That he is based on real people makes this monster even more terrifying, and the film itself even more essential.

	CHARACTER	MOVIE	ACTOR
10	Mr. Potter	It's a Wonderful Life (1946)	Lionel Barrymore
9	Silva	Skyfall (2012)	Javier Bardem
8	Janine Cody	Animal Kingdom (2010)	Jacki Weaver
7	Dr. Szell	Marathon Man (1976)	Laurence Olivier
6	Scar	The Lion King (1994)	Jeremy Irons
5	The Child Catcher	Chitty Chitty Bang Bang (1968)	Robert Helpmann
4	Noah Cross	Chinatown (1974)	John Huston
3	Colonel Hans Landa	Inglourious Basterds (2009)	Christoph Waltz
2	Khan Noonien Singh	Star Trek II: The Wrath of Khan (1982)	Ricardo Montalban
1	Edwin Epps	12 Years a Slave (2013)	Michael Fassbender

TOP 10

Whether the actor has a single line or plays an important second string character doesn't matter. They can appear as someone integral to proceedings or an irrelevant diversion. The only criteria for this list is that the part not be a lead, and that the actor do something remarkable with it.

SCENE-STEALING PERFORMANCES

10 MARGARET RUTHERFORD

The part of the irrepressibly mercurial medium who inadvertently causes havoc for a middle class couple could have been written for Rutherford.

9 EUGENE LEVY

This gross out comedy split audiences with it's crass but undeniably funny portrayal of high school boys looking for love. About the only thing everyone seems to agree on is that Eugene Levy is hilarious as Jim's lovably awkward Dad.

8 VIOLA DAVIS

When an actor can rely on their character being larger than life or somehow comical it's much easier for them to steal scenes. As the conflicted mother of a (possibly) sexually abused son, Davis has nothing but talent to rely on, and she doesn't come up short.

7 BOB PETERSON

More poignant than Pixar's usual fare, *Up* risks being hijacked by pathos at times. That it never quite happens is largely thanks to Dug, an infectiously exuberant talking dog who is just happy to have people to play with.

6 RALPH BROWN

Ralph Brown's iconic performance as the drug dealer to our eponymous heroes is unforgettable. Turning up out of the blue, he imparts profound wisdom, scathing analysis and utter gibberish in equal measure.

5 LEONARDO DICAPRIO

DiCaprio didn't become a mainstream icon until he starred in *Titanic* in 1997, but four years earlier he made a name for himself amongst movie buffs with an exceptional performance as a mentally handicapped young boy.

4 HEATH LEDGER

Even prior to his tragic death just a few months before the movie came out, Ledger's portrayal of Batman's nutty nemesis was tipped as something special. On release we realised just how special.

3 JUDI DENCH

With only eight minutes of screen time, Dame Judi Dench was a controversial winner of the best supporting actress Oscar for this performance. The fact she was able to do so much in such a short time is just one of the reasons she deserved it.

2 PETER SELLERS

Peter Sellers and director Stanley Kubrick would work together again on the more lauded *Doctor Strangelove*, but it's their first partnership that produced one of the definitive scene stealing performances. The sex obsessed writer Sellers plays here is equal parts hilarious and sinister, gliding in and out of scenes in pursuit of Lolita like a quietly determined shark.

1 ALEC BALDWIN

Baldwin steals the show so regularly he could have been the tribute for this list. If there's a single standout role it has to be Blake, the sharp suited motivational speaker who's sent by the owners of a real estate firm to shake things up amongst the sales team.

	ACTOR	CHARACTER	MOVIE
10	Margaret Rutherford	Madame Arcati	*Blithe Spirit (1945)*
9	Eugene Levy	Jim's Dad	*American Pie (1999)*
8	Viola Davis	Mrs. Miller	*Doubt (2008)*
7	Bob Peterson	Dug	*Up (2009)*
6	Ralph Brown	Danny	*Withnail and I (1987)*
5	Leonardo DiCaprio	Arnie Grape	*What's Eating Gilbert Grape (1993)*
4	Heath Ledger	The Joker	*The Dark Knight (2008)*
3	Judi Dench	Queen Elizabeth	*Shakespeare In Love (1998)*
2	Peter Sellers	Clare Quilty	*Lolita (1962)*
1	Alec Baldwin	Blake	*Glengarry Glenross (1992)*

TOP 10

With such an abundance of prominent war movies it seems a good idea to perform a flanking manoeuvre on the genre. By limiting the list to movies showing war from a perspective different to the norm, it might highlight both some original choices and contrasting viewpoints.

WAR MOVIES WITH A DIFFERENT PERSPECTIVE

10 HEAVEN AND EARTH (1993)

Based on the true story of Le Ly Hayslip (Hiep Thi Le), an ordinary villager struggling to survive the Vietnam war. She is forced to take on many different roles: revolutionary, wife, prostitute, drug courier and swindler in order to support herself and her child.

9 ENEMY AT THE GATES (2001)

During the Battle of Stalingrad an expanded game of cat and mouse is played out between two expert snipers, Russian Vasili Zaytsev (Jude Law), and German Erwin König (Ed Harris).

8 CULLODEN (1964)

The Battle of Culloden (in which British forces crushed the Scottish Jacobite uprising) is re-staged in this faux documentary and examined from both sides. Everything is presented as if cameras were filming a fly on the wall documentary on the battle.

7 COME AND SEE (1985)

After stumbling on a rifle a young and idealistic Belarusian boy decides to join the Soviet Army opposing Nazi Germany during WWII. Expecting heroism and honour he finds nothing but horror and misery.

6 SOLDIER OF ORANGE (1977)

As WWII breaks out a group of Dutch friends pick sides. Some are only too willing to fall in line with the Nazi ideology, others become fighters with the resistance.

5 TORA! TORA! TORA! (1970)

Uniquely shot as two separate productions (one in the U.S. the other in Japan, both using local crews) *Tora! Tora! Tora!* attempts to be the last word on the attack on Pearl Harbour, presenting the events as factually as possible and from the perspective of both sides.

4 DOWNFALL (2004)

Often cited as the first German movie to portray Hitler, *Downfall* is a study of the dictator's last weeks, holed up in his Berlin bunker. Star Bruno Ganz initially turned the role down, understandably uncomfortable with the idea of playing Hitler. Both his performance and the resulting film have become universally respected.

3 CROSS OF IRON (1977)

A fairly straight forward WWII movie, only told from the 'other' side. Issues of morality and honour are addressed in much the way they would be by the allied forces, and we learn class warfare and petty rivalries were as much of an issue for the Nazis as any other army.

2 LETTERS FROM IWO JIMA (2006)

Eastwood's brace of epic war films (the other being *Flags of Our Fathers* (2006)) show the battle of Iwo Jima from both sides. Here the action is seen from the Japanese viewpoint, in particular that of commanding officer General Kuribayashi (Ken Watanabe), who is at odds with the harshness and rigidity of the Japanese army.

1 DAS BOOT (1981)

The crew of a German U-Boat suffer incredible hardships as they attempt to stay alive. Lesser priorities include maintaining a sense of decency whilst trying to understand the philosophy of the Nazi regime they're forced to serve.

	MOVIE	DIRECTOR(S)
10	*Heaven and Earth (1993)*	Oliver Stone
9	*Enemy at the Gates (2001)*	Jean-Jacques Annaud
8	*Culloden (1964)*	Peter Watkins
7	*Come and See (1985)*	Elem Klimov
6	*Soldier of Orange (1977)*	Paul Verhoeven
5	*Tora! Tora! Tora! (1970)*	Richard Fleischer, Kinji Fukasaku and Toshio Masuda
4	*Downfall (2004)*	Oliver Hirschbiegel
3	*Cross of Iron (1977)*	Sam Peckinpah
2	*Letters from Iwo Jima (2006)*	Clint Eastwood
1	*Das Boot (1981)*	Wolfgang Peterson

TOP 10

The shadowy world in which the movie P.I. tends to operate can have a seductive appeal for an audience. P.I.'s travel light, play both sides as necessary and will make their own rules. They're free spirits, answering to nothing but their own personal morality. By virtue of his being a consulting detective rather than private investigator (though the difference is unclear), but more the fact he's such an obvious choice, this is a tribute to Sherlock Holmes.

PRIVATE INVESTIGATORS

10 EDDIE VALIANT
The late Bob Hoskins seems to have a whale of a time as Roger Rabbit's toon-hating, and extremely reluctant, partner.

9 HARRY ANGEL
Mickey Rourke crackles with charisma as Harry Angel, a downtrodden and bedraggled detective hired to find a long forgotten musician.

8 MIKE HAMMER
Mickey Spillane's Mike Hammer is brought to life in all his brutal, misanthropic glory in this second of many big screen incarnations. Although not the preferred choice of the author, Meeker is superb as Hammer, a P.I. more prone to violence and cynicism than eminent contemporaries such as Sam Spade and Philip Marlowe.

7 JEFF BAILEY
The archetypal 'you can't escape your past' film noir, director Jacques Tourneur and writer Daniel Mainwaring infuse the movie with a palpable forboding doom.

6 IRWIN M 'FLETCH' FLETCHER
Chevy Chases's iconic creation is a sublimely indifferent fruitcake of a detective. Constantly on the brink of bankruptcy, eviction and even imprisonment, Fletch's apparently incompetent investigation technique masks a sharp mind and astute moral compass.

5 JOHN SHAFT
Although the character's origins were seemingly forgotten as he morphed into James Bond over the course of the sequels, Shaft was originally an uncompromising private dick ('that's a sex machine to all the chicks', of course) fighting injustice on the streets of Harlem.

4 PHILIP MARLOWE
A sort of revisionist or neo noir, *The Long Goodbye* transposes Raymond

Chandler's illustrious detective from his 1940s natural habitat to the more pessimistic 1970s. His struggle to be a decent man in a selfish and corrupt time adds a unique and fascinating dimension.

3 JAKE GITTES

One of the great Jack Nicholson's seminal performances sees his Jake Gittes embroiled in a complicated murder plot related to the fraudulent machinations of the Los Angeles power elite of the late 1930s.

2 SAM SPADE

Bogart gives arguably the quintessential portrayal of the private dick in this John Huston directed classic about criminals squabbling over a priceless statuette. Spade is a wily sort, but even he struggles to keep it together when distracted by the obligatory femme fatale.

1 NICK CHARLES

After marrying beautiful heiress Nora (Myrna Loy), former detective Nick Charles is repeatedly drawn back into the criminal underworld when one eccentric old friend or another needs his help. The light-hearted wit with which he approaches each unwanted case, usually after having his arm twisted by the more adventurous Nora, is central to the appeal of these brilliantly funny movies.

	CHARACTER	MOVIE	ACTOR
10	Eddie Valiant	Who Framed Roger Rabbit (1988)	Bob Hoskins
9	Harry Angel	Angel Heart (1987)	Mickey Rourke
8	Mike Hammer	Kiss Me Deadly (1955)	Ralph Meeker
7	Jeff Bailey	Out of the Past (1947)	Robert Mitchum
6	Irwin M. 'Fletch' Fletcher	Fletch and Fletch Lives (1985 & 1989)	Chevy Chase
5	John Shaft	The original Shaft series (1971-1973))	Richard Roundtree
4	Philip Marlowe	The Long Goodbye (1973)	Elliot Gould
3	Jake Gittes	Chinatown (1974)	Jack Nicholson
2	Sam Spade	The Maltese Falcon (1941)	Humphrey Bogart
1	Nick Charles	The series (1934-1947)	William Powell

TOP
10

Playing God seems to be the prevalent pastime of the mad scientist, spooky old castles his preferred domain. Probably inspired by forerunners such as Archimedes and the mythological Daedalus, the mad scientist can exist almost anywhere on the good/evil spectrum with no prerequisite to be villainous, though trouble will inevitably result from his unholy tinkering with the nature of things. Tribute to Doctor Frankenstein.

MAD SCIENTISTS

10 DR. HANS ZARKOV
Topol's eccentric Hans Zarkov is concerned by the strange weather conditions on earth so he builds a spaceship in order to investigate a distant star system he believes to be the source of the storms.

9 DR. CATHETER
The sinister Dr, Catheter, head of research at the heartless Clamp corporation, gets his hands on Gizmo, the lovable mogwai from the first film. Lee wanted to crank up the comedy inherent in Catheter's cartoon villain persona but, fortunately for us, he's played straight down the line.

8 DR. HERBERT WEST
In Mad Scientist: The College Years a series of experiments that begin with student doctor Herbert West reanimating a dead cat leads to him decapitating a lecturer and bringing the head back to life.

7 THE INVENTOR
Like a tragic, goth Pinocchio, Edward Scissorhands was made to be like a real boy by the mercurial Inventor (one of Vincent Price's last roles). Unfortunately the Inventor died before Edward was finished, leaving him to take care of himself in a crumbling mansion... and with blades where his hands should be.

6 DR. MICHAEL HFUHRUHURR
Hfuhruhurr's complicated love life has already seen him widowed and then married to a gold digging schemer, but his real troubles start when he falls in love with a brain in a jar. Already famous for developing the 'cranial screw-top' brain surgery technique, Hfuhruhurr has a plan to implant the brain in a new body... if only he can find one.

5 DR. MOREAU
The original and best take on H.G. Wells' *The Island of Dr. Moreau*, about a scientist who splices humans with animals.

4 DR. FRANK-N-FURTER
Loony Frank-N-Furter, the transvestite spoof of Dr. Frankenstein, becomes jealous when his creation prefers the company of Janet (Susan Sarandon).

3 DR. EMMETT BROWN
Doc Brown's iconic DeLorean time machine is a symbol of the 80's, much like the denim ensemble worn throughout the movie by Marty McFly.

2 DR. PRETORIUS
Having succeeded in creating human life in miniature, Pretorius is eager to work with Dr. Frankenstein

and further develop his ideas. But even Frankenstein finds Pretorius' God delusion a little worrying.

1 DR. STRANGELOVE

This former Nazi scientist's big idea is to move civilisation underground in the face of a nuclear threat from Russia. The high proportion of women (who must all be attractive in order to help facilitate the rebuilding of the human race) to men clearly has nothing to do with his enthusiasm for the plan.

	CHARACTER	MOVIE	ACTOR
10	Dr. Hans Zarkov	*Flash Gordon (1980)*	Topol
9	Dr. Catheter	*Gremlins 2: The New Batch (1990)*	Christopher Lee
8	Dr. Herbert West	*Re-Animator (1985)*	Jeffrey Combs
7	The Inventor	*Edward Scissorhands (1990)*	Vincent Price
6	Dr. Michael Hfuhruhurr	*The Man With Two Brains (1983)*	Steve Martin
5	Dr. Moreau	*The Island of Lost Souls (1932)*	Charles Laughton
4	Dr. Frank-N-Furter	*The Rocky Horror Picture Show (1975)*	Tim Curry
3	Dr. Emmett Brown	*Back to the Future series (1985-1990)*	Christopher Lloyd
2	Dr. Pretorius	*The Bride of Frankenstein (1935)*	Ernest Thesiger
1	Dr. Strangelove	*Dr. Strangelove (1964)*	Peter Sellers

TOP 10

Two people taking it in turns to kick each other is not an inherently interesting spectacle for most moviegoers. But the martial arts genre has much more to offer, particularly if one delves into the best its Asian homelands have to offer.

MARTIAL ARTS MOVIES FOR PEOPLE WHO DON'T LIKE MARTIAL ARTS MOVIES

10 JUDO STORY (1943)
Through Judo, Sanshiro (Susumu Fujita), a youth with an attitude problem, learns about what's important in life.

9 LONE WOLF MCQUADE (1983)
In what is easily Chuck Norris's best movie (exactly what that means is a matter of opinion) the multiple karate champion plays eponymous Texas Ranger McQuade, a man out to avenge the death of his partner and bring down a ruthless drug dealer.

8 THE LEGEND OF DRUNKEN MASTER (1994)
Jackie Chan's last significant Hong Kong movie before his focus switched to a spell in Hollywood is chock-full of his trademark slapstick.

7 REDBELT (2008)
It might seem like renowned playwright David Mamet is out of his comfort zone with this story about a skilled martial arts trainer who vows never to fight again. But what little fighting there is is purely a dramatic device,

which puts Mamet on very familiar ground.

6 MR. VAMPIRE (1985)
Featuring villainous hopping zombie-vampires that can be stopped only by kung fu or a post-it note to the forehead, Mr. Vampire is a fine example of the wacky imagination at play in the Hong Kong action cinema of the 1980s.

5 POLICE STORY (1985)
Fast paced action packed and brimming with charm, *Police Story* is essentially a traditional crime caper but with the added acrobatics of a Jackie Chan on top form.

4 KUNG FU HUSTLE (2004)
This manic cross between the cartoons of Chuck Jones, classic martial arts cinema and the Three Stooges is impossible not to love. Writer,

JACKIE CHAN

UN FILM

producer, director and star Stephen Chow's second movie to break out in the west is a brilliantly constructed fable about heroic martial artists saving the put upon residents of a slum from the villainous Axe Gang.

3 KILL BILL: VOL. 1 & 2 (2003 & 2004)
After being left for dead by her partner and colleagues, a supremely talented assassin

sets off in search of retribution. Channelling the 1970s exploitation craze for violent revenge movies, and doing it with style, Tarantino's epic tale is a modern classic.

2 HERO (2002)
Nameless, the prefect of a small territory in ancient China, arrives at the palace of ruler Qin. Qin has been subject to a series of

assassination attempts by agents of his rivals, but Nameless claims to have beaten each in combat. The fights are presented as stand alone flash back sequences, with the grade and production design colour coordinated with visual cues to give each account a unique look and feel.

1 CROUCHING TIGER, HIDDEN DRAGON (2000)

Threads involving forbidden love, the theft of a priceless sword, bandit kidnappers, honour and vengeance are all successfully juggled by Ang Lee, a director more associated with traditional prestige films than Wuxia.

	MOVIE	DIRECTOR	STARRING	MIGHT APPEAL TO FANS OF
10	*Judo Story (1943)*	Akira Kurosawa	Susumu Fujita	Classical Japanese Cinema
9	*Lone Wolf Mc-Quade (1983)*	Steve Carver	Chuck Norris	Westerns
8	*The Legend of Drunken Master (1994)*	Chia-Liang Liu	Jackie Chan	Slapstick
7	*Redbelt (2008)*	David Mamet	Chiwetel Ejiofor	Drama
6	*Mr. Vampire (1985)*	Ricky Lau	Lam Ching-ying	Hopping Vampires
5	*Police Story (1985)*	Jackie Chan	Jackie Chan	Police Procedurals
4	*Kung Fu Hustle (2004)*	Stephen Chow	Stephen Chow	Chuck Jones Cartoons
3	*Kill Bill: Vol. 1 & 2 (2003 & 2004)*	Quentin Tarantino	Uma Thurman	Style and Revenge
2	*Hero (2002)*	Yimou Zhang	Jet Li	Arthouse Cinema
1	*Crouching Tiger, Hidden Dragon (2000)*	Ang Lee	Michelle Yeoh	Repressed Feelings

TOP 10

Although fascination with celebrity seems to have reached some sort of zenith in recent times, filmmakers have been preoccupied with analysing and deconstructing the nature of fame for decades. That in itself shows us the desire to be famous has probably been a problematic phenomenon for longer than many of us realise.

MOVIES ABOUT CELEBRITY

10 I'M STILL HERE (2010)

This fictional documentary follows Joaquin Phoenix as he claims to be retiring from acting to pursue his real dreams. Phoenix took method acting to a new level, spending a year pretending his attempt to make it as a rapper was genuine, and upsetting a lot of industry bigwigs in the process.

9 BRIGHT YOUNG THINGS (2003)

Evelyn Waugh's account of the 1930's 'it crowd', adapted from his second novel *Vile Bodies*.

8 CELEBRITY (1998)

A vapid wannabe novelist tries to penetrate celebrity cliques in order to raise his own stock and enjoy some of the advantages reaped by the rich and famous. Unsurprisingly the attempts prove both fruitless and soul destroying.

7 THE BLING RING (2013)

The true story of a group of fame obsessed Californian students who took to burgling the homes of Hollywood stars in order to snatch a small taste of the lifestyle they so craved.

6 KING OF COMEDY (1982)

Made when both Scorsese and star Robert De Niro were at the peak of their powers, and addressing an issue more pertinent now than ever before, it's odd this dryly satirical masterpiece is still so neglected.

5 ALMOST FAMOUS (2000)

Teenage music fan and wannabe writer William Miller (Patrick Fugit) lands a dream assignment covering an up-and

-coming rock band for *Rolling Stone* magazine. But how will he react to being thrown head first into the world of celebrity narcissism?

4 BYE BYE BIRDIE (1963)

Inspired by the career of Elvis Presley, *Bye Bye Birdie* uses a musical comedy format to examine the nature of fame, though it's more interested in giving the audience a rollicking good time.

3 LA DOLCE VITA (1960)

La Dolce Vita spends a week following Rome based gossip magazine columnist Marcello (Marcello Mastroianni) as he fails to find anything rewarding or satisfying in his life. The emptiness of celebrity is laid bare with a crushingly authoritative certainty.

2 SUNSET BOULEVARD (1950)

Gloria Swanson plays Norma Desmond, once a giant of the silent film era but now largely forgotten and reduced to shuffling around her decrepit Hollywood mansion almost alone. Desperate for a comeback vehicle she gets her claws into distinctly average screenwriter Joe Gillis (William Holden), but her obsession leads to misery, madness and murder.

1 TO DIE FOR (1995)

An ambitious TV weather girl hatches a plan to kill her husband, who she perceives is standing in the way of the success to which she is entitled. This strikingly prescient movie takes a satirical look at the lengths people are prepared to go in order to achieve stardom.

	MOVIE	DIRECTOR
10	I'm Still Here (2010)	Casey Affleck
9	Bright Young Things (2003)	Stephen Fry
8	Celebrity (1998)	Woody Allen
7	The Bling Ring (2013)	Sofia Coppola
6	King of Comedy (1982)	Martin Scorsese
5	Almost Famous (2000)	Cameron Crowe
4	Bye Bye Birdie (1963)	George Sidney
3	La Dolce Vita (1960)	Federico Fellini
2	Sunset Boulevard (1950)	Billy Wilder
1	To Die For (1995)	Gus Van Sant

TOP
10

Whether examining the nature of prisons or merely using incarceration as part of a dramatic structure, prison movies provide all sorts of opportunities to present exciting escape attempts, oppressive regimes, social conflict and more. Although technically a different genre if we're being pedantic, POW movies are included here.

PRISON MOVIES

10 CHICKEN RUN (2000)
The first feature length movie from Wallace and Gromit creator Nick Park sees a farm full of chickens intent on escape.

9 LA GRANDE ILLUSION (1937)
A philosophical look at life in a German POW fortress during WWI. Von Rauffenstein (Erich von Stroheim) could be a worse commandant, but attempting to escape is a way of life for prisoners of war.

8 STALAG 17 (1953)
J J Sefton (William Holden), an American Sergeant, runs all the scams in WWII POW camp Stalag 17. But he's also more chummy with the guards than his fellow prisoners find comfortable. When they realise an informant has been tipping off the Germans to escape attempts, Sefton is put in the spotlight.

7 RESCUE DAWN (2006)
Dieter Dengler, a German pilot serving the U.S.A. in the Vietnam war is shot down and held captive in the jungles of Laos. Having already made an excellent documentary (1997's *Little Dieter Needs to Fly*) on Dengler's experiences, which included seeing his friend beheaded and trekking barefoot through miles of jungle, Werner Herzog is familiar enough with his subject to lace the film with authentic detail.

6 FEMALE PRISONER 701: SCORPION (1972)
Framed by her lover, a corrupt cop, Nami Matsushina (Meiko Kaji) becomes a liability in the brutal prison to which she's sentenced. Plans are afoot to have her killed, but she has her own plan to escape.

5 HUNGER (2008)
Republican inmates of Northern Ireland's notorious Maze prison embark on an idealogical hunger strike, led by the charismatic Bobby Sands (Michael Fassbender).

4 MIDNIGHT EXPRESS (1978)
The terrifying true story of Billy Hayes (Brad Davis), an American tourist caught trying to smuggle hashish out of Turkey. Sentenced to four years in the atrocious squalor of a Turkish prison, he soon realises the environment is

perilous and the system corrupt, and escape is his only option.

3 A PROPHET (2009)

Nineteen year old Algerian Malik El Djebena (Tahar Rahim) is sentenced to six years in a French prison for attacking police officers. Whilst inside he learns to play the complicated political game of survival and rises slowly through the ranks of the dominant Corsican mob.

2 ESCAPE FROM ALCATRAZ (1979)

Although officials like to say nobody ever escaped from Alcatraz, there's a good chance Frank Morris (here played by Clint Eastwood) managed it. He certainly got out and into the water, though whether he made it to shore alive is unclear.

1 THE SHAWSHANK REDEMPTION (1994)

Andy Dufrasne (Tim Robbins), an innocent man jailed for the murder of his wife, finds solace in friendship with a fellow inmate.

	MOVIE	DIRECTOR(S)
10	Chicken Run (2000)	Peter Lord and Nick Park
9	La Grande Illusion (1937)	Jean Renoir
8	Stalag 17 (1953)	Billy Wilder
7	Rescue Dawn (2006)	Werner Herzog
6	Female Prisoner 701: Scorpion (1972)	Shunya Ito
5	Hunger (2008)	Steve McQueen
4	Midnight Express (1978)	Alan Parker
3	A Prophet (2009)	Jacques Audiard
2	Escape from Alcatraz (1979)	Don Siegel
1	The Shawshank Redemption (1994)	Frank Darabont

TOP 10

The great French director Jean-Luc Godard once observed, 'all you need for a movie is a gun and a girl.' Whilst there's possibly a touch of hyperbole to the statement, there's also some truth. The gun is the ultimate dramatic device, introduce one to a scene, almost any scene, and the dynamic changes completely. But when everyone has a gun the drama is simply amplified... enormously. Tribute to Sergio Leone.

SHOOT-OUTS

10 THE MATRIX (1999)
Neo (Keanu Reeves) and Trinity (Carrie-Anne Moss) spring their leader Morpheus (Laurence Fishburne) from The Agents. Hyper real skills make for a breakneck battle while inordinate firepower guarantees the carnage.

9 BUGSY MALONE (1976)
Fat Sam's Speak Easy hosts the chaotic showdown between rival gangs in this kids classic. Bullets are replaced with custard, but apart from that it's authentic enough to expect Jimmy Cagney to pop up with a splurge gun.

8 SHOOT 'EM UP (2007)
Mr Smith saves a heavily pregnant woman from a hitman, only for the hitman's reinforcements to arrive just as the woman goes into labour. Smith simultaneously delivers the baby and fights off the bad guys.

7 HOT FUZZ (2007)
After uncovering a cult in a pleasant English town, cops Nicholas Angel (Simon Pegg) and Danny Butterman (Nick Frost) discover the conspiracy goes deeper than they ever imagined as half the town come out shooting.

6 THE UNTOUCHABLES (1987)
Referencing one of the most famous scenes in cinema (the 'Odessa Steps' sequence from *Battleship Potemkin*), this gunfight on the steps of Chicago's Union Station builds to the infamous 'baby carriage catch'.

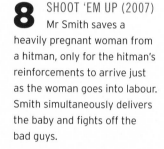

5 THE SHOOTIST (1976)
Dying of cancer, former gunslinger John Books (John Wayne) decides he has unfinished business. Knowing it will be his last day on earth he invites three men to a saloon in order to settle some scores with them.

4 HARD BOILED (1992)
In one three minute take, two cops take out a small army of gun smugglers hiding out in a hospital. It's scenes like this that gave director John Woo his reputation for being the foremost action-filmmaker of his generation.

3 DESPERADO (1995)
With a guitar case full of guns and a blind determination to avenge the death of his loved one, el Mariachi (Antonio Banderas) shoots his way from saloon to saloon in a timeless movie heavily influenced by Western tropes.

2 HEAT (1995)
Bank robber Neil McCauley (Robert De Niro) wants to make one last, big hit before retirement. Caught in the act, McCauley and his gang shoot their way through LA while being pursued by cop Vincent Hanna (Al Pacino).

1 THE WILD BUNCH (1969)
From the opening frames of *The Wild Bunch* the viewer senses this is how it has to end. Pike (William Holden) fronts the final stand against a corrupt element of the Mexican army after one of his posse is murdered.

	MOVIE	DIRECTOR(S)	BETWEEN	LOCATION
10	The Matrix (1999)	Andy Wachowski and Lana Wachowski	Goodies and baddies	The Matrix
9	Bugsy Malone (1976)	Alan Parker	Rival gangs	Chicago Speak Easy
8	Shoot 'Em Up (2007)	Michael Davis	Gangsters and a drifter	Warehouse
7	Hot Fuzz (2007)	Edgar Wright	Cops and cultists	Quaint English town
6	The Untouchables (1987)	Brian De Palma	Government agents and Al Capone	Chicago's Union Station
5	The Shootist (1976)	Don Siegel	Dying gunslinger and bad guys	Saloon in Carson City
4	Hard Boiled (1992)	John Woo	Cops and gun smugglers	Hospital
3	Desperado (1995)	Robert Rodriguez	Desperado and general scum	Mexican Saloon
2	Heat (1995)	Michael Mann	Cops and bank robbers	Downtown Los Angeles
1	The Wild Bunch (1969)	Sam Peckinpah	Bank robbers and the Mexican army	Mexican town Agua Verde

TOP
10

Although not the mainstream mainstay they once were, concert films are still the purest means of combining music with moving imagery. And, with such a diverse and extensive back catalogue, they will always be of value to music and movie fans alike.

CONCERT MOVIES

10 THE CONCERT FOR BANGLADESH (1972)
Some of the biggest stars of the day are brought together by Beatle George Harrison for a benefit concert in aid of refugees of the Bangladesh Liberation War.

9 STOP MAKING SENSE (1984)
Shot over three nights at the Pantages Theater in Hollywood, *Stop Making Sense* helped revolutionise the way sound is recorded for movies. It also represents a bold new approach to concert films in the way the audience are integrated and the footage shot.

8 THE WHITE STRIPES UNDER GREAT WHITE NORTHERN LIGHTS (2009)
At the height of their popularity The White Stripes play a series of gigs across Canada, some in stadiums, some in bus shelters and cafes.

The relationship between band members Meg and Jack White is as fascinating as their unique performing style.

7 NEIL YOUNG: HEART OF GOLD (2006)
During an emotionally charged summer for Neil Young (his life was being threatened by a cerebral aneurysm and his father had just died), concerts at the Ryman Auditorium in Nashville were filmed by concert film legend Jonathan Demme. At the request of the director, Young abandons plans to play only material from his new album and performs a second set of classic songs. The audience should thank Demme.

6 HEIMA (2007)
Ethereal Icelandic post-rock peddlers Sigur Rós play a triumphant series of homecoming shows over the summer of 2006.

5 ZIGGY STARDUST AND THE SPIDERS FROM MARS (1973)
When the film was recorded at London's Hammersmith Apollo in July 1973, David Bowie had already performed the show 60 times over the previous two months. What was meant to be the midway point of a world tour ended up being the final performance of his Ziggy Stardust persona.

4 THE SONG REMAINS THE SAME (1976)
After several failed attempts to pin down a Led Zeppelin gig on film, it was finally nailed over the summer of 1973. A series of typically mystical and far out interludes break up some incredible concert footage from New York's enormous Madison Square Garden.

3 MONTEREY POP (1968)
This hugely influential movie provides a snapshot of life at the heart of the

counterculture when optimism was still its dominant force.

2 GIMME SHELTER (1970)

The final stage of the Rolling Stones' 1969 U.S. tour is chronicled by eminent documentarians Albert and David Maysles. The tour includes the infamous Altamont concert which saw the tragic death of fan Meredith Hunter, thanks (in part) to the decision to have the Hells Angels provide security.

1 THE LAST WALTZ (1978)

A simply stunning array of musicians accompany The Band for their 1976 farewell concert at the Winterland Ballroom in San Francisco (where they had debuted just seven years earlier). The likes of Bob Dylan, Van Morrison, Neil Young, Eric Clapton, Muddy Waters and dozens of others join the group for an incredibly atmospheric 'live' performance.

	MOVIE	ACT(S)	DIRECTOR(S)
10	The Concert for Bangladesh (1972)	George Harrison, Bob Dylan, Eric Clapton etc.	Saul Swimmer
9	Stop Making Sense (1984)	Talking Heads	Jonathan Demme
8	The White Stripes Under Great White Northern Lights (2009)	The White Stripes	Emmett Malloy
7	Neil Young: Heart of Gold (2006)	Neil Young	Jonathan Demme
6	Heima (2007)	Sigur Rós	Dean DeBlois
5	Ziggy Stardust and the Spiders from Mars (1973)	Ziggy Stardust and the Spiders from Mars	D.A. Pennebaker
4	The Song Remains the Same (1976)	Led Zeppelin	Peter Clifton and Joe Massot
3	Monterey Pop (1968)	Otis Redding, Jimi Hendrix, The Who etc.	D.A. Pennebaker
2	Gimme Shelter (1970)	The Rolling Stones	The Maysles Bros.
1	The Last Waltz (1978)	The Band and friends	Martin Scorsese

TOP 10

Whether or not young children can genuinely act, or are merely following instructions, is a question such performers have always faced. Can children truly understand character motivations and emotions? When the end result is as good as these entries does it even matter?

PERFORMANCES BY CHILDREN

10 CLAUDIA
The eternally young Claudia is saved from a grim death at the hands of the plague when she is bitten by, and turned into, a vampire.

9 COLE SEAR
Haley Joel Osment was nominated for a best supporting actor Academy Award for his sensitive portrayal of Cole Sear, a downcast little boy with the ability to see dead people walking among us.

8 DAVID ZELLABY
Every woman of childbearing age in the British village of Midwych suddenly falls simultaneously pregnant. The resulting children, each of which has a shock of white hair and unnervingly calm disposition, soon start to exhibit strange characteristics. The deeply creepy David spearheads the campaign to undermine or destroy those who challenge them in their mysterious objectives.

7 CLARK 'MOUTH' DEVEREAUX
In the 80's if you needed a cocky but appealing youth to do some light charming, you went to Corey Feldman. He never quite managed the transition to adult star, relegated as he is to the bottom end of the B-movie quality spectrum.

6 OLIVE HOOVER
Precocious Olive drives the narrative in this quirky tale of a family of misfits on a road trip to a child beauty pageant.

5 PHILLIPE
Phillipe, the son of a French diplomat in London, idolises butler Baines (Ralph Richardson), who recognises how lonely the boy is and regales him with fantastical tales. After an argument leads to an accident, Baines' wife dies in a fall witnessed by the boy, but confused over what he saw Phillipe wrongly forms the impression Baines killed her. There's wonderful nuance in Davies' performance, managing to portray Phillipe's isolated vulnerability without it ever becoming mawkish.

4 OLIVER TWIST
As the angelic orphan Oliver Twist is bounced from one exploitative surrogate to another, Davies perfectly captures his naive vulnerability. The most celebrated section of the film sees him paired with another top notch child performance in Anthony Newley's Artful Dodger. Both would find considerable success in different roles, with Davies becoming a successful TV producer and Newley a pop star.

3 ANTOINE DOINEL
With mother, stepfather and teachers unable, or

unwilling, to offer Antoine the simple affection the troubled adolescent needs, we must watch a profound tragedy unfold as he's trapped by a system that will unfairly brand him for life.

2 IRIS
Jodie Foster's lauded performance as child prostitute Iris is a touchstone for all young actors.

1 MATHILDA
Like so many on this list, Mathilda is a troubled child searching for a father figure outside her family. She finds one in the unlikely form of Leon, a taciturn neighbour who just happens to be a mob hitman.

	CHARACTER	MOVIE	ACTOR
10	Claudia	*Interview With the Vampire (1994)*	Kirsten Dunst
9	Cole Sear	*The Sixth Sense (1999)*	Haley Joel Osment
8	David Zellaby	*Village of the Damned (1960)*	Martin Stephens
7	Clark 'Mouth' Devereaux	*The Goonies (1985)*	Corey Feldman
6	Olive Hoover	*Little Miss Sunshine (2006)*	Abigail Breslin
5	Phillipe	*The Fallen Idol (1948)*	Bobby Henrey
4	Oliver Twist	*Oliver Twist (1948)*	John Howard Davies
3	Antoine Doinel	*The 400 Blows (1959)*	Jean-Pierre Leaud
2	Iris	*Taxi Driver (1976)*	Jodie Foster
1	Mathilda	*Leon aka The Professional (1994)*	Natalie Portman

TOP 10

Time to put pen to paper and create your own top 10 list of spy movies...

10

9

8

7

6

5

4

3

2

1

Spies come in many guises. Cold war agents sneaking micro film across borders, swaggering action men leaping from trains, desk-bound suits pulling strings from afar. The shadowy world of espionage is an excellent breeding ground for fascinating movie characters.

SPIES AND SECRET AGENTS

10 ALEC LEAMAS
A proper cold war spy thriller with Richard Burton as the maybe double agent at the heart of a complicated conspiracy. Based on the novel by legendary author John Le Carre, Burton won a BAFTA for his hypnotic performance.

9 JANE SMITH
The improbable story of a husband and wife who are both freelance spies/assassins, but neither of whom knows the truth about the other. Although presented as an action movie it's actually more of a rollicking romcom. With guns.

8 OSBOURNE COX
Disillusioned CIA analyst Osbourne Cox is trying to write his memoirs. In the space of a few days he's sacked, divorced and then blackmailed by a moronic personal trainers who believe they have acquired a data disc of national importance.

7 MRS. ISELIN
Brainwashing, Frank

Sinatra and one of the most memorably chilling performances in cinema from Angela Lansbury. *The Manchurian Candidate* suggests even the family matriarch can be corrupted beyond recognition by communism.

6 HAUPTMANN GERD WIESLER
In 1984 East Berlin the Stasi monitor anyone extolling values different from their own. One agent begins to question whether the playwright he is assigned to spy on might be fighting for a worthy cause and helps him evade capture.

5 JASON BOURNE
Before the Bourne series movie spies were usually either cold war relics or unconvincing suave operators. With it's incredible kinetic energy and characters that avoid black and white moral

classification, Bourne reinvented spy movies.

4 HARRY PALMER
Although offered up as a sort of working class, down to earth James Bond, Harry Palmer's first adventure is every bit as far fetched as those of his better known colleague, with the plot involving mind control and 'psychic driving'.

3 GEORGE SMILEY
The head of the British secret service must discover the identity of a Soviet mole. Oldman's superb performance is clearly based on that of Alec Guinness, who played Smiley on the small screen some 30 years earlier.

2 T.R. DEVLIN
Cary Grant isn't the most convincing of spies, but that does nothing to harm Hitchcock's 1946 classic. As Devlin he falls in love with Alicia (Ingrid Bergman) who is charged with infiltrating a Nazi organisation intent on mass murder.

1 JAMES BOND
There are pretenders to Bond's throne but for the last 50 years nobody has managed to topple the king. If anything his appeal is stronger than ever, with 2012's *Skyfall* earning more at the box office than any other Bond movie to date.

	CHARACTER	MOVIE	ACTOR
10	Alec Leamas	*The Spy Who Came in from the Cold* (1965)	Richard Burton
9	Jane Smith	*Mr. and Mrs. Smith* (2005)	Angelina Jolie
8	Osbourne Cox	*Burn After Reading* (2008)	John Malkovich
7	Mrs. Iselin	*The Manchurian Candidate* (1962)	Angela Lansbury
6	Hauptmann Gerd Wiesler	*Lives of Others* (2006)	Ulrich Mühe
5	Jason Bourne	*The Bourne series* (2002-2007)	Matt Damon
4	Harry Palmer	*The Ipcress File* (1965)	Michael Caine
3	George Smiley	*Tinker Tailor Soldier Spy* (2011)	Gary Oldman
2	T.R. Devlin	*Notorious* (1946)	Cary Grant
1	James Bond	*Various*	Various

TOP 10

Naval gazing is a favourite pastime of filmmakers so perhaps it's no surprise that there have been so many great movies made about the industry. More surprising is the way most of them paint it as caustic and exploitative, regardless of where and when they were made.

MOVIES ABOUT MOVIES

10 A COCK AND BULL STORY (2005)
Winterbottom's approach to filming Tristram Shandy, the famously unfilmable novel, is to make a movie of the attempt to make a movie. It gets even more complicated with stars Steve Coogan and Rob Brydon playing versions of themselves.

9 SUNSET BOULEVARD (1950)
One of the most universally beloved movies to emerge from the Hollywood studio system. The desperate craving for attention of a forgotten silent era star becomes a biting allegory for the sham that is fame and celebrity in the movies.

8 THE ARTIST (2011)
Sharing a similar setup to *Singin' in the Rain*, *The Artist* also touches on some of the same issues. Strikingly original stylistic touches helped make this bitter/sweet love story an international phenomenon, taking home seven Oscars.

7 STARDUST MEMORIES (1980)
You can't get much more meta than this. Allen's film is about a filmmaker who is plagued by accusations his new films aren't as good as his old, with the film itself parodying Fellini's *8½* in style, another film about another filmmaker.

6 THE PLAYER (1992)
This pitch black comedy documents the lengths to which people will go for success. Altman ruthlessly skewers Hollywood types for their lack of creativity and honesty - so much so it's hard to see how the director ever found work again.

5 SINGIN' IN THE RAIN (1952)
Hollywood of the late 1920's is the setting for this musical comedy masterpiece. Almost unbelievably it wasn't a success at first, with audiences taking their time to discover the charms of Gene Kelly's fabled centrepiece routine.

4 MULHOLLAND DRIVE (2001)
The famously baffling *Mulholland Drive* could be about many things. One thread that people seem to agree about sees enthusiastic ingenue Betty (Naomi Watts) reduced to an emotional wreck by her attempts to crack Hollywood.

3 ED WOOD (1994)
Fans of Tim Burton's recent garish offerings (*Alice in Wonderland, Dark Shadows*) might be surprised by this subdued and affectionate tribute to Ed Wood, the cross-dressing WWII hero who arguably made the worst movies in history.

2 8½ (1963)
Guido (Marcello Mastroianni), a
successful filmmaker, has 'director's block' and
is lacking enthusiasm for his latest movie. As his
marriage crumbles he seems to lose interest in
reality and retreats into a series of existential
flashbacks.

1 SULLIVAN'S TRAVELS (1941)
An intelligent and commercial movie
about the difference between making intelligent
movies and commercial ones. Specifically the
value in doing what you do well, rather than
doing something you think might be more
worthy badly.

	MOVIE	DIRECTOR(S)
10	A Cock and Bull Story (2005)	Michael Winterbottom
9	Sunset Boulevard (1950)	Billy Wilder
8	The Artist (2011)	Michel Hazanavicius
7	Stardust Memories (1980)	Woody Allen
6	The Player (1992)	Robert Altman
5	Singin' in the Rain (1952)	Stanley Donen and Gene Kelly
4	Mulholland Drive (2001)	David Lynch
3	Ed Wood (1994)	Tim Burton
2	8 ½ (1963)	Federico Fellini
1	Sullivan's Travels (1941)	Preston Sturges

TOP 10

Visual effects are the processes used to create imagery 'out of camera', i.e. not live on a set (special effects). This list focuses on modern methods, which essentially means computer generated imagery (CGI), though other techniques can be involved.

VISUAL EFFECTS SEQUENCES

10 THE PSEUDOPOD
A diving team searching for a lost nuclear submarine encounter an apparently alien life at the bottom of the sea. In the most memorable sequence, early CGI is used to show an NTI (non-terrestrial intelligence) using water to form shapes and faces.

9 ALL EATEN AWAY
This otherwise fairly forgettable genre movie has one legendary VFX sequence at it's centre. The scene in which Kevin Bacon's Sebastien Caine first becomes invisible, one grisly layer of tissue at a time, still inspires young effects artists today.

8 THE POD RACE
Even those disappointed to the point of being offended by the Star Wars prequels reserve praise for the pod race. Lucas indulges his love of motor racing in a breathtaking action sequence featuring 500mph hovering jets racing on a treacherous circuit.

7 THE T-1000 DOESN'T BURN
We watch with baited breath, waiting to see if the T-1000 shape shifting robot has survived a firey crash. From the flames strides a humanoid shape with a metallic skin. This enduring scene demonstrates just how effective a tool CGI will become.

6 PEARL HARBOUR ATTACK
Like a couple of other entries on this list, *Pearl Harbour* is not a standout movie. The sequence in which the eponymous port is attacked by Japanese forces during WWII,

however, is most definitely a standout scene.

5 PARIS CUBED

As Ariadne (Ellen Page) starts to understand the control she can wield over a dreamscape, she literally folds Paris into a cube before our eyes. The sequence isn't the most difficult to achieve but has an enduring, mind bending impact on the viewer.

4 LIGHT CYCLE RACE

The first film to use CGI extensively, ironically *Tron* was ruled ineligible for an Academy Awards effects nomination because it was considered cheating to use a computer. The heavily stylised sequence is still visually stunning and utterly exciting.

3 GOLLUM ARGUES WITH SMEAGOL

A rare example of a real actor contributing at least as much to a CGI character as the computer wizards. Andy Serkis' physical portrayal (later mapped onto the CGI character) proved essential to the appeal of the famously wretched Gollum.

2 BRACHIOSAURUS REVEAL

The relatively benign scene in which the human characters first see a dinosaur. There are more showy sequences but the daylight and lack of diversions mean there's nowhere for the effects to hide. For anyone who saw it on release, it's unforgettable.

1 SATELLITE AVALANCHE

Several sequences from Alfonso Cuaron's majestic space drama could qualify for this list. But the opening 13 minute shot of debris crippling a space shuttle stands out for its beauty and technical complexity, not to mention it's unprecedented length.

	SEQUENCE	FILM	DIRECTOR	CGI BY
10	The Pseudopod	*The Abyss (1989)*	James Cameron	Steve Johnson's XFX
9	All eaten away	*Hollow Man (2000)*	Paul Verhoeven	SPI
8	The pod race	*Star Wars: Episode I - The Phantom Menace (1999)*	George Lucas	ILM
7	The T-1000 doesn't burn	*Terminator 2: Judgement Day (1991)*	James Cameron	ILM
6	Pearl Harbour Attack	*Pearl Harbour (2001)*	Michael Bay	ILM
5	Paris cubed	*Inception (2010)*	Christopher Nolan	Double Negative
4	Light cycle race	*Tron (1982)*	Steven Lisberger	MAGI
3	Gollum argues with Smeagol	*The Lord of the Rings: The Two Towers (2002)*	Peter Jackson	Weta
2	Brachiosaurus reveal	*Jurassic Park (1993)*	Steven Spielberg	ILM
1	Satellite avalanche	*Gravity (2013)*	Alfonso Cuaron	Framestore

TOP 10

Loneliness is a complicated and powerful emotional response, but it's one that can be well suited to being explored by cinema. These entries run the gamut of characters defined by their estrangement from conventional society.

MOVIES ABOUT ALIENATION

10 IN A LONELY PLACE (1950)
Humphrey Bogart was known for playing cynical characters, but there was usually a veil of artifice between them and the audience. With his realistic portrayal of an alcoholic murder suspect, Bogart won uncommon plaudits for his work.

9 GHOST WORLD (2001)
Two girls spend the summer after high school trying to decide who they are going to be. Terminal outsiders, they have a few unremarkable adventures, face difficulties getting on in life and, eventually, challenges to their friendship.

8 PINK FLOYD – THE WALL (1982)
An almost dialogue free mixture of animation and live action, *Pink Floyd - The Wall* is an introspective nightmare of a movie. Pink (Bob Geldof) suffers spiritual desolation resulting from the disconnect between artists and their audiences.

7 MY OWN PRIVATE IDAHO (1991)
Mike (River Phoenix) and Scott (Keanu Reeves) form a strong bond as they attempt to earn a living for themselves as street hustlers. Having sunk to rock bottom, Mike realises he must find the mother who abandoned him years before.

6 STEPPENWOLF (1974)
This adaptation of Hermann Hesse's abstract tale of alienation is not always completely successful. Nonetheless there is enough of the great author's metaphysical analysis to make the movie a powerful and engrossing experience.

5 LOST IN TRANSLATION (2003)
After a chance meeting in Tokyo, two isolated Americans become friends. The loneliness is palpable in Sofia Coppola's directorial follow-up to *The Virgin Suicides*, both films that touch on the loneliness of characters surrounded by people.

4 ERASERHEAD (1977)
Supposedly about a loner left to care for his child, the reality is Lynch doesn't care about *Eraserhead*'s narrative. He's more interested in delivering a hypnagogic assault of loosely connected surreal meditations on loneliness and misery.

3 LA STRADA (1954)
A bestial circus strongman buys a naive young girl to keep him company and help with his act. Her misery is unrelenting until a rival of the strongman starts to convince her there might be an alternative to a life of desolate servitude.

2 THE PASSENGER (1975)

On a whim journalist David Locke (Jack Nicholson) assumes the identity of a recently dead arms dealer who had been staying in the same hotel. Locke's increasing estrangement from society leads to various analogous incidents.

1 TAXI DRIVER (1976)

Travis Bickle (Robert De Niro) is amongst the most notorious of cinema's alienated souls. His disillusioned Vietnam veteren freewheels aimlessly around New York, treading a fine line between crusading vigilante and violent misanthrope. By the end of the film we're still no closer to understanding which he is.

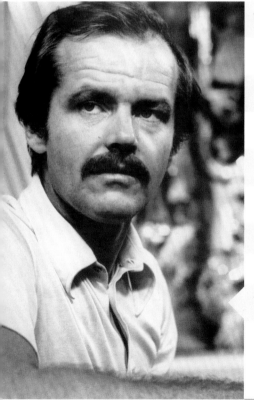

	MOVIE	DIRECTOR
10	In a Lonely Place (1950)	Nicholas Ray
9	Ghost World (2001)	Terry Zwigoff
8	Pink Floyd The Wall (1982)	Alan Parker
7	My Own Private Idaho (1991)	Gus Van Sant
6	Steppenwolf (1974)	Fred Haines
5	Lost in Translation (2003)	Sofia Coppola
4	Eraserhead (1977)	David Lynch
3	La Strada (1954)	Federico Fellini
2	The Passenger (1975)	Michelangelo Antonioni
1	Taxi Driver (1976)	Martin Scorsese

TOP 10

The cool kid in school had nothing on this mixture of confident, stylish and unnaturally appealing characters. To avoid making the other men and women on the list seem a bit drab, James Bond is excluded as the tribute.

COOLEST CHARACTERS

PAM GRIER
is

Jackie Brown

a Quentin Tarantino film

CHRISTMAS DAY   MIRAMAX

10 TONY STARK
Stark is the charismatic, gregarious billionaire genius behind the Iron Man superhero. With friends at the highest level of both the U.S. government and Norse mythology (his fellow Avenger is Thor), address books probably don't get any more impressive.

9 JACKIE BROWN
Ageing flight attendant Jackie Brown oozes the sort of nonchalant class that can only come from experience. Even when she becomes embroiled in the machinations of a murderous gun dealer her feathers barely show a ruffle.

8 MARK HUNTER
During the day Mark Hunter is an easily forgettable high school kid in small town Arizona. But by night he becomes the pirate radio DJ Hard Harry, an ethical agitator committed to exposing the hypocrisy and injustice at the heart of his school.

7 SLIM BROWNING
Bacall was just 19 when she made her debut in Howard Hawks' adaptation of Ernest Hemingway's (famously least favourite) novel. Playing a freespirited American roaming Martinique, if Bacall even understood what naivety is it doesn't show for a second.

6 MICHEL POICCARD
Michel is a dynamic young petty thief who, after stealing a car, is promoted to murderer when he kills the policeman pursuing him. Murder isn't cool, but Jean-Paul Belmondo can do what he likes.

5 WILLIAMS
Jive-talking, afro-wearing karate expert Williams somehow manages to make even Bruce Lee look uncool. Although *Enter the Dragon* was Kelly's biggest movie by far he starred in a series of cult actioners in the 1970s, cementing the title of cinema's first African American martial arts star.

4 PETER VENKMAN
The casual indifference with which Venkman greets the objects of his ire, be they supercilious city officials, intolerant professors or disorderly ghosts, is the basis of his profound cool. But peel away the insouciant front and he's a caring, affable raconteur... sort of.

3 TYLER DURDEN
Tyler Durden is confident, good-looking, stylish, cool and tough, all qualities that a modern emasculated man might project onto a fantasy persona. Which, funnily enough, is just what has happened here.

2 VIC VEGA AKA MR. BLONDE
If we skip over Mr. Blonde's psychopathic penchant for torture, the gritty nonchalance we're left with makes him the coolest character in American cinema.

1 JEF COSTELLO
In attempting to describe a threshold for obscenity, U.S. Supreme Court Judge Potter Stewart famously said ,"I know it when I see it". It comes down to the same thing with Jef Costello - it's hard to quantify his cool, you just know he's got more of it than anyone else. Any attempt to explain it is doomed; the only way to understand is to see *Le Samourai*.

	CHARACTER	MOVIE	ACTOR
10	Tony Stark	*Iron Man series (2008-ongoing)*	Robert Downey Jr.
9	Jackie Brown	*Jackie Brown (1997)*	Pam Grier
8	Mark Hunter	*Pump Up the Volume (1990)*	Christian Slater
7	Slim Browning	*To Have and Have Not (1944)*	Lauren Bacall
6	Michel Poiccard	*Breathless (1960)*	Jean-Paul Belmondo
5	Williams	*Enter the Dragon (1973)*	Jim Kelly
4	Peter Venkman	*Ghost Busters (1984)*	Bill Murray
3	Tyler Durden	*Fight Club (1999)*	Brad Pitt
2	Vic Vega aka Mr. Blonde	*Reservoir Dogs (1992)*	Michael Madsen
1	Jef Costello	*Le Samourai (1967)*	Alain Delon

TOP 10

Although colour movies have dominated the landscape for half a century or so, black & white has never really gone away. Although technical and financial limitations no longer necessitate monochrome cinematography, creative choices apparently still lead to it.

CONTEMPORARY BLACK AND WHITE

10 THE AMERICAN ASTRONAUT (2001)
Filmed for around $1 million, McAbee's avant garde space-western is a strange beast. The unique approach to the visual style relies on more than monochrome photography, with paintings used in FX shots and props made from junk.

9 THE WHITE RIBBON (2009)
Hanake won the Palme d'Or at Cannes for his darkly fascinating portrayal of life in a German village just prior to WWI. The film addresses the nature of evil, specifically how it can takes root before developing into established forms.

8 FRANCES HA (2012)
Frances Halladay is a struggling dancer living in New York. When her best friend moves out of their shared apartment, Frances starts an uneventful journey of personal

discovery. As ever, New York looks incredible in black & white.

7 LA HAINE (1995)
This blistering social commentary had a profound impact on release in its native France. It examines the lives of young immigrants living in a notorious Parisian housing project, and presents an uncompromising vision of their struggles.

6 THE MAN WHO WASN'T THERE (2001)
The Man Who Wasn't There is an unusually downbeat entry in the Coen Bros' impressive canon. But the stark, crisp photography from first rate cinematographer Roger Deakins is amongst the most beautiful he's ever achieved.

5 DOWN BY LAW (1986)
Ostensibly a story about a prison break, this unusual movie eschews all

established conventions. Really it's a study of the dynamic between the three protagonists, whose behaviour and philosophising reveal interesting human truths.

4 ED WOOD (1994)

This very personal study of the characters and particularly movies that inspired a young Tim Burton echoes the feel of the subject perfectly. Clearly Bela Lugosi doesn't look right in colour, even when portrayed by a modern actor.

3 PI (1998)

Aronofsky's surreal, Kafkaesque debut follows an obsessive number theorist who may have stumbled onto an explanation of mankind's purpose on earth. Or it might just be a really good way of rigging the stock market.

2 THE ARTIST (2011)

This hugely popular French silent movie uses monochrome in a similar way to Ed Wood. It's less an aesthetic choice than a means of mimicking the techniques and limitations of the era the filmmakers want to evoke.

1 SCHINDLER'S LIST (1993)

It can be interesting to consider why the decision to shoot in a certain way was made. Here the monochrome look is reverential, it's as if Spielberg is so respectful of the ordeal he's documenting that garish colour seemed crass.

	MOVIE	DIRECTOR
10	The American Astronaut (2001)	Cory McAbee
9	The White Ribbon (2009)	Michael Haneke
8	Frances Ha (2012)	Noah Baumbach
7	La Haine (1995)	Mathieu Kassovitz
6	The Man Who Wasn't There (2001)	Ethan & Joel Coen
5	Down by Law (1986)	Jim Jarmusch
4	Ed Wood (1994)	Tim Burton
3	Pi (1998)	Darren Aronofsky
2	The Artist (2011)	Michel Hazanavicius
1	Schindler's List (1993)	Steven Spielberg

TOP 10

Perhaps it's because the western is often considered the core cinematic form that it's been subverted so often over the years. Or perhaps it's because it provides such a good allegorical framework. Whatever the reason, there are some seriously wacky westerns out there.

WEIRD WESTERNS

10 ZACHARIAH (1971)
Loosely based on Hermann Hesse's novel *Siddhartha*, featuring music by the likes of Country Joe and the Fish, and starring incompetent, electric guitar wielding gunslingers, Zachariah unsurprisingly belongs to the sub-genre known as 'Acid Western'.

9 THE TERROR OF TINY TOWN (1938)
There's nothing unusual about a Western, which sees a cowboy coming to the aid of a beautiful woman. Likewise, musical westerns have a long and successful tradition. What makes *The Terror of Tiny Town* unique is the exclusively dwarf cast.

8 VALLEY OF GWANGI (1969)
Although little more than a variant on the King Kong story, *The Valley of Gwangi* has a loyal following thanks to it being the last movie to feature stop motion dinosaur effects by the legendary Ray Harryhausen. Its campy charm is not to be underestimated.

7 GREASER'S PALACE (1972)
Underground filmmaker Robert Downey (Sr.) tended to work in impenetrable allegories and this is fairly typical of his output. Jesse is on his way to Jerusalem when he falls foul of gangster Seaweedhead Greaser and the world is threatened by constipation.

6 7 FACES OF DR. LAO (1964)
When the mysterious Chinese circus master Dr. Lao (Tony Randall... seriously) arrives in the small town of Abalone he introduces the residents to all sorts of fantastical wonders and leaves them forever changed.

5 SUKIYAKI WESTERN DJANGO (2007)
Essentially a Japanese Western with elements of Samurai movies blended in, this madly frenetic offering from notorious fruitcake director Takashi Miike features Quentin Tarantino as an elderly gunman in a plot that's basically Yojimbo on steroids.

4 STRAIGHT TO HELL (1987)
One of the most eclectic casts ever assembled (Elvis Costello, Grace Jones, Dennis Hopper, Courtney Love, Jim Jarmusch...) rampage through this bizarre remake of 1967's *Django, Kill!* Loaded with symbolism and at times utterly impenetrable, it's classic Alex Cox.

3 TEARS OF THE BLACK TIGER (2000)
Beautiful pastel imagery abounds in this stylised and poetic minor masterpiece

from first time director Sasanatieng. Although fairly traditional in its plot (part touching romance, part tale of bandits terrorising a rural community) the atmosphere is completely unique.

2 DEAD MAN (1995)

This Johnny Depp vehicle is, on one hand, a funny and accessible fish out of water tale. It's also a consciously postmodern existential parable infused with the poetry of Blake and preoccupied with the marginalisation of the indigenous American. Something for everyone, then.

1 EL TOPO (1970)

El Topo (or The Mole) is a legendary slice of far out flower power craziness. A huge hit on the 'Midnight Movies' circuit (largely thanks to John Lennon's vocal support) it's only relatively recently become available again to anyone brave enough to endure it.

	MOVIE	DIRECTOR	WEIRD HOW?
10	Zachariah (1971)	George Englund	It's a surreal collision of styles
9	The Terror of Tiny Town (1938)	Sam Newfield	Everyone in it is a dwarf
8	Valley of Gwangi (1969)	Jim O'Connolly	It's about a dinosaur hunter
7	Greaser's Palace (1972)	Joshua Logan	It's a counter culture Christ parable
6	7 Faces of Dr. Lao (1964)	George Pal	It stars a supernatural Chinese guy
5	Sukiyaki Western Django (2007)	Takashi Miike	It's a wacky cultural mashup
4	Straight to Hell (1987)	Alex Cox	It's brimming with arthouse weird
3	Tears of the Black Tiger (2000)	Wisit Sasanatieng	It's a Western from Thailand
2	Dead Man (1995)	Jim Jarmusch	It's preoccupied with existentialism
1	El Topo (1970)	Alejandro Jodor-owsky	It's completely crazy

TOP
10

Be warned, some of these movies go well beyond traditional melodramatic tear-jerkers. When profound suffering is documented by filmmakers with exceptional ability, it can prove to be an overwhelming combination. If in doubt, stay well away from number one.

MOVIES THAT WILL MAKE YOU CRY

10 AN AFFAIR TO REMEMBER (1957)

Nicolò (Cary Grant) and Terry (Deborah Kerr) meet and almost instantly fall in love but are each already in relationships. They agree to meet in six months time if their feelings remain. When Terry cannot make the meeting due to an accident, Nicolò assumes she has moved on.

9 MY LEFT FOOT (1989)

The true story of Christy Brown, who was born with a form of cerebral palsy which left him able to control only his left foot. Daniel Day-Lewis won his first Academy Award for his portrayal of the Irish artist.

8 CINEMA PARADISO (1988)

A young boy in a small Italian town is enchanted by the cinema and forms a close friendship with the local projectionist. Later, grown up

and a successful filmmaker, he returns to the town and reminisces about the past.

7 TITANIC (1997)

The phenomenal commercial success of *Titanic* has come to overshadow many of its qualities, one of which is the way we are drawn into the tragic love affair between working class Jack Dawson (Leonardo DiCaprio) and upper crust Rose DeWitt Bukater (Kate Winslet).

6 THE DIVING BELL AND THE BUTTERFLY (2007)

Like *My Left Foot*, *The Diving Bell and the Butterfly* is a true story of the human spirit triumphing over physical adversity. Jean-Dominique Bauby suffers a massive stroke which renders him unable to move. Using just his left eye he manages to develop a system of communication.

5 LIFE IS BEAUTIFUL (1997)

This story of a father trying to make life in a WWII concentration camp bearable for his young son is perfectly concocted to tug on our heart strings.

4 OLD YELLER (1957)

Farm boy Travis Coates (Tommy Kirk) reluctantly adopts a yellow coated mongrel stray. Over time the dog proves itself by saving the family from various threats, leading he and Travis to form a close bond. But after Yeller is bitten by a rabid wolf the family face a heartbreaking dilemma.

3 BAMBI (1942)

Destined to become Great Prince of the Forest, Bambi, a good natured fawn, is tutored by his brave father and nurtured by his loving mother. That is until she's shot dead in front of him. Although

Bambi eventually recovers and grows safely to adulthood, audiences are usually left sobbing.

2 LOVE STORY (1970)

Widely criticised for being emotionally manipulative and overly sentimental, *Love Story* nevertheless became a massive hit. The story follows Jenny (Ali MacGraw) and Oliver (Ryan O'Neal), a young couple in the throws of true love, beset by tragedy when they discover Jenny is terminally ill.

1 GRAVE OF THE FIREFLIES (1988)

Kobe, Japan during WWII. A young brother and sister struggle to survive in the fire-bombed remnants of the city when their mother is killed and Aunt abandons them. As death from malnutrition looms they discover Japan has surrendered and their sailor father is dead.

	MOVIE	DIRECTOR(S)	WHY SO WEEPY?
10	An Affair to Remember (1957)	Leo McCarey	Difficult love affair
9	My Left Foot (1989)	Jim Sheridan	Spirit over adversity
8	Cinema Paradiso (1988)	Giuseppe Tornatore	Tragic accident
7	Titanic (1997)	James Cameron	Tragic love
6	The Diving Bell and the Butterfly (2007)	Julian Schnabel	Spirit over adversity
5	Life is Beautiful (1997)	Roberto Benigni	Holocaust suffering
4	Old Yeller (1957)	Robert Stevenson	Pet dog euthanasia
3	Bambi (1942)	James Algar and Samuel Armstrong	Orphaned fawn
2	Love Story (1970)	Arthur Hiller	Tragic love
1	Grave of the Fireflies (1988)	Isao Takahata	Wartime suffering

TOP 10

If James Bond movies have taught us nothing else it's that every memorable villain needs an equally engaging henchman. Someone to do the dirty work... and be killed by the hero in the middle of the third act.

HENCHMEN

10 MR. IGOE
If you are of a certain age Mr. Igoe is likely seared into your consciousness. He's not the stock grumpy tough guy you normally find in kids movies. Instead he channels something genuinely unnerving with a psychotic determination.

9 MINI-ME
The result of an attempt to clone Austin Powers' nemesis, Dr. Evil, Mini-Me seems to combine features of

several henchmen from the James Bond series. And in spite of being just 81cm tall, he still got Britney Spears' phone number.

8 LEONARD
Although he would go on to great success, Martin Landau started out playing heavies. In *North by Northwest* he works for Vandamm (James Mason) and is unforgettably charged with killing Roger Thornhill (Cary Grant).

7 KLYTUS
Henchman to Ming the Merciless, expert in brainwashing, genius level intelligence, and a fondness for torture and a shiny metal face: Klytus had it all. Believe it or not he was played by Jason King himself, Peter Wyngarde.

6 JUAN WILD
Although Juan Wild's part is small it's memorable. When Lee Van Cleef's Colonel Mortimer strikes a match on the hunchback's hump, a tense round of oneupmanship ensues, telling Mortimer all he needs to know about Wild.

5 CLARENCE BODDICKER
Boddicker is instrumental in the plans of corrupt corporation president Dick Jones (Ronny Cox). A thoroughly nasty piece of work, his grizzly demise is surely cathartic for even the most squeamish of audience members.

4 MR. JOSHUA
Before Gary Busey was known for being slightly crazy in real life he played the unforgettable, and slightly crazy, Mr. Joshua. The final showdown with Mel Gibson's Riggs is amongst the most exciting fight scenes of the era.

3 WEZ
Vernon Wells was born to play bad guys. Making his second appearance as a henchman, this time as memorable mohican-sporting biker punk Wez, Wells lights up the screen as he brings all kinds of crazy to this dystopian actioner.

2 THE MINIONS
Originally meant to be more humanlike in appearance, budget constraints lead to the minions bizarre look. In spite, or perhaps because, of their appearance they proved hugely successful with fans and even feature in their own movie.

1 NICK NACK
Any number of the henchmen to have faced off against James Bond could have made this list. Nods must go to Oddjob and Jaws in particular. But Nick Nack is the most intriguing thanks to his undoubted intelligence and a penchant for manipulating even his boss.

	CHARACTER	MOVIE	ACTOR
10	Mr. Igoe	*Innerspace (1987)*	Vernon Wells
9	Mini-Me	*Austin Powers series (1999-2002)*	Verne Troyer
8	Leonard	*North by Northwest (1959)*	Martin Landau
7	Klytus	*Flash Gordon (1980)*	Peter Wyngarde
6	Juan Wild	*For a Few Dollars More (1965)*	Klaus Kinski
5	Clarence Boddicker	*Robocop (1987)*	Kurtwood Smith
4	Mr. Joshua	*Lethal Weapon (1987)*	Gary Busey
3	Wez	*Mad Max 2 (1981)*	Vernon Wells
2	The Minions	*Despicable Me (2010)*	Pierre Coffin
1	Nick Nack	*The Man With the Golden Gun (1974)*	Herve Villechaize

TOP 10

A character paradigm that has lead to some of cinema's most memorable performances. Free from any responsibility to traditional behavioural codes, that their free will can be as intoxicating as their profligacy is disturbing. Tribute to Darth Vader.

COMING OF AGE MOVIES

1960s small town California.

6 **RUMBLE FISH (1983)** This moody, monochrome look at the troubled lives of a gang of street thugs gave breakout opportunities to 1980s heavyweights like Matt Dillon and Mickey Rourke.

5 **THE LAST PICTURE SHOW (1973)** A dying Texas town is the melancholic setting for this rambling examination of the trials and tribulations of teenage life in post war America. Centred around a pool hall and cinema, a group of young friends laugh, love and fight as they try to enjoy their last summer of adolescence.

10 **KIDS (1995)** Surely amongst the most controversial coming-of-age movies, Kids' naturalistic depiction of sexually active drug using teens caused a furore on release.

9 **SHOW ME LOVE (1998)** Two girls, one popular and outgoing, the other a depressed recluse, feel trapped by the Swedish town in which they live. Gradually they fall into a relationship and find they're stronger together.

8 **THE SQUID AND THE WHALE (2005)** Pretentiously intellectual parents subject their sons to baffling, hypocritical pseudo-philosophy as a means of helping them deal with their divorce.

7 **AMERICAN GRAFFITI (1973)** Often cited as an inspiration for the hit sitcom *Happy Days*, *American Graffiti* is George Lucas's sentimentalised account of teen life in early

4 **ADVENTURELAND (2009)** During the summer of 1987 college grad James Brennan (Jesse Eisenberg) is forced to work at a rundown theme park in order to raise money for school. There he falls in love with Em Lewin (Kristen Stewart) and traditional experiences, like learning to value what is usually taken for granted, are enjoyed by all.

3 JUNO (2007)

Once in a while a coming of age movie comes along that somehow defines an epoch and sets the direction of the genre for years to come. That's probably the case with each of the top three here, but none more so than this timely tale of Juno (Ellen Page) and Paulie (Michael Cera), teen friends who must deal with the challenges of Juno's accidental pregnancy.

2 REBEL WITHOUT A CAUSE (1955)

The daddy of the genre, *Rebel Without a Cause* is as pertinent now as it was sixty years ago. Just as Jim Stark (James Dean) seeks approval from his peers in lieu of a loveless home life, so too do kids today. His troubled past is inevitably revisited as he grapples to make sense of adulthood.

1 STAND BY ME (1986)

In 1959 small-town Oregon, four 12-year-old friends set off on foot to find a dead body rumoured to be nearby. On their journey they are nearly killed more than once and face particular challenges from local bullies, but it all adds to the series of valuable life lessons they learn.

	MOVIE	DIRECTOR
10	Kids (1995)	Larry Clark
9	Show Me Love (1998)	Lukas Moodyson
8	The Squid and the Whale (2005)	Noah Baumbach
7	American Graffiti (1973)	George Lucas
6	Rumble Fish (1983)	Francis Ford Coppola
5	The Last Picture Show (1973)	Peter Bogdanovich
4	Adventureland (2009)	Greg Mottola
3	Juno (2007)	Jason Reitman
2	Rebel Without a Cause (1955)	Nicholas Ray
1	Stand By Me (1986)	Rob Reiner

TOP
10

With nothing but imagination to limit their appearance and portrayal, many animated characters have inevitably become amongst the most memorable and enjoyable committed to screen.

ANIMATED CHARACTERS

10 PUSS IN BOOTS
This foil-wielding fugitive feline proved so popular in the *Shrek* sequel that he was given his own spinoff movie. Much of his appeal lies in Banderas's excellent voice work, which reveals Puss as a cocky but loveable matador type.

9 KANEDA
In post-apocalypse Tokyo, Kaneda leads a biker gang that gets tangled up in a government conspiracy. When Tetsuo, his best friend, develops strange powers, Kaneda must prevent him destroying Tokyo.

8 JACK SKELLINGTON
Jack Skellington, aka The Pumpkin King of Halloween Town, discovers a secret door leading to the enchanting Christmas Town, and determines to conquer it. But he's not a bad guy, he just needs his enthusiasm for Halloween back.

7 ELSA, SNOW QUEEN OF ARANDELLE

Born with strange cryokinetic powers that enable her to produce ice and snow, Princess Elsa accidentally injures her younger sister before shutting herself off from the kingdom to prevent doing further harm. This classic Disney tale of love overcoming adversity became one of the most successful movies of all time.

6 GROMIT

Clearly the brains behind the operation, Gromit might share his master's love of cheese but is a far better prepared and more insightful chap. His amiable, sympathetic demeanour have charmed audiences around the world.

5 CRUELLA DE VIL

One of Disney's most memorable characters and certainly greatest villains. Cruella's desire to butcher dozens of puppies for their skins is a remarkably dark plot, but the style with which she is brought to life makes it palatable for all.

4 BALOO

Everyone's favourite breezy bear is a lesson in characterisation. Instantly likeable and pleasingly lackadaisical, and with an endearing instinct to protect young Mowgli, he's almost the perfect guardian for an orphaned man cub. Almost.

3 BUZZ LIGHTYEAR
Buzz Lightyear, Space Ranger was designed as a contrast and modern equivalent to Woody, a traditional cowboy doll. The chemistry the two share became the legendary basis of the *Toy Story* series' phenomenal success.

2 HOMER SIMPSON
Described as one of the most influential people of the last quarter century, the epitome of American humour and everything that's good about TV, the legend that is Homer Jay Simpson could easily have been number one on this list.

1 TOTORO
Totoro, the gentle forest spirit (and mascot of legendary Japanese animation house Studio Ghibli) who helps and inspires two young sisters, has to be one of cinema's most magical creations. In his limited time on screen he prints himself indelibly into the psyche, the most heartwarming animated character of all.

	CHARACTER	MOVIE	VOICE ACTOR(S)
10	Puss in Boots	*Shrek and Puss in Boots films (2004-2011)*	Antonio Banderas
9	Kaneda	*Akira (1988)*	Mitsuo Iwata and Cam Clarke
8	Jack Skellington	*The Nightmare Before Christmas (1993)*	Danny Elfman and Chris Sarandon
7	Elsa, Snow Queen of Arandelle	*Frozen (2013)*	Idina Menzel
6	Gromit	*Wallace and Gromit series (1989-2008)*	None
5	Cruella De Vil	*101 Dalmations (1961)*	Betty Lou Gerson
4	Baloo	*The Jungle Book (1967)*	Phil Harris
3	Buzz Lightyear	*Toy Story series (1995-2010)*	Tim Allen
2	Homer Simpson	*The Simpsons Movie (2010)*	Dan Castellaneta
1	Totoro	*My Neighbour Totoro (1988)*	None

TOP 10

Special mention should be made of *Cinema Paradiso* (1988). With the local church demanding the eradication of all kisses from movies played at the town theatre, the projectionist spends years editing together each excised embrace. When the compilation is finally run intact - in one of the most moving scenes in cinema - we're presented with a blizzard of previously suppressed unadulterated passion.

KISSES

10 CECILIA TALLIS AND ROBBIE TURNER

Seldom can a kiss ever have had such terrible and unforeseeable repercussions. A misunderstanding over what a young girl saw leads to a lifetime of misery for at least three protagonists.

9 JOHN PRENTICE AND JOEY DRATON

Often incorrectly cited as the first interracial kiss in the movies, the mainstream success of *Guess Who's Coming to Dinner,* and the fact it addressed the issue of race so acutely, make this a powerful moment in many ways.

8 ENNIS DEL MAR AND JACK TWIST

When sheep herders Ennis and Jack finally meet up again after years apart, the passion is palpable and the kiss intense. A touching moment of pure satisfaction in a relationship riddled with apparently unsurmountable challenges.

7 JOHNNY AND BABY

This perennial tale of forbidden dancing, and even more forbidden love, crackles with Johnny and Baby's chemistry. The key moment is a close call between the kiss that marks the dawn of their relationship and the spectacular finale.

6 BOB HARRIS AND CHARLOTTE

Not a kiss of passion or love but a kiss that marks a special, platonic but emotional connection. The air of authenticity is perhaps a result of Johansson not knowing Murray would kiss her, a surprise deliberately saved for the final take.

5 LADY AND TRAMP
The image of two characters eating spaghetti, unwittingly locking lips over a shared strand, has become shorthand for romantic attraction. It's easy to forget it was first done by two dogs in a back street behind a restaurant.

4 CHARLES AND CARRIE
"Is it still raining? I hadn't noticed." Words that can bring a tear to the eye... in more ways than one. Whether Carrie is a romantic swept up

in an amorous clinch, or an irritatingly banal stereotype getting wet, is up to the viewer.

3 ROMEO AND JULIET
Baz Luhrmann's spirited Shakespeare tribute features a young couple of such celestial perfection it almost seems wrong for them to kiss. But kiss they do, and quite often. The definitive instance, however, has to be on the balcony.

2 HOLLY GOLIGHTLY AND PAUL VARJAK
After spending the whole film sparring

with one another and dancing around their obvious attraction, Paul and Holly finally demolish the metaphorical wall between themselves and embrace... but only after they've found Holly's cat.

1 RHETT BUTLER AND SCARLETT O'HARA
Leaving to take part in the civil war, Rhett doesn't think he'll be back. Scarlett is furious because she shares his concern, making the kiss they also share poignant rather than passionate, tempered by fear rather than fervor.

	KISSERS	MOVIE	ACTORS
10	Cecilia Tallis and Robbie Turner	Atonement (2007)	Keira Knightley and James McAvoy
9	John Prentice and Joey Draton	Guess Who's Coming to Dinner (1967)	Sidney Poitier and Katharine Houghton
8	Ennis del Mar and Jack Twist	Brokeback Mountain (2005)	Heath Ledger and Jake Gyllenhaal
7	Johnny and Baby	Dirty Dancing (1987)	Patrick Swayze and Jennifer Grey
6	Bob Harris and Charlotte	Lost in Translation (2003)	Bill Murray and Scarlett Johansson
5	Lady and Tramp	Lady and the Tramp (1955)	Barbara Luddy and Larry Roberts (voices)
4	Charles and Carrie	Four Weddings and a Funeral (1994)	Hugh Grant and Andie McDowell
3	Romeo and Juliet	William Shakespeare's Romeo + Juliet (1996)	Leonardo DiCaprio and Claire Danes
2	Holly Golightly and Paul Varjak	Breakfast at Tiffany's (1961)	Audrey Hepburn and George Peppard
1	Rhett Butler and Scarlett O'Hara	Gone with the Wind (1939)	Clark Gable and Vivien Leigh

TOP 10

This small British production house had varying success producing a range of traditional fare from the mid 1930s into the late 1950s. But it was a string of sci-fi and horror hits starting with *The Quatermass Xperiment* in 1955 that steered it in the direction for which it will be forever remembered.

HAMMER HORROR

10 DR. JEKYLL AND SISTER HYDE (1971)

You can tell the movies which came towards the end of Hammer's most successful period by their increasingly wacky concepts. One of their final successes, the title says it all, frankly.

9 THE ABOMINABLE SNOWMAN (1957)

This low budget thriller was made just as Hammer was finding its feet with monster movies. It's big on character study and small on monsters, but that's no bad thing when you have the likes of Peter Cushing to play with.

8 VAMPIRE CIRCUS (1972)

Although it was not well received at the time, *Vampire Circus* is now widely recognised as a successful attempt to breathe new life into the horror genre. It's more cerebral approach and unusual look mark it out as unique in the Hammer cannon.

7 CURSE OF THE WEREWOLF (1961)

A young Oliver Reed stars as the titular lupine aggressor in this notably severe take on the werewolf myth.

6 THE DEVIL RIDES OUT (1968)

Friends Duc de Richleau (Christopher Lee) and Rex Van Ryn (Leon Greene) become embroiled in a Satanic cult that's seeking to summon up the Angel of Death.

5 QUATERMASS AND THE PIT (1967)

The third and final instalment in the Quatermass series of movies (there was also a TV series) sees an alien spacecraft unearthed during work on London's tube network. Quatermass is summoned and his discoveries lead to no less than a new theory as to how human life first came to be.

4 THE CURSE OF FRANKENSTEIN (1957)

Hammer's first big horror hit was for some time the most successful British movie to have been shot in the country. It departs significantly from the Universal series in terms of characterisation, visual design and the use of colour, not to mention a strikingly different looking monster (necessary for legal reasons). But it also injects a dry British wit that results in some big laughs.

3 THE NANNY (1965)

Hollywood icon Bette Davis stars as the psychopathic nanny to a troubled 10-year-old boy. The movie is devoid of supernatural elements, which was perhaps key to it achieving near universal acclaim from critics, who tended to look down on Hammer productions.

2 THE PLAGUE OF THE ZOMBIES (1966)
The esteemed doctor Sir James Forbes (André Morell, who could class up a John Waters movie) answers a plea for help from a former student now practicing medicine in a Cornish village. An outbreak of zombies is causing problems, could it be something to do with the local squire's recent trip to Haiti?

1 HORROR OF DRACULA (1958)
Although Hammer would end up scraping the bottom of the Dracula barrel, their first stab at the Transylvanian Count is a masterpiece of the horror genre. Christopher Lee excels in the lead and was arguably the first to make the vampire both humanistic and sexy, traits that are at the core of the modern explosion in vampire fiction.

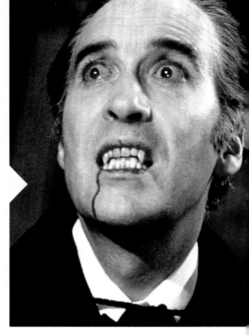

	MOVIE	DIRECTOR
10	Dr. Jekyll and Sister Hyde (1971)	Roy Ward Baker
9	The Abominable Snowman (1957)	Val Guest
8	Vampire Circus (1972)	Robert Young
7	Curse of the Werewolf (1961)	Terence Fisher
6	The Devil Rides Out (1968)	Terence Fisher
5	Quatermass and the Pit (1967)	Roy Ward Baker
4	The Curse of Frankenstein (1957)	Terence Fisher
3	The Nanny (1965)	Seth Holt
2	The Plague of the Zombies (1966)	John Gilling
1	Horror of Dracula (1958)	Terence Fisher

TOP
10

The very best documentaries should highlight some kind of hidden truth, not necessarily in their subject, but perhaps in ourselves. In fact at this level the subject is largely unimportant, the wider implications of its study being key.

ESSENTIAL DOCUMENTARIES

10 HARLAN COUNTY U.S.A. (1976)

Eminent documentarian Barbara Kopple is on comfortable ground with this look at the 1973 'Brookside Strike', in which 180 Kentuckian coal miners were refused contracts after joining their union.

9 THE TIMES OF HARVEY MILK (1984)

America's first openly gay elected political representative, and the story of his tragic murder, is the subject of this fascinating study.

8 ANVIL! THE STORY OF ANVIL (2008)

While many contemporaries such as Bon Jovi and Whitesnake went on to find chart success, it didn't quite happen for Canadian rockers Anvil. Still cited as an inspiration to bands like Metallica, this real life Spinal Tap is a touching tribute to the good guys who never made it big.

7 TAXI TO THE DARK SIDE (2007)

Winner of the 2007 Academy Award for documentary feature, and holder of a 100% positive rating on review aggregator website Rotten Tomatoes, Gibney's examination of the U.S.A.'s policy on torture is a sobering experience.

6 MAN ON WIRE (2008)

In 1974 French high-wire artist Philippe Petit strung a rope between the twin towers of New York's World Trade Centre and spent an hour walking from one side to the other. The documentary structure is adapted to something akin to a heist movie, with Petit the charismatic mastermind and the towers themselves, loaded with symbolism post 9/11, his objective.

5 THIS IS NOT A FILM (2012)

Found guilty of creating, "propaganda against the

regime", filmmaker Jafar Panahi is under house arrest awaiting news on an appeal. While there he cleverly sidesteps a ban on filmmaking, giving interviews or generally communicating by using a camera phone to document his struggle.

4 THE THIN BLUE LINE (1988)

When someone asks for concrete evidence of a 'message movie' changing something for the better, you could do worse than point them to *The Thin Blue Line*. What starts as an investigation into the circumstance of the killing of a Dallas police officer results in the supposed killer (who had been sentenced to death) being completely exonerated by evidence collected by director Erroll Morris and his collaborators.

3 THE INTERRUPTERS (2011)

The spotlight is shone on the work of three 'Violence Interruptors' (reformed thugs charged with defusing tension in violent inner-city communities) as they attempt to disband gangs in Englewood and the neighbouring communities of Chicago's South Side.

2 THE SORROW AND THE PITY (1969)

This four hour account of France's collaboration with Nazi Germany during WWII is unlikely to be an easy watch for anyone. But what it reveals about the capacity of ordinary people to do both terrible and wonderful things makes it essential.

1 GATES OF HEAVEN (1978)

A peek behind the curtain at a Californian pet cemetery. *Gates of Heaven* is the perfect example of why the supposed subject doesn't matter when a gifted documentarian stumbles on characters like these. Director Werner Herzog had to eat his shoe after betting Morris the film would never be shown.

	MOVIE	DIRECTOR(S)	SUBJECT
10	Harlan County U.S.A. (1976)	Barbara Kopple	Bitter miners strike
9	The Times of Harvey Milk (1984)	Rob Epstein	Politician Harvey Milk
8	Anvil! The Story of Anvil (2008)	Sacha Gervasi	Rock band
7	Taxi to the Dark Side (2007)	Alex Gibney	Torture of terror suspects
6	Man on Wire (2008)	James Marsh	Philippe Petit
5	This is Not A Film (2012)	Jafar Panahi and Mojtaba Mirtahmasb	Jafar Panahi
4	The Thin Blue Line (1988)	Errol Morris	A murder
3	The Interrupters (2011)	Steve James	Chicago violence
2	The Sorrow and the Pity (1969)	Marcel Ophüls	French collaborators WW2
1	Gates of Heaven (1978)	Errol Morris	A pet cemetery

TOP 10

Movies have long been a means of addressing the elephant in the room, that ticking clock that we know will slowly wind down and mandate our eventual death. Movies that look at how we deal with this inevitability can offer profound insights into the value of life, and suggestions for what we might do with it.

MOVIES ABOUT MORTALITY

10 SEVEN POUNDS (2008)

Will Smith is Tim Thomas, an engineer so grief stricken after causing the deaths of seven people he literally dedicates his life to saving seven others.

9 ABOUT SCHMIDT (2002)

Soon after retiring, insurance actuary Warren Schmidt (Jack Nicholson) realises he's wasted his life. With his wife recently deceased he sets off on a road trip with the aim of stopping his daughter marrying the fiancée he deems unsuitable.

8 THE MEANING OF LIFE (1983)

Monty Python's final movie is a series of sketches tied together by the theme of life. From the birth of a child in a hospital more interested in appearances and procedures than patient wellbeing, to the death of a group of friends

poisoned by tinned salmon mousse, the absurdities of life are mercilessly skewered.

7 THE SEA INSIDE (2004)

Quadriplegic Ramón Sampedro (Javier Bardem) campaigns for euthanasia to be legalised in his native Spain. One of his main adversaries is local woman Rosa (Lola Dueñas), who is determined to show him life can still be worth living in his condition.

6 THE STRAIGHT STORY (1999)

When his long estranged brother Lyle (Harry Dean Stanton) suffers a stroke, elderly Alvin Straight (Richard Farnsworth) drives his mower 240 miles to see him. On the way he subtly imparts much wisdom to those he encounters, not to mention the audience.

5 A MATTER OF LIFE AND DEATH (1946)

Towards the end of WWII, Squadron Leader Peter Carter (David Niven) is struggling back towards base in his damaged Lancaster bomber when it becomes apparent he won't make it. Although technically dead, it turns out Heaven has cocked up the paperwork, and Carter is given another chance at life.

4 WILD STRAWBERRIES (1957)

Whilst making the long journey to an awards ceremony in his honour, cantankerous Professor Isak Borg (Victor Sjöström) starts to reminisce on his life. He sees cathartic parallels to the lives of the various hitchhikers he picks up and eventually finds peace.

3 TOKYO STORY (1953)

A retired couple from rural southwest Japan visit

their adult son and daughter in bustling Tokyo. But the children have been swept up in the stresses of city life and pay scant attention to their parents. Only Noriko (Setsuko Hara), the widow of a second dead son, treats them with respect.

2 IKIRU (1952)
After being diagnosed with cancer, a middle aged bureaucrat realises he has done nothing good with his life and sets out to remedy the situation by building a park for local children.

1 THE SEVENTH SEAL (1957)
Returning from the Crusades, a Swedish knight encounters Death and challenges him to a game of chess. Allegory abounds for the following 90 minutes.

	MOVIE	DIRECTOR(S)
10	Seven Pounds (2008)	Gabriele Muccino
9	About Schmidt (2002)	Alexander Payne
8	The Meaning of Life (1983)	Terry Jones and Terry Gilliam
7	The Sea Inside (2004)	Alejandro Amenábar
6	The Straight Story (1999)	David Lynch
5	A Matter of Life and Death (1946)	Michael Powell and Emeric Pressburger
4	Wild Strawberries (1957)	Ingmar Bergman
3	Tokyo Story (1953)	Yasujir Ozu
2	Ikiru (1952)	Akira Kurosawa
1	The Seventh Seal (1957)	Ingmar Bergman

TOP 10

Without wanting to wallow in negativity, it's no small wonder movies adapted from video games have such a bad reputation. It's even debatable whether a first class movie has ever resulted from a game. But in a sea of subpar cinema, there are some that plumb particularly bewildering depths.

WORST VIDEO GAME ADAPTATIONS

elements-of-film-noir-and-supernatural-tones.

7 SUPER MARIO BROS. (1993)

Super Mario Bros. features Bob Hoskins and John Leguizamo as Brooklyn plumbers who must rescue Princess Daisy from Dennis Hopper's evil King Koopa. And there's some stuff about dinosaurs and saving the world too.

10 LARA CROFT: TOMB RAIDER (2001)

With both the game and lead actress boasting megastar credentials it's no surprise the *Tomb Raider* movie was a hit. But, commercial success or not, it's a first degree stinker with a leaden script, clichéd action and ridiculous plot.

9 DOOM (2005)

Coming along years after the *Doom* craze had passed, the movie of the

classic first person shooter missed the boat in terms of finding its audience. Talk of a franchise seems to have been premature with no word yet on the sequel.

8 MAX PAYNE (2008)

Max Payne the man is a New York Detective investigating the murder of his wife and child. *Max Payne* the movie is a confused mess of police-procedural-meets-revenge-fantasy-with-

6 WING COMMANDER (1999)

What was once a video game with niche appeal became a movie with no appeal when *Wing Commander* swooped onto the big screen. The stock plot offers no surprises with the poor actors unable to do anything interesting with it.

5 STREET FIGHTER (1994)

At the time this garish calamity became a byword for overblown, star-driven disasters, and time hasn't been kind to it since. Unable to tap into the martial arts or video games market, it's now almost disappeared from memory.

4 MORTAL KOMBAT: ANNIHILATION (1997)
Sporting a much smaller budget than *Street Fighter*, this sequel to *Mortal Kombat* manages to drop all the balls it's predecessor just about managed to keep in the air. Unbelievably, a series of these things followed.

3 DOUBLE DRAGON (1994)
Based on a title that even non-gamers might have affectionate memories of, *Double Dragon* is a martial arts movie that, like *Street*

Fighter, is aimed squarely at the kids. That won't help your enjoyment of it, regardless of age.

2 BLOODRAYNE (2005)
We're now entering a legendary realm in the world of terrible movies: the Uwe Boll video game adaptation. Widely considered the worst filmmaker ever, Boll churns out nonsense like this period-vampire fiasco every few months.

1 ALONE IN THE DARK (2005)
Alone in the Dark possibly marks the apex of Boll's diabolical filmography. It sees a paranormal detective searching for a murderer, though Boll's crimes against cinema might be a more worthy subject for investigation.

	MOVIE	DIRECTOR(S)	ROTTEN TOMATOES' FRESH RATING	IMDb SCORE
10	*Lara Croft: Tomb Raider (2001)*	Simon West	19.00%	5.7/10
9	*Doom (2005)*	Andrzej Bartowiak	19.00%	5.2/10
8	*Max Payne (2008)*	John Moore	16.00%	5.4/10
7	*Super Mario Bros. (1993)*	Annabel Jankel and Rocky Morton	16.00%	4.0/10
6	*Wing Commander (1999)*	Chris Roberts	11.00%	4.0/10
5	*Street Fighter (1994)*	Steven E. de Souza	13.00%	3.7/10
4	*Mortal Kombat: Annihilation (1997)*	John R. Leonetti	6.00%	3.6/10
3	*Double Dragon (1994)*	James Yukich	0.00%	3.5/10
2	*BloodRayne (2005)*	Uwe Boll	4.00%	2.8/10
1	*Alone in the Dark (2005)*	Uwe Boll	1.00%	2.3/10

TOP 10

A classic movie tough guy needs to be more than just capable of winning a fight. Technical skill and canny strategising are not what it's about (hence no Bruce Lee). But a tough guy must have an imposing presence, be able to take anything you throw at them, and possess a steely determination in confrontational situations.

TOUGH GUYS

10 CHIANG TAI
Bolo Yeung will be instantly recognisable to fans of martial arts movies. For thirty years the former bodybuilder was the go-to guy if a production needed a physically intimidating Asian villain, though it was a heroic role as Chinese Hercules that gave him his signature character.

9 CONAN
Conan has been around since the 1930s in various books, TV shows and comics. But it's Schwarzenegger's muscle bound iteration of the sword and sorcery poster boy that personifies the character for most.

8 MAC 'TRUCK' TURNER
After an injury puts paid to his football career, Truck turns to bounty hunting for a living. But when a criminal he's pursuing is killed, a hit is put out on his life and Truck must fend off a gang of murderous hoodlums.

7 PAUL KERSEY
Paul Kersey demonstrates how almost anyone can be a tough guy when inner rage overcomes physical limitations. Like the Incredible Hulk, emotion makes Kersey capable of extraordinary feats.

6 BRITT
Unlike most of the Magnificent Seven, who sign up to protect a Mexican village from bandits because they need the money, Britt does so because he fancies a fight. That alone should make anyone going up against him think twice.

5 REISMAN
There aren't many actors who could convincingly keep order amongst one of the most deplorable groups of reprobates ever assembled on screen. Lee Marvin shows he can do it with one arm tied behind his back.

4 MACHETE
Danny Trejo served multiple prison sentences and established himself as a fearsome boxer before getting his foot on the Hollywood ladder. For the last forty years he's largely played villains, but ironically found his greatest success as the heroic Machete, a socially conscious Mexican outlaw.

3 PHILO BEDDOE
Eastwood plays Orangutan-owning Philo Beddoe, a truck driver who makes money on the side in bare-knuckle brawls. This is a movie that shows men fighting as they used to in old Hollywood: with endless swings to the jaw accompanied by the deafening crack of an over exuberant sound designer.

2 MATT HUNTER

As a multiple karate champion and legend of the sport, Norris might be the only actor in history who would stand a chance against the fictional names on this list. The all-American Uzi-wielding Matt Hunter is possibly his toughest character: singlehandedly fending off a Russian invasion is no small feat.

1 THOMAS DUNSON

The image perpetuated by the Duke and the studios he's worked for makes him a shoo in for the top spot. It's hard to pick the toughest character he played because they were all basically the same, but you definitely wouldn't want to mess with Dunson.

	CHARACTER	ACTOR	MOVIE
10	Chiang Tai	Bolo Yeung	Chinese Hercules (1973)
9	Conan	Arnold Schwarzenegger	Conan the Barbarian (1982)
8	Mac 'Truck' Turner	Isaac Hayes	Truck Turner (1974)
7	Paul Kersey	Charles Bronson	Death Wish (1974)
6	Britt	James Coburn	The Magnificent Seven (1960)
5	Reisman	Lee Marvin	Dirty Dozen (1967)
4	Machete	Danny Trejo	Machete series (2010-ongoing)
3	Philo Beddoe	Clint Eastwood	Every Which Way But Loose (1978)
2	Matt Hunter	Chuck Norris	Invasion U.S.A. (1985)
1	Thomas Dunson	John Wayne	Red River (1948)

TOP
10

Macguffin is a term popularised by Alfred Hitchcock and used to describe any plot device that takes the form of an object, person or piece of information which is desired by the movie's protagonists. It might be a briefcase full of money being sought by both police and criminals. Or it could be plans for a weapon being fought over by rival agents, or occasionally it's nature may not be revealed at all. All that matters is that everyone wants it, and therefore it drives the plot.

MACGUFFINS

10 THE GENESIS DEVICE

The Genesis Device is a combination machine and chemical process that reorganises matter on a planetary scale. As such it has a high value as both a terraforming tool and weapon.

9 1964 CHEVY MALIBU

Los Angeles repossession companies compete to locate and recover a car driven by a mysterious man. The huge bounty leaves it obvious to all concerned that the mysterious contents of the car are of significant value.

8 BICYCLE

When the bicycle that's crucial to his new job is stolen, Antonio (Lamberto Maggiorani) searches high and low for it with increasing desperation.

7 BRIEFCASE

With the rich environment Tarantino creates it's easy to forget what actually drives the plot. Bu whatever is in crime boss Marcellus Wallace's (Ving Rhames) briefcase, it must be very important.

6 THE HOLY GRAIL

Charged by God (represented here by an animation of cricketer W G Grace) with recovering the chalice into which Christ bled, King Arthur (Graham Chapman) and his knights' set off on their quest. The Python's take on the legend of the Holy Grail is every bit as preposterous as you might expect.

5 THE MALTESE FALCON

In the 16th century the Maltese Knights Templar gifted Charles V of Spain a priceless gold statue of an eagle. Four hundred years later San Francisco crooks are killing to get their hands on it.

4 A BOX

Private Eye Mike Hammer is one of many parties chasing a valuable and dangerous box. About all we know for sure is that the box can kill and nobody connected with it can be trusted.

3 MILITARY SECRETS

As war looms in Europe, the balance of power could depend on who gets hold of plans for a high-tech new engine. One of Hitchcock's finest films, this is a fast-paced thriller that travels the length and breadth of Britain.

2 THE ARK OF THE COVENANT
With Hitler instructing his agents around the world to round up every important artefact they can find, the race is on to discover the location of the chest which stores the ten commandments.

1 THE ONE RING
The treacherous ring, formed by the dark Lord Sauron to gain dominion over the free peoples of Middle-earth, is sought by all who dwell there. Only those who are true of heart can handle it safely, and even then only for a short time.

	MACGUFFIN	MOVIE	WHY IS IT SO POPULAR?
10	The Genesis Device	*Star Trek II and III (1982, 1984)*	It can create or destroy worlds
9	1964 Chevy Malibu	*Repo Man (1984)*	It contains aliens. Maybe
8	Bicycle	*Bicycle Thieves (1948)*	Our hero needs it to work
7	Briefcase	*Pulp Fiction (1994)*	Valuable contents
6	The Holy Grail	*Monty Python and the Holy Grail (1975)*	It's Christ's cup
5	The Maltese Falcon	*The Maltese Falcon (1941)*	It's a priceless statuette
4	A Box	*Kiss Me Deadly (1955)*	It has great power
3	Military Secrets	*The 39 Steps (1935)*	Plans for a new engine
2	The Ark of the Covenant	*Raiders of the Lost Ark (1981)*	It held the ten commandments
1	The One Ring	*The Lord of the Rings series (2001-2003)*	It's imbued with great power

TOP 10

With so many great movie car chases to choose from, and two or three so comprehensively dominating the landscape, there was need for some brutal culling here. So *Bullitt* (1968), *The French Connection* (1971) and *The Italian Job* (1969) are the joint subjects of this list's tribute.

CAR CHASES

10 TOMORROW NEVER DIES (1997)
Trapped in a multi-storey car park, James Bond (Pierce Brosnan) is under fire from evil media tycoon Elliot Carver's (Jonathan Pryce) goons. Ducking down in the back seats to avoid gunfire, Bond uses the car's remote control to evade capture.

9 THE BOURNE IDENTITY (2002)
Bourne approaches this life and death escape in the same calm, analytical fashion he does everything else. Nods to *The Italian Job* are inevitable as he careers around Zürich in a Mini Mayfair.

8 TO LIVE AND DIE IN LA (1985)
This complicated chase was made more difficult to film by virtue of it taking place against oncoming traffic. Director William Friedkin had the idea after falling asleep at the wheel and waking up on the wrong side of the road.

7 DEATH PROOF (2007)
Tarantino pays homage to the 1970s exploitation movies he loves in this retro chase, during which the protagonists switch roles when psycho Stuntman Mike (Kurt Russell) realises the girls he's trying to intimidate are no shrinking violets.

6 RONIN (1998)
With long, unbroken shots and the camera mounted low on the car, we feel as if we're on board as it screams around the twisty roads of the south of France.

5 THE MATRIX RELOADED (2003)
Trinity (Carrie-Anne Moss) and Morpheus (Laurence Fishburne) bend metal, and the laws of physics, trying to escape from Agents. The Wachowski's constructed a 1.5 mile long section of freeway just for this nine minute scene.

4 GONE IN 60 SECONDS (1974)
Professional car thief Vicinski Pace (H.B. Halicki) has just one car left to steal in order to meet a highly profitable order for 48 specific vehicles. After identifying the yellow Ford Mustang, a double cross by his partner leaves him surrounded by police. And a 34 minute chase through six cities ensues.

3 THE TRANSPORTER (2002)
The mysterious Frank (Jason Statham) demonstrates his incredible skills behind the wheel when he acts as getaway driver for three bank robbers.

2 FAST FIVE (2011)
Out for revenge on crime boss Herman Reyes (Joaquim de Almeida), street racing bandits Dom (Vin

Diesel) and Brian (Paul Walker) decide to steal a bank vault containing much of his cash. They tear through the street of Rio dragging the safe, the size of a small truck, behind them whilst being chased by both police and Reyes' men.

1 VANISHING POINT (1971)

Former race car driver Kowalski makes a bet that he can drive from Denver to San Francisco by 3pm the following day. En route he evades numerous attempts by the police to catch him. *Vanishing Point* is one long car chase, as well as an allegory demonstrating how anti-establishment ideology is crushed by authoritarianism.

	MOVIE	PRINCIPAL CARS	DIRECTOR
10	*Tomorrow Never Dies (1997)*	BMW 750 and Mercedes S-Class	*Roger Spottiswoode*
9	*The Bourne Identity (2002)*	Mini Mayfair and Citroën ZX	*Doug Liman*
8	*To Live and Die in LA (1985)*	Chevy Impala and Chevy Malibu	*William Friedkin*
7	*Death Proof (2007)*	Dodge Charger and Chevy Nova	*Quentin Tarantino*
6	*Ronin (1998)*	Mercedes 450 SEL and Audi S8	*John Frankenheimer*
5	*The Matrix Reloaded (2003)*	Ducati 996 and Cadillac Escalade	*Andy Wachowski and Lana Wachowski*
4	*Gone in 60 Seconds (1974)*	Ford Mustang	*H.B Halicki*
3	*The Transporter (2002)*	BMW 735i	*Louis Leterrier and Corey Yuen*
2	*Fast Five (2011)*	Dodge Charger SRT-8	*Justin Lin*
1	*Vanishing Point (1971)*	Dodge Challenger	*Richard C. Sarafian*

Whilst it seems inconceivable anyone could not love musicals, rumour has it such people are out there somewhere. This list is designed to bring them around slowly. Each entry is a bona fide musical, but one generally free from much of the genre's cliché and cumbersome pageantry.

MUSICALS FOR PEOPLE WHO DON'T LIKE MUSICALS

10 TOMMY (1975)
The Who's take on the musical follows the mixed fortunes of a deaf and blind boy who happens to be a pinball wizard.

9 EVERYONE SAYS I LOVE YOU (1996)
Woody Allen's usual tales of men and women falling in and out of love, only this time with added melodrama, Paris and, of course, music.

8 THE HAPPINESS OF THE KATAKURIS (2001)
The Katakuris, owners of a quiet hotel in rural Japan, face a quandary when their only guest dies. Wanting to avoid negative publicity they conceal the death, but then the next guest also expires. Billed as *The Sound of Music* meets *Psycho*, this bizarre black comedy comes with a gore warning.

7 WILLY WONKA AND THE CHOCOLATE FACTORY (1971)
Songs like 'The Candy Man Can' and 'Pure Imagination' helped *Willy Wonka & the Chocolate Factory* to an Academy Award nomination for original score as well as becoming instant classics of the musical genre.

6 ONCE (2006)
Touching tale of an

unnamed Irish busker (Glen Hansard) who falls in love with an also unnamed immigrant (Markéta Irglová). With Dublin the beautiful backdrop, they write and perform songs that detail their complicated love lives.

5 THE ROCKY HORROR PICTURE SHOW (1975)
The musical is just one of many genres *The Rocky Horror Picture Show* can claim to belong to. But, with songs like 'Sweet Transvestite' and 'Planet Schmanet Janet', it's a musical like no other.

4 YELLOW SUBMARINE (1968)
Based loosely on the Beatles song written by Lennon & McCartney, the movie details the Fab Four's mission to rid Pepperland of Blue Meanies. They accompany Captain Fred in the titular vessel and come across no end of peculiarities, which frequently lead the band into song.

3 SOUTH PARK: BIGGER, LONGER & UNCUT (1999)
The foul mouthed kids of South Park found success on the big screen with their maiden musical outing. The typically divisive plot has America go to war with Canada and Saddam Hussein in a loving relationship with Satan.

2 MOULIN ROUGE (2001)
One man's gaudy monstrosity is another's glossy masterpiece. Musical styles are mashed together remorselessly in a chaotic explosion of colour and sound.

1 THE BLUES BROTHERS (1980)

On a mission from God to raise money for the orphanage in which they grew up, Jake and Elwood Blues (John Belushi and Dan Aykroyd) go on a musical odyssey before staging a triumphant comeback show. Cameo appearances come from the likes of big stars like James Brown, Ray Charles, Aretha Franklin and Cab Calloway.

	MOVIE	DIRECTOR	STARRING	MIGHT APPEAL TO FANS OF
10	Tommy (1975)	Ken Russell	Roger Daltrey and Ann-Margret	1970's Rock
9	Everyone Says I Love You (1996)	Woody Allen	Woody Allen and Goldie Hawn	Woody Allen
8	The Happiness of the Katakuris (2001)	Takashi Miike	Kenji Sawada and Keiko Matsuzaka	Japanese Craziness
7	Willy Wonka and the Chocolate Factory (1971)	Mel Stuart	Gene Wilder and Peter Ostrum	Generic Craziness
6	Once (2006)	John Carney	Glen Hansard and Marketa Irglova	Romance
5	The Rocky Horror Picture Show (1975)	Jim Sharman	Tim Curry and Susan Sarandon	Classic Horror and Sci-fi
4	Yellow Submarine (1968)	George Dunning	Paul Angelis and John Clive	Psychedelia, The Beatles
3	South Park: Bigger, Longer & Uncut (1999)	Trey Parker	Matt Stone and Trey Parker	Swearing
2	Moulin Rouge (2001)	Baz Luhrmann	Nicole Kidman and Ewan McGregor	Bright Colours
1	The Blues Brothers (1980)	John Landis	John Belushi and Dan Aykroyd	Comedy, Good Music

TOP
10

How important a character is, and whether their death is significant, are not factors relevant to this list. Funny, horrific, profound or unexpected, all that matters is the character met an unforgettable end.

MEMORABLE DEATHS

1968; dispatching him in such a way makes a compelling point.

6 **JILL MASTERSON**
Using the unusual method of painting the entire body so it can't breathe (?!), Masterson is murdered in this grisly way for her indiscretion with James Bond.

10 **RUSSELL FRANKLIN**
You know there's something odd about the framing of the shot as Samuel L. Jackson's executive stands by an access port in an underwater research station. But nobody could be expecting a genetically engineered super-shark to leap out of the opening and snatch him up in its jaws.

9 **SGT. ELIAS**
Shot by a rival officer, we last see Elias on his knees, arms aloft, as the Viet Cong approach from all sides.

8 **BUTCH CASSIDY AND THE SUNDANCE KID**
After living on borrowed time just a little too long, Butch and Sundance are cornered by the Bolivian army.

7 **BEN**
Holed up in a farmhouse trying to avoid the zombie apocalypse, Ben's cool head and quick thinking sees him survive the night. At least until a mob of locals arrive to take out the zombies and mistake him for one. Casting an African American as the heroic lead was a bold move in

5 **FIRST SCANNER**
Intending to merely demonstrate his telepathic capability to assembled guests, this unnamed 'Scanner' is unwittingly engaged in a psychic battle with the far stronger Darryl Revok (Michael Ironside). The result, a brief but graphic shot of an exploding head, is one of the most iconic moment in 80's sci-fi.

4 **KANE**
Having been attacked by an alien life form that 'impregnated' him with it's offspring, Kane is sitting down

to his first meal for days when he goes into labour. After frantic convulsions a tiny monster bursts from his chest and scurries off, leaving poor Kane dead in a pool of blood.

3 TONY MONTANA

It's a mystery how he lasts as long as he does, but when it comes the death of Tony Montana is every bit as dramatic as we'd expect. Atop a high balcony that opens up onto his tasteless mansion, Tony sprays an invading mercenary army with bullets, but he doesn't notice one stealthy character approaching from behind.

2 JACK DAWSON

Although it's not clear why Jack doesn't clamber onto the same piece of floating debris that saves Rose (Kate Winslet), his death, drowning in icy waters, is no less poignant as a result.

1 MR. CREOSOTE

After making his way through a meal fit for several kings, the grotesquely obese Mr. Creosote declines the meal's denouement: a wafer thin mint. After pressure from the waiter, who seems to understand the effect it will have, the greedy gastronome relents, and bursts in an explosion of semi-digested food.

	CHARACTER(S)	MOVIE	ACTOR(S)	HOW
10	Russell Franklin	Deep Blue Sea (1999)	Samuel L. Jackson	Lunging super-shark
9	Sgt. Elias	Platoon (1986)	Willem Dafoe	A lot of gunfire
8	Butch Cassidy and The Sundance Kid	Butch Cassidy and The Sundance Kid (1969)	Paul Newman and Robert Redford	Even more gunfire
7	Ben	Night of the Living Dead (1968)	Duane Jones	Mistaken for zombie and shot
6	Jill Masterson	Goldfinger (1964)	Shirley Eaton	Suffocation
5	First Scanner	Scanners (1981)	Louis Del Grande	Telekinesis
4	Kane	Alien (1979)	John Hurt	Alien birth
3	Tony Montana	Scarface (1983)	Al Pacino	Shot
2	Jack Dawson	Titanic (1997)	Leonardo DiCaprio	Drowned
1	Mr. Creosote	The Meaning of Life (1983)	Terry Jones	Wafer thin mint

TOP
10

With literally endless possibilities, and no two movies agreeing on how the law of causality is affected by it, there is endless opportunity for movies to explore time travel. As a result there's a bit of everything here.

TIME TRAVEL MOVIES

10 TWELVE MONKEYS (1995)

James Cole (Bruce Willis), a convicted criminal, is sent back through time to learn about a virus that wiped out 99% of earth's population and forced the survivors underground.

9 HOT TUB TIME MACHINE (2010)

Three friends, each experiencing different challenges in their lives, return to a favoured old haunt for a night of drinking. But, wouldn't you know it, their hot tub malfunctions and takes them back in time.

8 LES VISITEURS (1993)

Godefroy de Papincourt (Jean Reno) is a medieval knight accidentally sent over 800 years into the future by an incompetent sorcerer.

7 BILL AND TED'S EXCELLENT ADVENTURE (1989)

Bill (Alex Winter) and Ted (Keanu Reaves) are moronic high school kids with a dreadful rock band, Wyld Stallyns. When the duo look set to fail history (resulting in Ted's threatened with military school), a time traveller from the future takes them to witness some of history's key moments first hand. It transpires that, one day, Wyld Stallyns' music will become a cornerstone of civilisation, and the band must be prevented from breaking up at all costs.

6 SLAUGHTERHOUSE-FIVE (1972)

Kurt Vonnegut's surreal anti-war novel was adapted, to the author's great satisfaction, in 1972. It details the experiences of the curious Billy Pilgrim (Michael Sacks), an optometrist from New York who becomes unstuck in time

(his words) and experiences his life out of sequence.

5 ARMY OF DARKNESS (1992)

Our hero Ash (Bruce Campbell) is sucked through a vortex and dumped into the dark ages with nothing but a chainsaw, a shotgun and a 1973 Oldsmobile Delta 88. Whilst there he gets involved with saving mankind from evil before conjurors attempt to send him back to the future.

4 LOOPER (2012)

Looper's inventive premise has criminals in the future sending assassination targets back through time to be disposed of without risk of interference from the authorities.

3 TIME BANDITS (1981)

Dwarves steal a map from the Supreme Being (Ralph Richardson) and use it to find hidden passageways through time in order to steal treasure.

2 THE TERMINATOR (1984)

A future war between man and machine spills over into 1984 when a ruthless android is sent back through time to kill the mother of a freedom fighter.

1 PRIMER (2004)

Four computer scientists stumble onto the means to travel through time. Where some time travel movies address causality and the grandfather paradox (the impact changing a detail in the past could have on the present) and alternate realities, *Primer* focuses on little else. It's an impossibly convoluted plot that cries out for close examination.

	MOVIE	JOURNEY	DIRECTOR
10	Twelve Monkeys (1995)	2035 to 1990	Terry Gilliam
9	Hot Tub Time Machine (2010)	2010-1986	Steve Pink
8	Les Visiteurs (1993)	1123 to 1992	Jean-Marie Poiré
7	Bill and Ted's Excellent Adventure (1989)	1988 to all over the place	Stephen Herek
6	Slaughterhouse-Five (1972)	1945 to the past and the far future	George Roy Hill
5	Army of Darkness (1992)	1987 to 1300	Sam Raimi
4	Looper (2012)	2074 to 2044	Rian Johnson
3	Time Bandits (1981)	Everywhere	Terry Gilliam
2	The Terminator (1984)	2029 to 1984	James Cameron
1	Primer (2004)	2003 to... it's complicated!	Shane Carruth

TOP
10

Samurai movies (known in Japan as *chanbara*, an onomatopoeic reference to the sound of clashing swords) were, and to an extent remain, hugely popular in Japan. *Chanbara* play a similar role within Japanese culture as the Western does in the U.S.A., with both likely to investigate themes of honour, revenge, responsibility and loyalty. This is a tribute list to *Seven Samurai*, unquestionably the high water mark for the genre.

SAMURAI MOVIES

10 THE TWILIGHT SAMURAI (2002)
Director Yôji Yamada might think he was born into the wrong age: the Jidaigeki (period) Samurai movies he has made seem to belong to the genre's 60's heyday, though the passing of time allows for a unique perspective.

9 YOJIMBO (1961)
After Seven Samurai this is probably the best, and best known, of master filmmaker Akira Kurosawa's chanbara. Both films were also

remade as successful westerns (*A Fistful of Dollars* and *The Magnificent Seven*).

8 GOY KIN (1969)
When a ruthless clan master kills a village of peasants in order to cover up his theft of a shipment of gold, one of his samurai is determined to see him pay.

7 SAMURAI REBELLION (1967)
Two of chanbara's biggest stars (Mifune and Tatsuya Nakadai) share the screen in this touching tale. When the

local daimyo (lord) orders the son of one of his samurais to turn over his wife to him, a bloody conflict becomes inevitable.

6 13 ASSASSINS (2010)
Political machinations lead to a strike force of top samurai being gathered together to assassinate the sadistic half brother of the Shogun. This remake of a popular 1963 movie of the same name is one of Takashi Miike's most critically praised recent offerings.

5 HARAKIRI (1962)
A simple story about a young ronin obliged to commit seppuku (suicide by self-disembowelment). The beauty of the black and white cinematography is in stark contrast with the uglier aspects of the Tokugawa era in which the movie is set.

4 LADY SNOWBLOOD: BLIZZARD FROM THE NETHERWORLD (1973)

A clear influence on Quentin Tarantino's *Kill Bill* movies and Chan-wook Park's 'vengeance trilogy', Lady Snowblood is the stylish tale of a now adult woman conceived and born purely to seek revenge for the butchering of her mother's family.

3 LONE WOLF AND CUB: SWORD OF VENGEANCE (1972)

Footage from this first entry in the legendary *Lone Wolf and Cub* series was cut together with the second and released as *Shogun Assassin* (1980). This is the more authentic experience, but *Shogun Assassin* is perhaps the more accessible entry to the genre.

2 ZATOICHI (2003)

A modern take on the classic Japanese legend of the blind swordsman, *Zatoichi* finds director/writer/producer/star Kitano in playful mood and on blistering form. It's hard to imagine anyone not being seduced by this stunningly crafted masterpiece.

1 THE SWORD OF DOOM (1966)

Ryu Tsukue is a villainous samurai of extraordinary ability. His rejection of Bushido, the moral code by which a samurai lives, leaves him an unethical monster and eventually provokes his descent into madness.

	MOVIE	DIRECTOR	STARRING
10	The Twilight Samurai (2002)	Yôji Yamada	Hiroyuki Sanada
9	Yojimbo (1961)	Akira Kurosawa	Toshir Mifune
8	Goy kin (1969)	Hideo Gosha	Tatsuya Nakadai
7	Samurai Rebellion (1967)	Masaki Kobayashi	Toshir Mifune
6	13 Assassins (2010)	Takashi Miike	Koji Yakusho
5	Harakiri (1962)	Masaki Kobayashi	Tatsuya Nakadai
4	Lady Snowblood: Blizzard from the Netherworld (1973)	Toshiya Fujita	Meiko Kaji
3	Lone Wolf and Cub: Sword of Vengeance (1972)	Kenji Misumi	Tomisabur Wakayama
2	Zatoichi (2003)	Takeshi Kitano	Takeshi Kitano
1	The Sword of doom (1966)	Kihachi Okamoto	Tatsuya Nakadai

LION D'A
FEST

TOP
10

Time to put pen to paper and create your own top 10 list of gangster movies...

10

9

8

7

6

5

4

3

2

1

TOP
10

The screen gangster may have evolved since the likes of Paul Muni and Jimmy Cagney ruled the roost with flashy, stylish performances. But even as they have become generally more believable, and even vulnerable, the gangster's ultimate appeal has remained undimmed. The list is a tribute to *The Godfather* series.

GANGSTERS

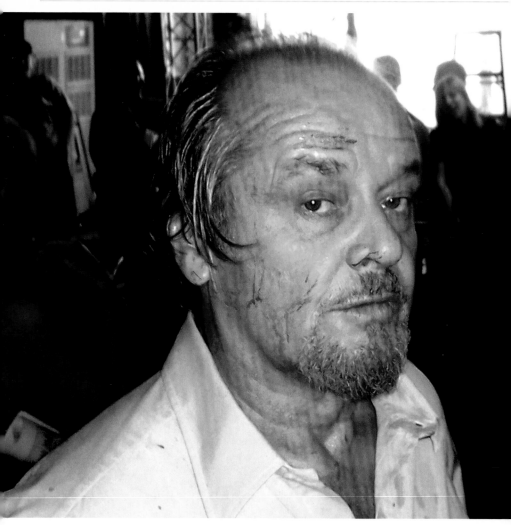

10 DOUGHBOY

Low-level hood Doughboy saunters around his South Central Los Angeles neighbourhood with a bottle of booze sticking out of one pocket and a gun the other. Rapper Ice Cube's first film role is a character he would have been familiar with, assuming the tales recounted in his music have some truth to them.

9 LEO O'BANNON

Leo is the head of an Irish-American mob organisation that controls an unnamed city in the prohibition era America. But his judgement is starting to slip and he ends up in a needless turf war with an up-and-coming Italian crime family.

8 HAROLD SHAND

Successful London gangster Harold Shand is trying to legitimise his business interests. On the brink of securing major overseas investment, a series of bombings and murders by unknown assailants seem to target his empire, throwing everything he's worked for into chaos.

7 FRANK COSTELLO

Martin Scorsese's remake of the Chinese thriller *Infernal Affairs* (2002) beefs up the role of the top gangster somewhat, but that's only sensible when you've bagged Jack Nicholson for the role.

6 MAX BERCOVICZ

This epic, sweeping take on the rise of organised crime in New York is the only significant non-Western directed by Italian Sergio Leone. That the nuance of American criminality is so faithfully rendered is even more impressive when you consider the big man couldn't speak English.

5 RAY VERGO

Prolific character actor Henry Silva has played a lot of gangsters over the years – there's no denying his face lends itself to the roles – but he'd never been given the sort of chance he has here to flesh out a full character, idiosyncrasies and all. Watching him do it is a pleasure.

4 MALIK EL DJEBENA

Set in a French prison, *A Prophet* follows young Algerian Malik as he becomes embroiled in gang, and then starts to ascend through the ranks.

3 RICO AKA LITTLE CAESER

A small fry gangster sets his sights on becoming the big fish in the pond.

2 TOMMY DEVITO

Pesci, sadly, is now more interested in crooning, but in his day he was amongst the best and most underrated working actors. His second collaboration with Martin Scorsese (after 1980's *Raging Bull*) sees him in his defining role, the ambitious but doomed mafioso Tommy.

1 TOM POWERS

Cagney was the ultimate gangster in the gangster movie's ultimate era. Bootlegger Tom Powers rises through the world of organised crime, becoming more brazen and aggressive as he goes. Even in 1931 it must have been obvious where things would end.

	CHARACTER	MOVIE	ACTOR
10	Doughboy	Boyz n the Hood (1991)	Ice Cube
9	Leo O'Bannon	Miller's Crossing (1990)	Albert Finney
8	Harold Shand	The Long Good Friday (1980)	Bob Hoskins
7	Frank Costello	The Departed (2006)	Jack Nicholson
6	Max Bercovicz	Once Upon a Time in America (1984)	James Woods
5	Ray Vergo	Ghost Dog: The Way of the Samurai (1999)	Henry Silva
4	Malik El Djebena	A Prophet (2009)	Tahar Rahim
3	Rico aka Little Caeser	Little Caeser (1931)	Edward G. Robinson
2	Tommy DeVito	Goodfellas (1990)	Joe Pesci
1	Tom Powers	The Public Enemy (1931)	James Cagney

TOP
10

Whether preparing for it, trying to avoid it or just wanting to survive it, war is an inherently dramatic event on which to hang a story. And, like any high stress situation, it has a habit of creating fascinating characters.

MILITARY MEN

10 RICHARD
We only catch up with Richard as he's discharged from the British army and returns to his home town of Matlock, Derbyshire. Learning of the brutal bullying his younger, mentally-impaired brother has been subjected to by a local gang, he sets out on a bloody trail of vengeance.

9 COLONEL DAX
In the WWI trenches, Dax commands a regiment of French troops who were handed a politically motivated suicide mission. With many of his men inevitably killed, survivors are picked at random to face a symbolic court martial for cowardice. Dax causes amused bewilderment amongst his senior officers when he insists on representing the men in court. But he crosses a line when the injustices of the case reach his moral tipping point and he speaks out.

8 PRIVATE JOHN WINGER
Failed cab driver John Winger joins the army expecting training to be like a stay at a fitness resort.

7 COLONEL NICHOLSON
The principled Nicholson loses sight of what's important in a Japanese POW camp during WWII. With the Japanese forcing his men to build a bridge, Nicholson determines it should be the best bridge possible.

6 CAPTAIN VIRGIL HILTS
The token American in this British favourite is also the most memorable character.

5 GENERAL GEORGE S. PATTON
Taking charge of a demoralised American II Corps in North Africa during WWII, Patton soon whips them into shape. But his successes on the battlefield are always undermined by his

outspokenness off it, and although his cunning is crucial to winning the war he ends it without a command.

4 GROUP CAPTAIN LIONEL MANDRAKE

The stiff RAF Captain Mandrake is one of the three roles played by Sellers in this black comedy.

3 LIEUTENANT COLONEL WILLIAM KILGORE

The iconic Kilgore, a man who loves the smell of napalm in the morning, commands an attack helicopter squadron.

Initially reluctant about escorting protagonist Captain Willard (Martin Sheen) through the mouth of the Nung river - an area occupied by the Viet Cong - he finally agrees due to the excellent surfing conditions there.

2 SERGEANT WILLIAM JAMES
Arriving as replacement team leader of a bomb disposal unit in Iraq, James soon gains a reputation for recklessness that puts his tight knit team on edge.

1 GUNNERY SERGEANT HARTMAN
Former U.S. Marine R L Ermey was initially hired as a technical advisor until director Stanley Kubrick saw a tape of what he could do. The amateur even saw much of his improvised dialogue incorporated into the script.

	CHARACTER	MOVIE	ACTOR
10	Richard	Dead Man's Shoes (2004)	Paddy Considine
9	Colonel Dax	Paths of Glory (1957)	Kirk Douglas
8	Private John Winger	Stripes (1981)	Bill Murray
7	Colonel Nicholson	Bridge on the River Kwai (1957)	Alec Guinness
6	Captain Virgil Hilts	The Great Escape (1963)	Steve McQueen
5	General George S. Patton	Patton (1970)	George C. Scott
4	Group Captain Lionel Mandrake	Dr. Strangelove (1964)	Peter Sellers
3	Lieutenant Colonel William Kilgore	Apocalypse Now (1979)	Robert Duvall
2	Sergeant William James	The Hurt Locker (2008)	Jeremy Renner
1	Gunnery Sergeant Hartman	Full Metal Jacket (1987)	R. Lee Ermey

TOP 10

It's interesting to chart the progress of women's rights through the depiction of the on-screen womaniser. Whilst a lothario of the 60's and 70's was generally complimented on his prowess, by the 90's and beyond he is seen as an almost tragic, emotionally immature figure. In *James Bond* (this list's tribute) you can even see it happen through the portrayal of a single character.

WOMANISERS

10 JACK
Jack, once a reasonably successful actor, and old college buddy Miles (Paul Giamatti) head off on a tour of California wine country prior to the former's imminent marriage. But Jack's less interested in the wine than finding some female company, and he isn't afraid to trade on his past fame to get some.

9 DAVE GARVER
When disc jockey Dave Garver picks up a woman in a bar, he becomes the target of her crazed obsession. She stalks him, vandalises his house, disrupts important events and threatens to kill his girlfriend.

8 JACK JERICHO
Jack runs into more than he bargained for with his latest squeeze Randy (Molly Ringwald). Not only does she play things even cooler than Jack, which inevitably makes him fall for her even harder,

but, thanks to her gambling father Flash (Dennis Hopper), Randy is also in trouble with the mafia.

7 GIACOMO CASANOVA
Less a biopic of the legendary Italian heartbreaker than an examination of the existential quandary a life of unrelenting satisfaction might lead to.

6 BLACK DYNAMITE
This comedic throwback to the blaxploitation movies of the 1970s features an exaggerated version of the sort of lothario such movies tended to glorify.

5 RAYMOND DELAUNEY
Pleasant young Henry Palfey (Ian Carmichael) always loses out in love to roguish cad Delauney – until he discovers a school that teaches seduction techniques.

4 MARCUS GRAHAM
A smarmy advertising executive keeps a string of girlfriends on call, all of whom think they're the apple of his eye. He starts to evaluate his character when a beautiful new boss starts objectifying him in the same way he has always done women.

3 ALFIE ELKINS
Cockney chancer Alfie sidles from relationship to relationship with little thought for the women involved. Having come close to taking responsibility for himself when one of his girlfriends falls pregnant, Alfie soon slips back into promiscuous ways.

2 FRANK T.J. MACKEY
Mackey is a minor celebrity in the male self-help world, selling videos and giving talks that explain how to pick up women. Tom Cruise stepped way outside his comfort zone to play this foul-mouthed, sexually aggressive narcissist.

1 GEORGE ROUNDY

A charismatic Beverley Hills hairdresser takes full advantage of his charms and opportunities by bedding a string of married clients as well as his various girlfriends. When he finally has an epiphany and suggests settling down with the woman he loves, she explains that he isn't marrying material.

	CHARACTER	MOVIE	ACTOR
10	Jack	Sideways (2004)	Thomas Haden Church
9	Dave Garver	Play Misty for Me (1971)	Clint Eastwood
8	Jack Jericho	The Pick-up Artist (1987)	Robert Downey Jr.
7	Giacomo Casanova	Fellini's Casanova (1976)	Donald Sutherland
6	Black Dynamite	Black Dynamite (2009)	Michael Jai White
5	Raymond Delauney	School for Scoundrels (1960)	Terry Thomas
4	Marcus Graham	Boomerang (1992)	Eddie Murphy
3	Alfie Elkins	Alfie (1966)	Michael Caine
2	Frank T.J. Mackey	Magnolia (1999)	Tom Cruise
1	George Roundy	Shampoo (1975)	Warren Beatty

TOP
10

To enjoy a good revelation it's obviously vital not to be aware what it is. It's always going to be difficult to discuss a twist without exposing it, so consider this a spoiler heavy list, the details of which should be avoided by anyone who hasn't seen the movie in question.

TWIST ENDINGS

10 APRIL FOOLS DAY (1986)

An apparently typical slasher movie setup (kids holidaying on an isolated island are picked off by an unseen killer, last remaining girl is driven half mad) is given a fantastically cruel and unexpected twist when it's revealed the host has staged the killings as a joke.

9 THE CRYING GAME (1992)

This psychological thriller set against the backdrop of Northern Ireland's troubles examines a succession of weighty subjects. The infamous twist comes when Fergus (Stephen Rea), and the audience, discover girlfriend Dil (Jaye Davidson) is actually transgender.

8 THE ORPHANAGE (2007)

Soon after moving to a former orphanage, the adopted son of a young couple goes missing. After spending months searching the whole country the mother discovers a hidden door, blocked by building equipment, to a basement. Inside is the body of their son.

7 CHINATOWN (1974)

Domineering patriarch Noah (John Huston) and his highly strung daughter Evelyn (Faye Dunaway) share a terrible secret. We suspect something is amiss from the start, but it's still a huge shock to learn Evelyn's daughter is the result of a sexual assault by Noah.

6 SOYLENT GREEN (1973)

In the near future much of society has collapsed after a population explosion exhausts food supplies. The state rations soylent green, an artificial foodstuff that proves

to be tackling not just the lack of food but the abundance of people... in the most disturbing way possible.

5 PLANET OF THE APES (1968)

Believing he is stranded on a distant planet ruled by apes, astronaut George Taylor (Charlton Heston) stumbles on a collapsed statue of Liberty, and realises he is actually on earth but in some terrible future in which mankind has been reduced to mute slavery.

4 FIGHT CLUB (1999)

Fight Club's nihilistic ethos really struck a chord with a disenchanted generation when it was released in 1999. The unexpected twist only helped it's appeal, as we discover that the two main characters are actually one and the same revolutionary psychopath.

3 LES DIABOLIQUES (1955)
A domineering schoolmaster is murdered when his mistress and wife take against him. When he reappears, weeks later, in a ghoulishly staged resurrection that scares his wife to death, we learn the initial 'murder' was a phony, with the death of the wife the ultimate goal.

2 PSYCHO (1960)
As with *Planet of the Apes*, it's hard to imagine anyone isn't aware of this twist. We learn Norman Bates' (Anthony Perkins) mother is long dead, and he isn't quite the gentle boy he seems... in fact he's responsible for all the brutal murders at the Bates Motel.

1 THE USUAL SUSPECTS (1995)
Fans still debate whether Kevin Spacey's unassuming conman, 'Verbal' Kint, really is Keyser Soze. It seems the revelation is so unexpected it makes us suspicious there might be more concealed within the labyrinthine plot. Maybe there is, but Verbal is Keyser Soze.

	MOVIE	DIRECTOR	THE TWIST (SPOILERS)
10	April Fools Day (1986)	Fred Walton	Nobody was killed, it was all a joke
9	The Crying Game (1992)	Neil Jordan	Gender confusion
8	The Orphanage (2007)	J.A. Bayona	He was trapped in the basement
7	Chinatown (1974)	Roman Polanski	He's her grandfather and her father
6	Soylent Green (1973)	Richard Fleischer	It's made of people
5	Planet of the Apes (1968)	Franklin J. Schaffner	It's the future and you're still on Earth
4	Fight Club (1999)	David Fincher	They're the same person
3	Les Diaboliques (1955)	Henri-Georges Clouzot	It was all a very complicated trick
2	Psycho (1960)	Alfred Hitchcock	Mother's dead and it was all Norman
1	The Usual Suspects (1995)	Bryan Singer	Verbal is Keyzer Soze

TOP 10

Occasionally a director and actor capable of getting the very best from each other are lucky enough to strike up an ongoing relationship. Sometimes they share a common ethos, sometimes there's a chasm between them and it's the conflict that produces the magic.

ACTOR-DIRECTOR PARTNERSHIPS

be making very different movies without them.

6 ALEC GUINNESS/ DAVID LEAN
Although the relationship deteriorated significantly, these two screen titans produced magic to the end.

5 DIANE KEATON/ WOODY ALLEN
Allen and Keaton collaborated before, during and after their relationship.

10 JACK LEMMON/ BILLY WILDER
Lemmon and Wilder made many of Hollywood's best comedies, with something interesting going on beneath the surface of each.

9 MARCELLO MASTROIANNI/ FEDERICO FELLINI
Fellini cast Mastroianni in two of the most important films of the 1960s.

8 JOHN WAYNE/JOHN FORD
Together Ford and Wayne forged the most identifiable screen persona in American cinema.

7 MAX VON SYDOW/ INGMAR BERGMAN
These two mined the bleakest depths of the human condition so others don't have to. Judd Apatow and Seth Rogen might

4 SETSUKO HARA/ YASUJIR OZU
Ozu's square, static lens, the simple straight lines of classical Japanese homes, the understated, humanistic acting. It all comes together perfectly to leave the viewer feeling almost soothed or contented. Hara usually played the daughter in Ozu's films, which were often about the everyday challenges facing ordinary families in a changing

Japan. The stunning actress made few films, never married and retired young, ensuring she would become an inviolable, legendary figure to a generation of Japanese.

3 KLAUS KINSKI/WERNER HERZOG

The mercurial, uncontrollable Kinski and the impulsive, determined Herzog had one of the most explosive friendships in cinema. Each

collaboration resulted in sworn testimonials they would never speak again – but both understood the symbiotic relationship they shared, each pushing, or antagonising, the other on to further greatness. But it took a toll and they worked together infrequently, with Kinski's death in 1991 putting paid to any future plans the most electrifying duo in cinema history may have had.

2 ROBERT DE NIRO/MARTIN SCORSESE

Scorsese and De Niro first worked together on 1973's *Mean Streets*, the sort of tale of New York gangsters the pair would become so indelibly linked to. But it was *Taxi Driver* that propelled both into the higher strata of the Hollywood system, earning as it did plaudits from all quarters. They went on to collaborate on films such as *Raging Bull* (1980), *The King of Comedy* (1982), *Goodfellas* (1990) and *Cape Fear* (1991), and promise to do so again soon.

1 TOSHIR MIFUNE/AKIRA KUROSAWA

Mifune was a struggling actor when he attended a talent competition staged by Toho, the biggest Japanese studio of the day. Kurosawa, already a reasonably established director, was in attendance and found himself mesmerised. The two men would make a series of films adored by critics and fans alike, including *Rashômon* (1950), *Throne of Blood* (1957), *Yojimbo* (1961) and of course *Seven Samurai* (1954), one of the most celebrated films in history.

	ACTOR/ DIRECTOR	COLLABORATIONS	HIGHLIGHT
10	Jack Lemmon/Billy Wilder	7	*The Apartment (1960)*
9	Marcello Mastroianni/Federico Fellini	6	*8 ½ (1963)*
8	John Wayne/ John Ford	21	*The Searchers (1956)*
7	Max Von Sydow/ Ingmar Bergman	13	*The Seventh Seal (1957)*
6	Alec Guinness/ David Lean	6	*Bridge on the River Kwai (1957)*
5	Diane Keaton/ Woody Allen	8	*Annie Hall (1977)*
4	Setsuko Hara/ Yasujir Ozu	6	*Tokyo Story (1953)*
3	Klaus Kinski/ Werner Herzog	6	*Fitzcarraldo (1982)*
2	Robert De Niro/ Martin Scorsese	9	*Taxi Driver (1976)*
1	Toshir Mifune/ Akira Kurosawa	16	*Seven Samurai (1954)*

TOP
10

Sometimes you just need to think of a movie and a song inextricably linked to it will be stuck in your head for the rest of the day. To allow some other folk a chance, Quentin Tarantino, the arch master of this phenomenon, is the subject of this list's tribute.

POP SONGS IN MOVIES

10 TAKE ME HOME, COUNTRY ROADS
This lesser known anime from Studio Ghibli reflects the curious love many Japanese share for the John Denver tune. Shizuku, the film's heroine, is translating it into Japanese for her school graduation, and it recurs throughout, playing a prominent and touching role.

9 IN YOUR EYES
The image of John Cusack (as lovelorn Lloyd Dobler) standing in front of his ex-girlfriend's house with a boom box above his head is unforgettable. As is the Peter Gabriel favourite blasting over the soundtrack. One of the most identifiable scenes in 80's cinema.

8 IMAGINE
It might be a bit on the nose but the use of John Lennon's anti-war classic is

unforgettable for those who have seen the film. You can tell who they are because they're likely to start weeping at just the thought of this beautifully simple composition.

7 IN DREAMS
David Lynch is known for his knack of taking the wholesomely mundane and twisting it into something nightmarish. Here Orbison's ethereal recording takes on a sinister quality as it's injected into the darkly oppressive atmosphere of the film.

6 HURDY GURDY MAN
Donovan's usual folk style was discarded in favour of the exotically hypnotic sound of this unusual 1968 hit tune. As with Lynch's use of Roy Orbison's 'In Dreams', here director David Fincher reveals hidden dimensions to the song that will stay with you forever.

5 I GOT YOU BABE
If you ever travel to Punxsutawney to report on a weather forecasting rat and get stuck in a time loop, pray this isn't the song you wake up to every morning. Before he even gets out of bed, Bill Murray's Phil is pushed to the brink of insanity... day after day after day.

4 LUST FOR LIFE
Played over the bravura opening titles to Danny Boyle's

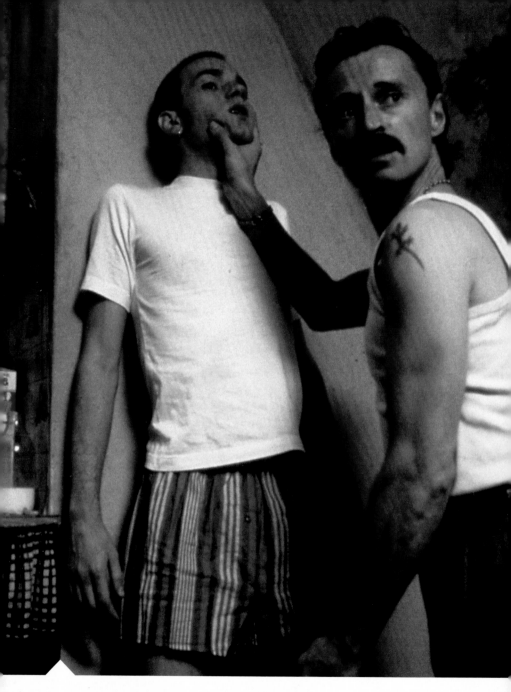

tale of heroin addiction in
late 80's Edinburgh, Lust
for Life's thundering and

uncompromising sound
immediately connected with
the 90's youth generation in

much the same way it had that
of the 70's.

3 BE MY BABY

This song kicks in on a slow-mo glide up to the composed face of Harvey Keitel's Charlie. Cut to De Niro's Johnny Boy, Charlie's wayward friend, flashing money that isn't his. One of the most perfect marriages of scene and song in the movies.

2 OLD TIME ROCK N ROLL

These days Tom Cruise is probably more famous for jumping on Oprah's sofa in a state of euphoria than for jumping on his parent's sofa in his underpants, but this scene cannot be overlooked. Perhaps not the most intellectually rewarding use of song, though.

1 BOHEMIAN RHAPSODY

An immediate hit in the UK, 'Bohemian Rhapsody' initially failed to find success in America. It wasn't until it's legendary use in *Wayne's World* that it became popular. Arguably unique both as a pop song and in how effectively it was incorporated into a movie's joke.

	SONG	ORIGINAL PERFORMER	MOVIE
10	Take Me Home, Country Roads	John Denver	*Whisper of the Heart (1995)*
9	In Your Eyes	Peter Gabriel	*Say Anything (1989)*
8	Imagine	John Lennon	*The Killing Fields (1984)*
7	In Dreams	Roy Orbison	*Blue Velvet (1986)*
6	Hurdy Gurdy Man	Donovan	*Zodiac (2007)*
5	I Got You Babe	Sonny and Cher	*Groundhog Day (1993)*
4	Lust for Life	Iggy Pop	*Trainspotting (1996)*
3	Be My Baby	The Ronettes	*Mean Streets (1973)*
2	Old Time Rock N Roll	Bob Seger	*Risky Business (1983)*
1	Bohemian Rhapsody	Queen	*Wayne's World (1992)*

TOP 10

There have been surprisingly few dramatic movies that tackle the fashion world directly. Most successful attempts to get under it's skin have used the documentary format, perhaps because the industry features real people who are just as colourful as those we invent.

MOVIES ABOUT FASHION

10 SEX AND THE CITY (2008)

Carrie Bradshaw (Sarah Jessica Parker) perseveres with her seesawing love life in this adaptation of the popular TV show, supported (as usual) by her friends - who have accidently scuppered her marriage plans.

9 VALENTINO: THE LAST EMPEROR (2008)

The documentary covers a year in Valentino's life including a retrospective of his work and preparation for the new show.

8 THE BITTER TEARS OF PETRA VON KANT (1972)

Fictional drama about cruel and abrasive fashion designer Petra von Kant (Margit Carstensen), who falls in love with aspiring model Karin (Hanna Schygulla). The two embark on an emotionally charged affair that,

unsurprisingly, ends in tears.

7 GIA (1998)

This biopic of model Gia Carangi marks Angelina Jolie's first lead performance. She is excellent as Gia, the stunning model who shot to stardom in the late 70's, but was blacklisted by the industry after cocaine and heroin problems affected her behaviour. She died tragically of an AIDS related illness at just 26.

6 THE SEPTEMBER ISSUE (2009)

A documentary on the effort involved in producing *Vogue* magazine's September issue, it's most important of the year. Having wisely decided to focus on Grace Coddington, the fascinating creative director of the magazine, rather than it's notorious but less interesting editor Anna Wintour, Fontaine latches onto the key to the film's appeal and runs with it.

5 COCO BEFORE CHANEL (2009)

Biopic of the designer starring the irrepressible Audrey Tautou.

4 THE DEVIL WEARS PRADA (2006)

A naïve girl bags her dream job as assistant to the editor of a fashion magazine. Unfortunately the editor in question is Miranda Priestly (Meryl Streep), a notoriously vicious bully.

3 ZOOLANDER (2001)

The fashion world is sent up mercilessly in this riotous spoof about the rivalry between two equally superficial male models. Derek Zoolander is at the top of the tree when hungry newcomer Hansel MacDonald (Owen Wilson) knocks him off his perch. Meanwhile, evil fashionistas plot to assassinate the Malaysian prime minister, who plans to cut the cheap labor relied upon by the fashion industry. But when Derek is brainwashed as part of the conspiracy, some of his harshest critics unite to save him and prevent the assassination.

2 WHO ARE YOU, POLLY MAGOO? (1966)

Polly Magoo (Dorothy McGowan) is an American supermodel being followed around Paris by a documentary crew. The fashion industry is brutally satirised for its triviality and emptiness, something McGowan must be familiar with, having been a successful model herself.

1 FUNNY FACE (1957)

Audrey Hepburn is Jo Stockton, a book shop clerk who inadvertently winds up in the background of a fashion photographers shoot. Obviously everyone who sees the pictures insists she must become a model.

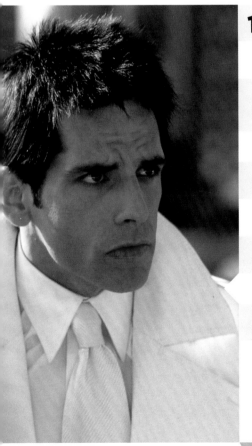

	MOVIE	DIRECTOR
10	Sex and the City (2008)	Michael Patrick King
9	Valentino: The Last Emperor (2008)	Matt Tyrnauer
8	The Bitter Tears of Petra von Kant (1972)	Rainer Werner Fassbinder
7	Gia (1998)	Michael Cristofer
6	The September Issue (2009)	R.J. Cutler
5	Coco Before Chanel (2009)	Anne Fontaine
4	The Devil Wears Prada (2006)	David Frankel
3	Zoolander (2001)	Ben Stiller
2	Who Are You, Polly Magoo? (1966)	William Kein
1	Funny Face (1957)	Stanley Donen

TOP 10

Existentialism can be a tricky term to define and seems to mean different things to different people. Here it's taken to refer loosely to any attempt to make sense of our place within a seemingly meaningless universe, or perhaps a way of examining our personal experiences as individuals and how they make us what we are. To those familiar with his work, it's perhaps needless to say that this is a tribute to Ingmar Bergman.

MOVIES DEALING WITH EXISTENTIALISM

10 THE TRUMAN SHOW (1998)
A man discovers his entire life is a TV reality show.

9 BEING JOHN MALKOVICH (1999)
Puppeteer Craig Schwartz (John Cusack) discovers a portal straight into the mind of actor John Malkovich.

8 ORDINARY PEOPLE (1980)
When the oldest son of an affluent family dies, his brother, father and mother all struggle to deal with the fallout.

7 UNTIL THE END OF THE WORLD (1991)
With a failed nuclear satellite causing widespread contamination and the destruction of most electronic devices, two men with a machine that can read brain impulses hole up in an Australian cave with other survivors.

6 I HEART HUCKABEES (2004)
Existential detectives Bernard and Vivian Jaffe (Dustin Hoffman and Lily Tomlin) are employed by Albert (Jason Schwartzman), a troubled environmental campaigner, to solve what he believes is a profound mystery: seeing the same stranger three times in one day.

5 AU HASARD BALTHAZAR (1966)
Insecure farm girl Marie (Anne Wiazemsky) and her donkey Balthazar lead comparable lives. Neither is in a position to respond to the way they're treated and, inevitably, both are exploited and abused.

4 TASTE OF CHERRY (1997)
A middle aged Iranian man decides to kill himself, but needs to find someone willing to bury him. To that end he travels the country asking people for help. Each explains why, from their perspective, they are not comfortable with the task.

3 AMERICAN BEAUTY (1999)
Lester Burnham (Kevin Spacey) is concealing a midlife crisis from his family. As he becomes obsessed with his teenage daughter's best friend he embraces his breakdown and the second youth that comes with it.

2 THE QUIET EARTH (1985)
All but a few of mankind are wiped out when an experiment into energy sharing goes wrong. Scientist Zac Hobson (Bruno Lawrence) is drawn to the brink of madness by guilt and introspection. He eventually finds other survivors and an interesting social dynamic develops.

1 SOLARIS (1972)

The crew of a space station orbiting the planet Solaris each fall prey to psychological problems, as does Kelvin (Donatas Banionis), the psychologist sent to help them. An intelligence on the planet surface is capable of conjuring up fully formed people from our memory, and Kelvin is effectively given a choice whether to stay with a replica of the woman he loved and lost, or return to earth and a life where she remains dead. The film asks what makes a human being human, what role experience, emotion and memory play in our humanity, and what, if anything, differentiates a real person from another being that is technically identical.

	MOVIE	DIRECTOR
10	The Truman Show (1998)	Peter Weir
9	Being John Malkovich (1999)	Spike Jonze
8	Ordinary People (1980)	Robert Redford
7	Until the End of the World (1991)	Wim Wenders
6	I Heart Huckabees (2004)	David O. Russell
5	Au hasard Balthazar (1966)	Robert Besson
4	Taste of Cherry (1997)	Abbas Kiarostami
3	American Beauty (1999)	Sam Mendes
2	The Quiet Earth (1985)	Geoff Murphy
1	Solaris (1972)	Andrei Tarkovsky

Avarice is a concept central to more movies than might immediately come to mind. But although greed might be the catalyst for most plots involving crime, a movie won't make this list unless it specifically addresses the subject of greed. Tribute to Charles Foster (Citizen) Kane.

GREEDY BASTARDS

10 ALMOST EVERYONE
This all-star caper movie starts with a dying bank robber cryptically revealing the location of his spoils to four passing motorists. As word spreads, a scramble to find the loot leads to mayhem.

9 JORDAN BELFORT
The true story of a Long Island stockbroker who swindled millions out of investors in a securities scam and splashed it on a lavish lifestyle.

8 RANDOLPH AND MORTIMER DUKE
These tyrannical brothers are stalwarts of the New York stock exchange, with Louis Winthorpe III (Dan Aykroyd) their best investor. To amuse themselves the two men make a bet as to whether a tramp could perform as well as Winthorpe if given the same opportunity. To that end they engineer a scenario whereby panhandler Billy Ray Valentine (Eddie Murphy) is given Winthorpe's job, while Winthorpe himself is stitched up and left homeless. But the Dukes severely underestimate the pawns in their game.

7 TRINA
A lottery win leads to nothing but misery for all concerned. Trina, the one who bought the ticket, becomes so obsessed with money that she prefers to live in poverty than spend any of the huge stack of gold she has squiralled away.

6 GENJÛRÔ AND TÔBEE
In the late 16th century, two Japanese villagers work feverishly to make clay pots that can be sold for a profit in a nearby town. But with civil war raging and the army of cruel lord Shibata marauding, there are too many deadly perils for a man to become preoccupied with his own greed.

5 TUCO
Sergio Leone's epic western offers three men's

distinct approaches to the procurement of money. One is smart and greedy, one stupid and greedy, the third more circumspect. Only one man survives.

4 EBENEZER SCROOGE
The best version of Dickens immortal morality tale, starring the wonderful Alastair Sim as the seasonal grouch who learns the perils of greed on a snowy Christmas Eve.

3 DOBBS
In Mexico, 1925, three Americans strike gold. One of them in particular, Dobbs, is so busy worrying about the threat his colleagues pose to his share that he doesn't notice the real danger: his own paranoia and greed.

2 DANIEL PLAINVIEW
An oil man interested in nothing but money, Plainview symbolises the dark side of the pioneer spirit.

1 GORDON GEKKO
The character who, more than any other, has come to represent the cancerous greed of amoral stockbrokers. His motto ('greed is good') could have been the clarion cry of those bankers and brokers who brought about the recent economic crisis.

	CHARACTER(S)	MOVIE	ACTOR(S)
10	Almost Everyone	It's a Mad, Mad, Mad, Mad World (1963)	Lots of People
9	Jordan Belfort	The Wolf of Wall Street (2013)	Leonardo DiCaprio
8	Randolph and Mortimer Duke	Trading Places (1983)	Ralph Bellamy and Don Ameche
7	Trina	Greed (1924)	Zasu Pitts
6	Genjûrô and Tôbee	Ugetsu Monogatari (1953)	Masayaki Mori and Eitarô Ozawa
5	Tuco	The Good, the Bad and the Ugly (1966)	Eli Wallach
4	Ebenezer Scrooge	A Christmas Carol (1951)	Alastair Sim
3	Dobbs	The Treasure of the Sierra Madre (1948)	Humphry Bogart
2	Daniel Plainview	There Will Be Blood (2007)	Daniel Day-Lewis
1	Gordon Gekko	Wall Street (1987)	Michael Douglas

TOP
10

Not all the couples here have enjoyed a classic love story. But each is uplifting in its own way and inspiring 1 one degree or another; a reflection of the power cinema has to involve us in the emotions of two fictional people partaking in a fictional relationship.

COUPLES

10 TONY AND ALICE
An industrialist trying to force the eccentric Sycamore family from their home sees his son (James Stewart) fall in love with the Sycamore's daughter (Jean Arthur).

9 RHETT BUTLER AND SCARLETT O'HARA
These two are hardly an example of a happy, loving couple. But the saga of their relationship is so entrenched in film (not to mention literary)

history they had to take a place on this list.

8 BELLA SWANN AND EDWARD CULLEN
Every generation needs its iconic young couple who face terrible challenges to their love. The current pair just happen to be vampires.

7 HARRY BURNS AND SALLY ALBRIGHT
Can a man and a woman be friends without sex getting in the way? Harry and Sally

spend years researching the answer before falling in love.

6 TOULA AND IAN
Toula, from a family of proud Greeks living in Chicago, falls in love with Ian, a WASP she knows full well her father will not accept. After dating secretly, the power of their love overcomes the obstacles facing their relationship.

5 HAROLD AND MAUDE
Harold is a teenager obsessed with death. Maude is a 79 year old preoccupied with enjoying life. Their's is an unusual but delightful romance.

4 TONY AND MARIA
This thinly disguised take on Romeo & Juliet, with New York gangs replacing the feuding Veronese families, is still a remarkable work nearly 60 years since it was first staged.

3 ALEC HARVEY AND LAURA JESSON
The doctor and housewife meet by chance at a railway station and develop an instant attraction. Although both are married, they continue to see each other, even knowing their regular rendezvous can lead to nothing but heartache.

2 TOM AND GERRI HEPPLE
Writer/director Mike Leigh's eye for what makes ordinary people fascinating subjects has never been sharper. Over the course of a year, middle aged couple Tom and Gerri Hepple see various friends and relatives pass through their home, each living with loneliness of one kind or another. They do what they can to help, the strength of their bond apparently giving them emotional energy to spare.

1 JESSE AND CÉLINE
Across three films and 18 years, director Richard Linklater and his collaborators created two characters with an extraordinary emotional depth. In the first film they meet and spend a romantically charged night in Vienna before parting ways, perhaps forever. In the second the former lovers reconnect in Paris nine years later and again share a magical connection. In the third film they are married and facing the reality of life beyond their idyllic, early courtship. At every stage the relationship is utterly convincing, each line of dialogue credible, and every emotional reaction authentic.

	COUPLE	MOVIE	ACTORS
10	Tony and Alice	*You Can't Take it With You (1938)*	James Stewart and Jean Arthur
9	Rhett Butler and Scarlett O'Hara	*Gone With the Wind (1939)*	Clark Gable and Vivien Leigh
8	Bella Swann and Edward Cullen	*Twilight series (2008-2012)*	Kristen Stewart and Robert Pattinson
7	Harry Burns and Sally Albright	*When Harry Met Sally (1989)*	Billy Crystal and Meg Ryan
6	Toula and Ian	*My Big Fat Greek Wedding (2002)*	Nia Vardalos and John Corbett
5	Harold and Maude	*Harold and Maude (1971)*	Bud Cort and Ruth Gordon
4	Tony and Maria	*West Side Story (1961)*	Richard Beymer and Natalie Wood
3	Alec Harvey and Laura Jesson	*Brief Encounter (1945)*	Trevor Howard and Celia Johnson
2	Tom and Gerri Hepple	*Another Year (2010)*	Jim Broadbent and Ruth Sheen
1	Jesse and Céline	*Before Sunrise/ Sunset/Midnight (1995-2013)*	Ethan Hawke and Julie Delpy

TOP
10

Given moral standards differ significantly throughout the world, it's intriguing how a handful of movies have managed to create almost universal international controversy.

CONTROVERSIAL MOVIES

10 TRIUMPH OF THE WILL (1935)

This documentary covering the 1934 Nuremberg rally is respected by filmmakers and enthusiasts for it's undeniable qualities. But at the same time its politics is almost universally despised. Director Leni Riefenstahl claimed not to realise the Nazi agenda.

9 THE BIRTH OF A NATION (1915)

Another example of accomplished cinema compromised by its politics, even on release *Birth of a Nation* was considered morally reprehensible by many. Actors in black face play African Americans as ignorant and aggressive, while the Ku Klux Klan are presented as heroes.

8 ANTICHRIST (2009)

Probably the only entry that clearly set out to be controversial, provocateur extraordinaire Lars von Trier uses a horror movie structure to inflict as much unpleasantness on the audience as possible. Nonetheless the film is adored by many critics.

7 CANNIBAL HOLOCAUST (1980)
Amongst the nastiest in a wave of gratuitously obnoxious horror movies to come out of Italy in the period, *Cannibal Holocaust* managed to upset just about everybody. Gore and violence loses its edge over time but the animal cruelty remains problematic.

6 THE EXORCIST (1973)
Refused a home video release in the UK until 1999 and still banned in some countries, in a way it's hard to see exactly why *The Exorcist* caused such upset. Unlike other entries on this list, it seems to have been the sheer effectiveness of its scare tactics.

5 LAST TANGO IN PARIS (1972)
At the time it was unheard of for major stars to appear in a movie so sexually explicit, but that one should be involved in the now infamous 'butter scene' was unthinkable. Cynics might suggest the controversy helped an average movie do exceptional business.

4 LIFE OF BRIAN (1979)
At the heart of the controversy over *Life of Brian* was the perception that Christ himself was being mocked by the Monty Python team. They remain adamant they were actually satirising the most gullible of religious believers. Either way it's very funny.

3 THE PASSION OF THE CHRIST (2004)
The tradition of the Passion Play, in which Christ is depicted enduring trial, suffering

and crucifiction, is central to the faith of many Christian denominations. Mel Gibson's movie version was massively successful in the U.S. but provoked accusations of anti-semitism.

2 SALÒ, OR THE 120 DAYS OF SODOM (1975)

A uniquely depraved and interminably arduous watch, Salò focuses on the debauched antics of four politically powerful fascist libertines in WWII era Italy as they torture, rape and generally abuse a series of victims for sexual gratification.

1 THE LAST TEMPTATION OF CHRIST (1988)

The catalyst for the unprecedented controversy that swept the world on the release of Last Temptation is the final scene. In what seems to be a dream sequence, Christ descends from the cross, marries Mary Magdalene and lives out his life as a mortal.

	MOVIE	DIRECTOR	CONTROVERSIAL WHY?
10	Triumph of the Will (1935)	Leni Riefenstahl	Nazi propaganda
9	The Birth of a Nation (1915)	D.W. Griffith	Racism
8	Antichrist (2009)	Lars von Trier	Graphic gore, sexual explicitness, gratuitous violence
7	Cannibal Holocaust (1980)	Ruggero Deodato	Graphic gore, sexual violence, animal cruelty
6	The Exorcist (1973)	William Friedkin	Blasphemy, scariness
5	Last Tango in Paris (1972)	Bernardo Bertolucci	Sexual violence, sexual explicitness
4	Life of Brian (1979)	Terry Jones	Blasphemy
3	The Passion of the Christ (2004)	Mel Gibson	Anti-semitism, graphic gore, gratuitous violence
2	Salò, or the 120 Days of Sodom (1975)	Pier Paolo Pasolini	Sexual violence, sexual explicitness, general depravity
1	The Last Temptation of Christ (1988)	Martin Scorsese	Blasphemy

TOP
10

A hotbed of illicit activity; the place where lovers meet, the scene of raucous partying, a hangout for reprobate degenerates, movie bars have seen it all. Whether you'd like to actually drink in any of these gin joints is a matter of personal preference.

BARS

10 GREELY'S
Typical old west saloon with a particularly unpalatable proprietor.

9 COYOTE UGLY SALOON
Believe it or not the real Coyote Ugly is pretty much the same as the movie version. Half naked women dance on the bar, sing, chug drinks and do anything else they can think of to get patrons to part with their cash.

8 CLUB SUGAR RAY
In the only movie Eddie Murphy made with his hero Richard Pryor, the two men play a father and (adopted) son team running a speakeasy and gambling joint in prohibition era New York.

7 THE LAST RESORT
In 2084 The Last Resort is an expansive underground bar in Mars' red light district. It doubles as a front for the revolutionaries

seeking to overthrow the cruel governor, Vilos Cohaagen (Ronny Cox).

6 PLEASURE ISLAND POOL HALL
On Pleasure Island there is no

authority, no adults and no rules. Naughty children can do whatever they want, including drinking and smoking, at the pool hall (this was 1940). But beware, if you get carried away and make a jackass of yourself,

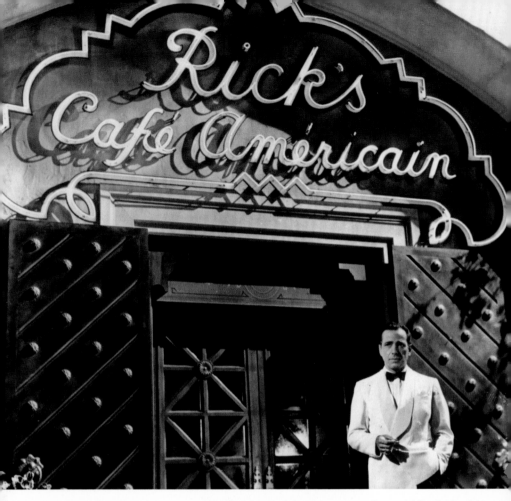

you will be turned into a donkey.

5 KOROVA MILK BAR
The Korova eschews traditional beverages in favour of milk laced with a variety of drugs. It also attracts quite a cross section of society, with dolled up opera singers sharing anthropomorphic tables with ultra-violent thugs.

4 THE GOLD ROOM
With the most cryptic of staff and a clientele of waltzing ghosts, the Gold Room will not be for everyone. Beware of any barman who materialises for a customer offering his soul for a glass of bourbon.

3 THE BLUE OYSTER
What we see of The Blue Oyster makes it seem a particularly welcoming place. But the gay bar is full of moustachioed, leather clad cliches, so if you're a macho police cadet it might not be quite up your street.

2 MOS EISLEY CANTINA
A disreputable bar at the centre of 'the most wretched hive of scum and villainy' is not a first date kind of place. But there are plenty of other big draws including excellent music, interesting customers, freedom from droids and seemingly regular outbursts of theatrical violence.

1 RICK'S CAFE AMERICAIN

Classier than anything we'd know as a cafe today, Rick's Cafe Americain featured a piano bar, full brass band, restaurant and casino. It was the place to go for corrupt officials, local dignitaries, and anyone interested in hushed conspiratorial whispering. Humphrey Bogart's permanently tuxedoed Rick kept order in the melting pot that was his little corner of wartime Morocco.

	BAR	MOVIE	LOCATION
10	Greely's	*The Unforgiven (1992)*	Big Whiskey, Wyoming
9	Coyote Ugly Saloon	*Coyote Ugly (2000)*	New York City
8	Club Sugar Ray	*Harlem Nights (1989)*	Harlem, New York
7	The Last Resort	*Total Recall (1990)*	Venusville, Mars
6	Pleasure Island Pool Hall	*Pinocchio (1940)*	Unknown
5	Korova Milk Bar	*Clockwork Orange (1971)*	Unidentified English city
4	The Gold Room	*The Shining (1980)*	The Overlook Hotel, Colorado
3	The Blue Oyster	*Police Academy (1984)*	Unidentified American city
2	Mos Eisley Cantina	*Star Wars: Episode IV – A New Hope (1977)*	Mos Eisley space port, Tatooine
1	Rick's Cafe Americain	*Casablanca (1942)*	Casablanca, Morocco

TOP 10

A dystopia is essentially any society in which we wouldn't want to live. Usually that means it's governed by some sort of oppressive, totalitarian regime. Or perhaps it has witnessed a nuclear holocaust, or been decimated in some other terrible fashion. But a society that is outwardly pleasant yet inwardly devoid of art, humour, personal freedom etc. can be just as much a dystopia. For obvious reasons these movies are generally set in the future.

DYSTOPIAN FUTURES

10 DEMOLITION MAN (1993)

Convicted of a crime for which he's innocent and placed in cryogenic status, John Spartan (Sylvester Stallone), a ruthless but brilliant cop, is thawed out to save the future from a threat of the past.

9 IDIOCRACY (2006)

The ingenious idea that drives *Idiocracy* supposes a world 500 years in the future in which human life has intellectually regressed. With everyone basically dumb, an average Joe frozen in 2006 wakes up to find himself an unparalleled genius.

8 DIVERGENT (2014)

Divergent's dystopia is a world in which all humans are unavoidably divided into factions based on certain human virtues.

7 FAHRENHEIT 451 (1966)

Guy Montag (Oskar Werner) is a firefighter, which in author Ray Bradbury's future means he's tasked with burning every book the oppressive state discovers. Eventually and inevitably he starts to glance at the books he destroys and wonders if he's doing the right thing.

6 AKIRA (1988)

Clearly heavily inspired by *Blade Runner*, *Akira*'s future Tokyo is a beautifully ugly battle ground seemingly populated by rival biker gangs and shadowy state authorities.

5 A BOY AND HIS DOG (1975)

Vic (Don Johnson) communicates telepathically with his dog Blood (Tim McIntire) as he searches for food in the wasteland that was once the U.S.A. This surreal, hilarious and completely unique movie was the only big screen outing for director L.Q. Jones, better known as an actor in TV Westerns such as *Rawhide*.

4 MAD MAX (1979)

With society hanging by a thread after oil supplies run out, the wife and son of Max (Mel Gibson), a tough but disillusioned cop, are murdered by marauding bikers. Having previously decided to quit the beleaguered police force, Max is compelled to suit up one last time and seek vengeance.

3 METROPOLIS (1927)
The movie that has surely influenced this subgenre more than any other, *Metropolis* is a grandiose critique on social injustice and authoritarian oppression.

2 BLADE RUNNER (1982)
With its soporific score, hypnotic visuals and mesmerising performances, *Blade Runner* is an immersive, almost abstract experience. Centring on Rick Deckard (Harrison Ford), a kind of official bounty hunter, the film questions just what it means to be human.

1 BRAZIL (1985)
The life of a low level bureaucrat spirals out of control when he tries to correct a simple error. *Brazil* has quite the most richly detailed, imaginatively realised and fantastically idiosyncratic futures the movies have yet to depict. The endless, inflexible and illogical bureaucracy is something we can probably all relate to nowadays.

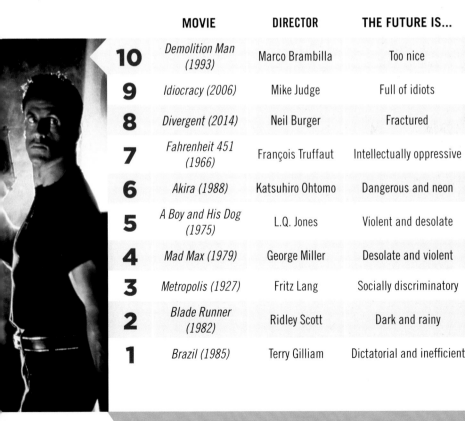

	MOVIE	DIRECTOR	THE FUTURE IS...
10	Demolition Man (1993)	Marco Brambilla	Too nice
9	Idiocracy (2006)	Mike Judge	Full of idiots
8	Divergent (2014)	Neil Burger	Fractured
7	Fahrenheit 451 (1966)	François Truffaut	Intellectually oppressive
6	Akira (1988)	Katsuhiro Ohtomo	Dangerous and neon
5	A Boy and His Dog (1975)	L.Q. Jones	Violent and desolate
4	Mad Max (1979)	George Miller	Desolate and violent
3	Metropolis (1927)	Fritz Lang	Socially discriminatory
2	Blade Runner (1982)	Ridley Scott	Dark and rainy
1	Brazil (1985)	Terry Gilliam	Dictatorial and inefficient

TOP
10

Thanks largely to the *Twilight* series of novels by Stephanie Meyer, vampires have experienced something of a renaissance. But for those who think the bloodsucking succubus is best personified by the likes of Edward Cullen or Bill Compton, read on for some even more interesting immortals. As none of its characters made this list, special mention should be made here of *Near Dark* (1987), one of the most popular revisionist vampire movies amongst fans.

VAMPIRES

10 EDWARD CULLEN
The modern vampire poster boy has to feature on this list. His relationship with Bella Swan (Kristen Stewart) is credited with injecting a significant romantic element into the vampire mythology, attracting the sort of young girls who had traditionally shown little interest in the genre.

9 MARTIN
This curious little movie from horror maestro George Romero deals with vampirism as the possible result of mental illness, asking whether the phenomenon might exist only in the mind.

8 CARMILLA KARNSTEIN
Ingrid Pitt, the first lady of Hammer horror, makes her vampire debut in this schlocky and undeniably sexist genre classic. She plays a beautiful young woman who imposes on the family caring for her

by sucking the life out of their daughter.

7 COUNT DRACULA
Dracula is evicted from his castle by the Romanian government, who plan to turn it into a gymnastics training centre. He travels to New York in search of a bride, but finds himself no more able to deal with the city's challenges than its mortal denizens. Bram Stoker actually gets a writing credit for this absurd comedy.

6 JERRY DANDRIDGE
The vampire myth is updated for the Spielberg generation in this family-friendly black comedy about a vampire who moves to the suburbs, and the little boy who becomes determined to expose him.

5 COUNT DRACULA
For many, Lugosi is still the definitive Dracula, and therefore the

definitive vampire. Although undoubtedly a supremely memorable and effective portrayal, it's also stagey, stiff and undeniably dated.

4 ELI
This dark, understated Swedish movie is a unique take on the subject, supposing vampires live undetected amongst us and face the same struggles we do.

3 MIRIAM BLAYLOCK
Another modern take, *The Hunger* sees Catherine Deneuve as Miriam Blaylock, a beautiful serial killer with a hunger for more than just blood.

2 COUNT DRACULA
The first of nine occasions on which Lee would play Dracula, Hammer's original movie made the actor's name whilst simultaneously typecasting him for life. There are clunky

moments but as a whole the performance and film are utterly unforgettable.

1 GRAF ORLOK

With the rights to *Dracula* prohibitively expensive, director F W Murnau decided to simply change the character's name and film the novel anyway. The result features what is still the most genuinely terrifying portrayal of a vampire ever committed to film.

	CHARACTER	MOVIE	ACTOR
10	Edward Cullen	*Twilight series (2008-2012)*	Robert Pattinson
9	Martin	*Martin (1976)*	John Amplas
8	Carmilla Karnstein	*The Vampire Lovers (1970)*	Ingrid Pitt
7	Count Dracula	*Love at First Bite (1979)*	George Hamilton
6	Jerry Dandridge	*Fright Night (1985)*	Chris Sarandon
5	Count Dracula	*Dracula (1931)*	Bela Lugosi
4	Eli	*Let the Right One In (2008)*	Lina Leandersson
3	Miriam Blaylock	*The Hunger (1983)*	Catherine Deneuve
2	Count Dracula	*Dracula: Prince of Darkness (1966)*	Christopher Lee
1	Graf Orlok	*Nosferatu (1922)*	Max Schreck

TOP 10

With few things more subjective than humour, establishing a 'house style' is uniquely valuable for a comedy act. Fans are assured they will get what they're looking for when they buy their ticket, and a guaranteed audience gives the act confidence and security.

COMEDY TROUPES AND DOUBLE ACTS

10 MARTIN & LEWIS
After struggling as nightclub singer (Dean Martin) and stage comic (Jerry Lewis), the two performers fell together in 1946. They immediately proved to be more than the sum of their parts, becoming a hugely successful act on stage, radio, TV and in movies.

9 CHEECH & CHONG
Successful stage shows and records inevitably lead to a big screen debut for these counter culture pinups. *Up In Smoke* was the smash hit comedy of 1978 and the catalyst for a series of increasingly freewheeling and self indulgent movies.

8 THE THREE STOOGES
The kings of slapstick made literally hundreds of shorts over a career that also took in vaudeville, TV, comic books, novelty records, radio and even video games. The secret to their longevity was surely their mass appeal and a willingness to change the lineup.

7 THE CHRISTOPHER GUEST TROUPE
The most respected comedy troupe of modern movies has to be Christopher Guest's assortment of actors. Many first came together for Rob Reiner's 1984 classic *This Is Spinal Tap*, later refining their style in movies like *Waiting for Guffman* (1997).

6 EDGAR WRIGHT, SIMON PEGG AND NICK FROST
Perhaps the one entry on this list that fans still expect to produce top drawer comedy gold. The British triptych, who started out together in TV's *Spaced*, have taken Hollywood by storm since their 'zomromcom' *Shaun of the Dead* was a big success in 2004.

5 THE MARX BROTHERS
From impoverished childhoods the Marx Brothers became big screen legends. Several 'minor' brothers would come and go over the years with some now forgotten. But Groucho, the most successful Marx, remains immediately recognisable and extensively quoted.

4 RICHARD PRYOR AND GENE WILDER
Pryor's belligerent stage

persona and Wilder's sensitive acting style don't suggest themselves as ideal bedfellows. But the magic of their chemistry is undeniable, their complementary dynamic second to none. A unique, magical and all too infrequent double act.

3 ABBOT & COSTELLO
Once again the vaudeville stage proves a stepping stone to Hollywood. Abbot and Costello were possibly the most popular comedy act of the 40's and 50's, a heyday for such American performers. The humour might be slightly dated but the charm remains.

2 LAUREL & HARDY
The first double act to achieve megastar status, slim Englishman Stan Laurel and chubby American Oliver Hardy defined not only a style of comedy but the classic physical dynamic of the double act. Their influence is visible on big screen and small even today.

1 MONTY PYTHON
The alternately surreal, satirical, dark and ridiculous humour of Monty Python found them the greatest international success of any comedy act for decades. With comics from Steve Martin to Will Ferrell citing them as a major influence, their legacy will continue for many years to come.

	TEAM	MOVIE COLLABORATIONS (SO FAR)	ACTIVE IN MOVIES	HIGHLIGHT
10	Martin & Lewis	16	1949-1956	The Stooge (1952)
9	Cheech & Chong	8	From 1978	Up In Smoke (1978)
8	The Three Stooges	200 or more (In various iterations)	1930-1970	Disorder in Court (1936)
7	The Christopher Guest Troupe	5 (In various iterations)	From 1984	Best in Show (2000)
6	Edgar Wright, Simon Pegg and Nick Frost	3	From 2004	Shaun of the Dead (2004)
5	The Marx Brothers	13 (Groucho, Chico and Harpo)	1929-1949	A Night at the Opera (1935)
4	Richard Pryor and Gene Wilder	4	1976-1991	Silver Streak (1976)
3	Abbot & Costello	36	1941-1956	Abbot and Costello Meet Frankenstein (1948)
2	Laurel & Hardy	100 or more	1926-1950	The Music Box (1932)
1	Monty Python	4	1971-1983	Life of Brian (1979)

TOP 10

Time to put pen to paper and create your own top 10 list of comedy movies...

10
9
8
7
6
5
4
3
2
1

TOP
10

The movies have always been preoccupied with military conflict, both historical and fictional. It offers great dramatic possibilities whilst presenting easy to understand black hat/white hat morality, and it can make for the most thrilling of climaxes.

BATTLES

10 THE CHARGE OF THE CUIRASSIERS
In the age of CGI it's easy to take scenes like this for granted. The epic scale is the result of 20,000 extras and some exceptional filmmaking, with the historical accuracy of the battle also (apparently) second to none.

9 THE BATTLE OF THE HORNBURG (AKA HELM'S DEEP)
The first major battle of *The Lord of the Rings* trilogy sees a vastly outnumbered Rohirrim army retreat to the fortress of Helm's Deep to face off against evil wizard Saruman's Uruk-Hai force.

8 THE BATTLE FOR ARNHEM
An undermanned, underarmed allied parachute brigade try to take and hold a crucial bridge in the Dutch town of Arnhem. They're up against an entire division of SS tanks and allied incompetence has left them without backup.

7 BATTLE OF ROURKE'S DRIFT
During the Anglo-Zulu war a small British detachment find themselves hemmed in with 4,000 Zulus approaching.

6 FREEDONIA VS. SYLVANIA
The climax to what is possibly the Marx Bros' greatest film is a chaotic war scene in which nobody, with the possible exception of the audience, seems to know which way they're meant to be shooting.

5 THE BATTLE OF STIRLING BRIDGE
One of the bloodiest battles of the First War of Scottish Independence saw victory for William Wallace's forces both in real life and the movie. That's about where the similarities end, though. The movie version doesn't even feature a bridge!

4 THE BATTLE OF THE ICHIMONJI CLAN
This tale of the downfall of a once powerful Sengoku-era clan is loosely based on King Lear. After dividing his kingdom amongst his three sons, an ageing warlord watches as they betray him and each other in a desperate scrap for more power.

3 DEATH STAR ASSAULT
If you don't get sidetracked by the questionable logic of this sequence it's a real corker. The structure is perfect: we clearly understand what the rebels need to do to win, they attack in identifiable waves and suspense comes from cutting away to a computer graphic illustrating the rebel base slowly coming into range of the Death Star. Hitchcock would be proud.

2 THE BATTLE OF THERMOPYLAE

Every technical trick in the book is deployed to amp up the drama as a small band of battle-hardened Spartans attempt to see off a huge Persian army determined to conquer them.

1 OMAHA BEACH LANDING

The breathtaking opening scene to Steven Spielberg's epic war movie is as effective today as it was on release. The visceral horror of the violence is unforgettable whilst the dynamic editing creates an unparalleled kinetic energy. And unusually for such phrenetic filmmaking we can keep our bearings throughout the pandemonium.

	BATTLE	MOVIE	BELLIGERENTS
10	The Charge of the Cuirassiers	Waterloo (1970)	Britain and France
9	The Battle of the Hornburg (aka Helm's Deep)	The Lord of the Rings: The Two Towers (2002)	The forces of Saruman and the Rohirrim
8	The Battle for Arnhem	A Bridge Too Far (1977)	Allied Forces and Nazi Germany
7	Battle of Rourke's Drift	Zulu (1964)	Britain and the Zulus
6	Freedonia vs. Sylvania	Duck Soup (1933)	Fictional nations Freedonia and Sylvania
5	The Battle of Stirling Bridge	Braveheart (1995)	Elements of Scotland and elements of England
4	The battle of the Ichimonji clan	Ran (1985)	Different elements of the Ichimonji clan
3	Death Star Assault	Star Wars: A New Hope (1977)	Rebel and Imperial Forces
2	The Battle of Thermopylae	300 (2006)	Sparta and the Persian Army
1	Omaha Beach Landing	Saving Private Ryan (1998)	Allied Forces and Nazi Germany

TOP
10

For this list we're not interested in how accomplished a cop might be, how many citizens they've rescued or robberies they've solved. It's purely about how much we enjoy watching them.

COPS

10 CAPTAIN GEORGE ELLERBY

The highly capable Ellerby marks another scene stealing role for Alec Baldwin.

9 DETECTIVE POPEYE DOYLE

Gruff, violent, racist and alcoholic, Doyle is a dedicated New York cop on the trail of a huge heroin shipment.

8 JIM MALONE

Connery's Irish cop (his Scottish accent is never explained) signs up to become part of Federal Agent Elliot Ness' (Kevin Costner) elite Untouchables, a special unit dedicated to catching Al Capone.

7 INSPECTOR JACQUES CLOUSEAU

If the world class incompetent Clouseau solves a case, chances are it's by accident.

6 CAPTAIN HANK QUINLAN

By the time *Touch of Evil* was mooted, Welles' reputation in Hollywood was in tatters. Nonetheless he was able to convince Universal Pictures to let him write and direct, and he took the opportunity to make his character, a corrupt police captain, even more unpalatable. Quinlan manoeuvres his enormous, sweating frame like it's a weapon, his shabby appearance somehow adding to the menace.

5 OFFICER JOHN MCCLANE

New York cop John McClane must call on all his resourcefulness to overcome a team of exceptional thieves posing as terrorists.

4 DETECTIVE VIRGIL TIBBS

Tibbs, a well respected African American homicide detective from Philadelphia, is passing through Sparta Mississippi when racist Police Chief Bill Gillespie (Rod Steiger) arrests him for the murder of a local businessman. With the misunderstanding cleared up, the equally dubious men are forced to work together to find the real killer.

3 DETECTIVE AXEL FOLEY

Street smart Detroit cop Foley becomes embroiled

in a smuggling racket when an old friend is murdered and he follows a lead to California. But his wise-ass attitude and relaxed approach to the rules don't go down well in Beverley Hills.

2 SERGEANT FRANK DREBIN

Redesigned from the vaguely effective police sergeant of the preceding *Police Squad!* TV series, the Drebin of the *Naked Gun* movies is a completely inept dimwit.

1 CHIEF MARGE GUNDERSON

We're used to cops being complicated, conflicted characters. Inner demons seem to be handed out with the badge, and they usually wind up sharing more in common with the criminals they chase than the wife who has invariably left them. Margie is different. As if a pleasant, homely lady from a quaint town doesn't seem vulnerable enough when facing off against hardened killers, writer/directors the Coen brothers made her heavily pregnant. The simple values she brings to the job enable us to see the futility of crime in a new light, something neatly demonstrated in the last lines of the film when Margie asks her captured culprit, 'there's more to life than a little money, you know. Don'tcha know that?'

	COP	MOVIE	ACTOR
10	Captain George Ellerby	*The Departed (2006)*	Alec Baldwin
9	Detective Popeye Doyle	*The French Connection (1971)*	Gene Hackman
8	Jim Malone	*The Untouchables (1987)*	Sean Connery
7	Inspector Jacques Clouseau	*Pink Panther series (1963-1978)*	Peter Sellers
6	Captain Hank Quinlan	*Touch of Evil (1958)*	Orson Welles
5	Officer John Mc-Clane	*Die Hard series (1988-2013)*	Bruce Willis
4	Detective Virgil Tibbs	*In the Heat of the Night (1967)*	Sidney Poitier
3	Detective Axel Foley	*Beverly Hills Cop series (1984-1994)*	Eddie Murphy
2	Sergeant Frank Drebin	*Naked Gun series (1988-1994)*	Leslie Nielsen
1	Chief Marge Gunderson	*Fargo (1996)*	Frances McDormand

TOP
10

On your own or in a party. Allegory or straight story. Motorcycle or lawnmower! There's little to link these entries beyond the ever effective device of centring them around a journey.

ROAD TRIPS

10 NEW YORK TO CHICAGO

Marketing executive Neal Page is desperate to get home to his family at Thanksgiving. Del Griffith, a shower curtain ring salesman, might be heading the same way, but has rather less urgency about him. The two men team up when necessity overcomes Page's scepticism for the bumbling Griffith.

9 SYDNEY TO ALICE SPRINGS

A pair of drag queens and their transexual cohort Bernadette (Terence Stamp) head off into the Australian desert in their bus, Priscilla. They're contracted to perform in Alice Springs, assuming they make it to the end of their eventful journey.

8 FLORIDA TO HOLLYWOOD

The first *Muppets* movie sees Kermit head off to Hollywood in search of stardom. On the way he comes across various other well-loved muppets who join him in his quest.

7 RHODE ISLAND TO ASPEN

When cretinous limo driver Lloyd believes his client has mistakenly left her bag at the airport, he and his equally imbecilic friend Harry vow to return it to her.

6 MIAMI TO NEW YORK

Ellie, a wildly spoilt heiress, absconds from her family to marry a gold-digger of whom they disapprove. Making the journey to him in New York proves more difficult than expected and she's forced to rely on the help of Peter Warne, a newspaper reporter who recognises Ellie and wants an exclusive. Slowly, inevitably, they fall in love.

5 BUENOS AIRES, ARGENTINA TO
CARACAS, VENEZUELA

Ernesto 'Che' Guevara's 1952 travels through South America are often cited as a formative experience for the future revolutionary.

4 MONTANA TO NEBRASKA

Believing he's won a sweepstake, irascible pensioner Woody Grant convinces his estranged son David to drive him to collect his winnings. David uses the opportunity to try to understand his distant, selfish father for the first time.

3 OKLAHOMA TO ARIZONA

Thelma, housewife to a neglectful husband, and Louise, a disillusioned waitress, decide to blow the cobwebs from their hair by hitting the road. But when Louise kills a man who attempts to rape Thelma, things get serious.

2 LAURENS, IOWA TO BLUE RIVER, WISCONSIN

Elderly Alvin Straight uses the only means at his disposal, a lawn mower, to travel to visit the brother he hasn't spoken to for years.

1 CALIFORNIA TO NEW ORLEANS

Having smuggled a quantity of cocaine into Los Angeles from Mexico, bikers Wyatt and Billy are flush with cash and decide to make the long trip to the Mardi Gras in New Orleans. On the way they stay with hippies who are struggling to grow crops on arid land, before hooking up with free spirited alcoholic lawyer George (Jack Nicholson). It's George who voices the film's central message: no matter how much Americans talk about the importance of freedom, many feel threatened by those who truly have it.

	JOURNEY	MOVIE	PRINCIPAL TRAVELLERS
10	New York to Chicago	*Planes, Trains and Automobiles (1987)*	Neal Page (Steve Martin), Del Griffith (John Candy)
9	Sydney to Alice Springs	*The Adventures of Priscilla, Queen of the Desert (1994)*	Mitzi/Anthony (Hugo Weaving), Felicia/Adam (Guy Pearce)
8	Florida to Hollywood	*The Muppet Movie (1979)*	Kermit (Jim Henson), Miss Piggy (Frank Oz)
7	Rhode Island to Aspen	*Dumb and Dumber (1994)*	Lloyd (Jim Carrey), Harry (Jeff Daniels)
6	Miami to New York	*It Happened One Night (1934)*	Peter Warne (Clark Gable), Ellie Andrews (Claudette Colbert)
5	Buenos Aires, Argentina to Caracas, Venezuela	*The Motorcycle Diaries (2004)*	Ernesto Guevara de la Serna (Gael García Bernal), Alberto Granado (Rodrigo De la Serna)
4	Montana to Nebraska	*Nebraska (2013)*	Woody Grant (Bruce Dern), David Grant (Will Forte)
3	Oklahoma to Arizona	*Thelma and Louise (1991)*	Thelma (Geena Davis), Louise (Susan Sarandon)
2	Laurens, Iowa to Blue River, Wisconsin	*The Straight Story (1999)*	Alvin Straight (Richard Farnsworth)
1	California to New Orleans	*Easy Rider (1969)*	Wyatt (Peter Fonda), Billy (Dennis Hopper)

TOP 10

Although present in all sorts of genres and mediums, the femme fatale is most closely associated with film noir. Her most vital characteristic is the ability to ensnare and then lead a man to his doom, either moral or actual. She must be seductive but needn't be inherently villainous. A beautiful woman trapped in an impossible situation can be as dangerous as any criminal.

FEMME FATALES

woman need to be re-examined and Laura becomes the prime suspect in the murder.

7 JESSICA RABBIT
The animated nightclub singer and husband of Roger (Charles Fleischer), Jessica isn't bad, she's just drawn that way.

10 ANNA SCHMIDT
In post WWII Vienna, Harry Lime (Orson Welles), a black marketeer, is apparently killed in an accident, leaving his best friend Holly Martins (Joseph Cotton) to investigate the mysterious circumstances. Lime's girlfriend Anna appears to know more than she will admit about both the extent of Lime's nefarious trade and his accident.

9 LAURA DANNON
Writer/director Rian Johnson's directorial debut mischievously subverts the classic film noir archetypes, not least by transposing the action to an American high school. Laura, although only a schoolgirl, already has an inauspicious air about her before we learn just how mixed up she is in a drug theft and murder.

8 LAURA HUNT
Advertising executive Laura Hunt is believed to have been murdered when someone resembling her is found shot dead in her apartment. But when she reappears, the fate and identity of the dead

6 LYNN BRACKEN
With several rival police officers investigating a violent robbery, this sultry call girl is deployed by the perpetrators to confuse and compromise the investigation by getting between the cops.

5 KITTY MARCH
Tapped out cashier Chris Cross (Edward G. Robinson) falls for con artist Kitty who, believing him to be wealthy, wrings every penny she can from her lovelorn mark.

4 SUZANNE STONE MARETTO

Not the most subtle of femme fatales, frustrated but ruthless weather girl Suzanne Stone Maretto wants rid of her loving husband Larry (Matt Dillon). After seducing vulnerable high school student Jimmy Emmett (a young Joaquin Phoenix), Suzanne convinces he and his equally impressionable friends to kill Larry for her.

3 PHYLLIS DIETRICHSON

Quintessential femme fatale Phyllis Dietrichson is intent on escaping her marriage and collecting a big insurance payout by having her husband bumped off. Poor schmo Walter Neff is the unfortunate instrument of her greed, lured to his doom by Diethrichson's beauty.

2 CATHERINE TRAMELL

Sharon Stone's frequent state of undress, not to mention Michael Douglas's bare bottom, are about the only features that distinguish *Basic Instinct* from the classic noirs it apes.

1 JUDY BARTON

Emotionally torturing Jimmy Stewart should be a crime in itself, but it's her role in the murder of an industrialist's wife that sets Barton on the path to doom.

	CHARACTER	MOVIE	ACTOR
10	Anna Schmidt	The Third Man (1949)	Alida Valli
9	Laura Dannon	Brick (2005)	Nora Zehetner
8	Laura Hunt	Laura (1944)	Gene Tierney
7	Jessica Rabbit	Who Framed Roger Rabbit (1988)	Kathleen Turner
6	Lynn Bracken	L.A. Confidential (1997)	Kim Basinger
5	Kitty March	Scarlet Street (1945)	Joan Bennett
4	Suzanne Stone Maretto	To Die For (1995)	Nicole Kidman
3	Phyllis Dietrichson	Double Indemnity (1944)	Barbara Stanwyck
2	Catherine Tramell	Basic Instinct (1992)	Sharon Stone
1	Judy Barton	Vertigo (1958)	Kim Novak

TOP 10

A glance down this list should demonstrate just how great a movie psychopath can be. Whether quietly deranged or ostentatiously firing both barrels of crazy, these characters are amongst the most fun in cinema. This list is a tribute to the original psycho, Norman Bates.

PSYCHOPATHS

10 ZACHARIAH
Unnervingly rational Zachariah is one of the eponymous Seven Psychopaths in director Martin McDonagh's excellent satirical black comedy.

9 BEGBIE
Just one of the destructive forces hemming in protagonist Renton (Ewan McGregor), the witless Begbie is a hysterically aggressive, unprincipled lunatic.

8 JOHN RYDER
With no apparent motive, John Ryder drifts across America hitching rides before killing the unsuspecting drivers. After picking him up in the desert, Jim Halsey (C. Thomas Howell) manages at first to escape Ryder's clutches, but then falls victim to his murderous vendetta.

7 KAKIHARA
Kakihara, a sadomasochistic enforcer for the Japanese mob, both delivers and receives a series of terrible injuries in this ultra-violent crime movie about a deranged vigilante. The movie's Manga origins are apparent in its stylised brutality and idiosyncratic characters.

6 DON LOGAN
The tour de force performance from the always excellent Sir Ben Kingsley is the best thing about this British crime caper. Living an idyllic life on the Costa del Sol, retired crook Gal Dove (Ray Winstone) is the unfortunate object of Don's attention when the latter is sent to intimidate the former safecracker into returning to England for a job.

5 HARRY POWELL
Having convinced himself he's doing God's work by killing women, a misogynistic phony preacher ingratiates himself into the lives of his former prison cellmate's family. All that matters to Powell is the proceeds of their father's bank robbery, and he remorselessly pursues the children he believes know its location.

4 ANNIE WILKES
Kathy Bates' most famous role is this unhinged literary fan who captures and imprisons her favourite author. Displeased with the latest turn taken in a series of novels to which Annie is particularly attached, she forces him to rewrite to her specification.

3 PATRICK BATEMAN
The superficial excesses of the 80's are lampooned brilliantly in this study of a psychopathic investment banker who finds his recreation in grisly murder.

2 ASAMI YAMAZAKI
Intent on finding love seven years after the death of his wife, Aoyama (Ryu Isibashi) falls for the serene Asami

Yamazaki. But on realising he was once married, Asami snaps and poisons her new lover, before revealing a fondness for torture.

1 FRANK BOOTH

The savage, remorseless and utterly terrifying Frank Booth is one of the most memorable film characters of all time. His reprehensible crimes include kidnapping the husband and child of singer Dorothy Vallens (Isabella Rossellini) in order to make her compliant to his sadistic urges.

	CHARACTER	MOVIE	ACTOR
10	Zachariah	*Seven Psychopaths (2012)*	Tom Waits
9	Begbie	*Trainspotting (1996)*	Robert Carlyle
8	John Ryder	*Hitcher (1986)*	Rutger Hauer
7	Kakihara	*Ichi the Killer (2001)*	Tadanobu Asano
6	Don Logan	*Sexy Beast (2000)*	Ben Kingsley
5	Harry Powell	*Night of the Hunter (1955)*	Robert Mitchum
4	Annie Wilkes	*Misery (1990)*	Kathy Bates
3	Patrick Bateman	*American Psycho (2000)*	Christian Bale
2	Asami Yamazaki	*Audition (1999)*	Eihi Shiina
1	Frank Booth	*Blue Velvet (1986)*	Dennis Hopper

TOP 10

What at first might seem an illogical blend of genres makes some sense when you consider how much more palatable horror can be, and therefore how much further you can push it, when tempered with humour. These movies have to work as horror and conform to the tropes associated with horror comedy, so the likes of *Young Frankenstein* (1974) or *The Cat and the Canary* (1939), though brilliant, don't fit the criteria.

COMEDY HORROR MOVIES

10 SEVERANCE (2006)
Intriguing for the way it satirises callous corporations, this British movie suffers a little from a lack of subtlety and originality.

9 PIRANHA (1978)
A fairly run of the mill kids in peril from beasties B movie elevated to a greater status by perfectly judged tongue in cheek moments.

8 THE CABIN IN THE WOODS (2012)
Polished, studio-backed and with a big budget, *The Cabin in the Woods* attempts to be the last word on the titular cliché. The final act throws the rule book out of the window (and bounces it off a haunted tree).

7 SHAUN OF THE DEAD (2004)
A lovingly crafted ode

to George Romero, this zomromcom (zombie romantic comedy) sees unambitious Londoner Shaun (Simon Pegg) attempt to win back his girlfriend whilst fighting a zombie apocalypse.

6 BRAINDEAD AKA DEAD OR ALIVE (1992)
Before hitting the big league with *The Lord of the Rings*, director Peter Jackson had a neat line in absurdist horror. This ridiculously gory story has Mommy's boy Lionel (Timothy Balme) dealing with an outbreak of the living dead.

5 CEMETERY MAN (1994)
Essentially a zombie arthouse comedy, cemetery man Francesco Dellamorte (Rupert Everett) faces an army of the risen dead in a small Italian town. The movie is preoccupied with the concept of duality, a significant theme of the Dylan Dog comics on which it's based.

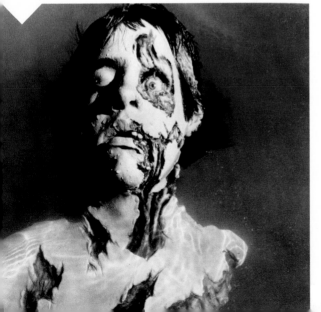

RE-ANIMATOR (1985)
4 Herbert West (Jeffrey Combs) is a brilliant student doctor who has devised a means to bring the dead back to life.

SCREAM (1996)
3 Having had a hand in popularising the slasher genre, director Wes Craven here deconstructs it to hilarious effect.

EVIL DEAD II (1987)
2 Like Peter Jackson, Sam Raimi started out making nasty but silly little horror movies before becoming a household name. This sequel (actually more a remake) to *Evil Dead* is the perfect blend of uncompromising horror and preposterous humour.

AN AMERICAN WEREWOLF IN LONDON (1981)
1 A couple of American backpackers are attacked by a werewolf on the Yorkshire moors of Northern England. One survives and turns into a werewolf, the other dies and turns into a comedian. Sort of.

	MOVIE	DIRECTOR
10	Severance (2006)	Christopher Smith
9	Piranha (1978)	Joe Dante
8	The Cabin in the Woods (2012)	Drew Goddard
7	Shaun of the Dead (2004)	Edgar Wright
6	Braindead aka Dead or Alive (1992)	Peter Jackson
5	Cemetery Man (1994)	Michele Soavi
4	Re-Animator (1985)	Stuart Gordon
3	Scream (1996)	Wes Craven
2	Evil Dead II (1987)	Sam Raimi
1	An American Werewolf in London (1981)	John Landis

TOP 10

Hollywood in particular has produced many musicals featuring fabulous dance numbers. But quality routines appear in dramatic and comedic movies too, and it's these that are often overlooked. This is a tribute to *Saturday Night Fever*.

DANCE SCENES (NOT FROM MUSICALS)

10 THE FISHER KING (1991)

Originally the scene where Parry (Robin Williams) and Lydia (Amanda Plummer) meet was based around a Grand Central Station busker. Eventually developed into an extensive waltz, the final scene is an elegant reminder of Gilliam's creativity.

9 AUSTIN POWERS IN GOLDMEMBER (2002)

The brilliantly fun opening sequence to the third Austin Powers movie consists of a succession of sight gags danced to Quincy Jones' 'Soul Bossa Nova'. A string of A-list cameos, including Jones himself, adds to the fun.

8 AIRPLANE (1980)

This *Saturday Night Fever* spoof sees pilot Ted Stryker don the infamous white suit and dance to a sped up version of The Bee Gees 'Stayin' Alive'. Things escalate into a brawl with a biker gang, though Ted doesn't seem to notice.

7 MODERN TIMES (1936)

The Nonsense Song performed by Charlie Chaplin in *Modern Times* is a largely improvised piece using random words from various languages. The accompanying dance is an equally bizarre pantomime routine.

6 MONTY PYTHON AND THE HOLY GRAIL (1975)

On their quest for the holy grail, King Arthur (Graham Chapman) and his knights finally reach Camelot. However, after witnessing the ridiculous 'Camelot Song' and its dance, Arthur decides it is a silly place and moves on.

5 ZATOICHI (2003)

The eponymous blind swordsman makes his way through a brutal feudal era Japan in a taciturn gloom. All things considered, the last thing we expect at the end of the movie is a bravura tap dancing routine to a thundering musical accompaniment.

4 DIRTY DANCING (1987)

All together: 'Now I've had the time of my life, No I've never felt this way before, Yes I swear it's the truth, And I owe it all to yoo-oo-ooou.' There's just no arguing with the emotional power of Johnny and Baby's climactic dance scene.

3 PULP FICTION (1994)

In a delicious nod to John Travolta's past notoriety playing a dancer, mob enforcer Vincent Vega is challenged by gangster's moll Mia Wallace to win a jive competition. The electric scene is played out to Chuck Berry's 'You Never Can Tell'.

2 BANDE À PART (1964)

Symbolic of their (in some cases newfound) free spirited attitudes, three friends give an impromptu performance of 'the Madison dance' in a French cafe. The atmosphere crackles with an unconstrained joie de vivre.

1 YOUNG FRANKENSTEIN (1974)

After successfully animating a creature made from the body parts of various corpses, Dr. Frankenstein decides to prove his creation can do anything a real human can... which leads to them putting on a stage show in top hat and tails.

	MOVIE	PERFORMED BY	DIRECTOR
10	The Fisher King (1991)	Commuters	Terry Gilliam
9	Austin Powers in Goldmember (2002)	Austin Powers (Mike Myers) and company	Jay Roach
8	Airplane (1980)	Ted (Robert Hays) and Elaine (Julie Hagerty)	Jim Abrahams, David Zucker and Jerry Zucker
7	Modern Times (1936)	A Factory Worker (Charlie Chaplin)	Charlie Chaplin
6	Monty Python and the Holy Grail (1975)	The Pythons	Terry Gilliam and Terry Jones
5	Zatoichi (2003)	Background Characters (lead by Japanese dance troupe The Stripes)	Takeshi Kitano
4	Dirty Dancing (1987)	Johnny (Patrick Swayze) and Baby (Jennifer Grey)	Emile Ardolino
3	Pulp Fiction (1994)	Vincent Vega (John Travolta) and Mia Wallace (Uma Thurman)	Quentin Tarantino
2	Bande à Part (1964)	Odile (Anna Karina), Arthur (Claude Brasseur) and Franz (Sami Frey)	Jean-Luc Godard
1	Young Frankenstein (1974)	Dr. Frankenstein (Gene Wilder) and The Monster (Peter Boyle)	Mel Brooks

TOP
10

In the 1950s Hollywood expertly tapped into America's growing fear of Communism with a succession of movies built around the same simple allegory. In place of Communists, aliens became the unknown evil invaders, and one of the most identifiable and formulaic subgenres exploded into life.

RED MENACE MOVIES (50'S SCI-FI)

10 THIS ISLAND EARTH (1955)
Aliens seeking our help in an intergalactic war turn out to be less trustworthy than we expected.

9 INVADERS FROM MARS (1953)
A popular concept in these movies sees ordinary people changed into emotionless automatons as aliens either replace or take control of them. The metaphor for creeping Communism is hardly subtle.

8 X THE UNKNOWN (1956)
It wasn't just fears of a red invasion these moviemakers stoked. The dangers associated with nuclear proliferation were ripe for exploitation too. Here a radioactive beast terrorises a Scottish army base, getting bigger and stronger as it absorbs more energy.

7 THE WAR OF THE WORLDS (1953)
H.G. Wells' celebrated story about an alien invasion in Southern England is successfully transposed to rural California. Some of the more subtle commentary is lost but the movie stands up remarkably well even today.

6 EARTH VS. THE FLYING SAUCERS (1956)
Dr. Russell Marvin (Hugh Marlowe) launches a series of satellites that mysteriously fall back to earth. When he captures the event on a strange recording, he realizes why.

5 20 MILLION MILES TO EARTH (1957)
An American spaceship returns from Venus carrying a small lizard like creature which immediately starts to grow exponentially.

4 THE THING FROM ANOTHER WORLD (1951)
Scientists at an Arctic research station are besieged by an alien monster after accidentally thawing it out. The presence of the great Howard Hawks (*Rio Bravo*, *The Big Sleep*) at the helm elevates a

typical screenplay to atypical heights. One of the most influential movies of the era and genre, it was remade by John Carpenter as *The Thing* in 1982.

3 THE BLOB (1958)
After seeing a meteorite land nearby, teenager Steve Andrews (Steve McQueen) and his girlfriend become embroiled in a blob of jello's attempt to take over the world. The fact it's so bizarrely scored (the title song is by Burt Bacharach) and improbably cast (McQueen was pushing 30 and looks even older) adds to the tongue in cheek appeal of a fun movie.

2 INVASION OF THE BODYSNATCHERS (1956)

One of the most important movies of the red menace wave, *Invasion of the Bodysnatchers* entered the public conscience like nothing else from the era. It's surprisingly heavy going, creating an overwhelming sense of our vulnerability and providing some very effective shocks. In the end the studio demanded the tone be lightened and commissioned reshoots.

1 THE QUATERMASS XPERIMENT AKA THE CREEPING UNKNOWN (1955)

The lone human survivor of a rocket ship crash begins mutating into a terrible monster. Adapted from an earlier TV series, this British contribution to the genre takes a slightly more (read very) cerebral approach.

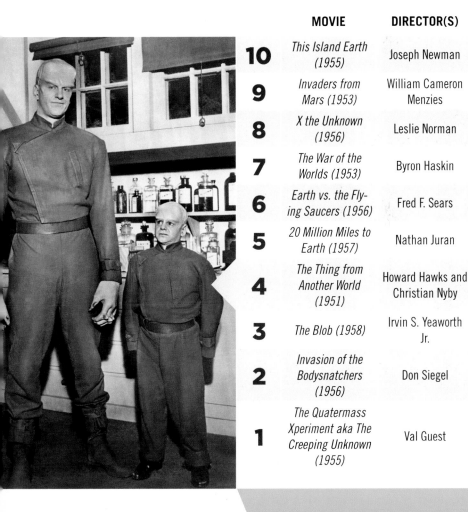

	MOVIE	DIRECTOR(S)
10	This Island Earth (1955)	Joseph Newman
9	Invaders from Mars (1953)	William Cameron Menzies
8	X the Unknown (1956)	Leslie Norman
7	The War of the Worlds (1953)	Byron Haskin
6	Earth vs. the Flying Saucers (1956)	Fred F. Sears
5	20 Million Miles to Earth (1957)	Nathan Juran
4	The Thing from Another World (1951)	Howard Hawks and Christian Nyby
3	The Blob (1958)	Irvin S. Yeaworth Jr.
2	Invasion of the Bodysnatchers (1956)	Don Siegel
1	The Quatermass Xperiment aka The Creeping Unknown (1955)	Val Guest

TOP 10

Attempting to adapt a successful TV series for the big screen is a notoriously tricky prospect. It's not just about making something that works at 60 minutes or less do the same over the course of a couple of hours. Audience expectations change when they pay money to sit in a darkened theatre.

BEST ADAPTATIONS OF A TV SERIES

10 BEAVIS AND BUTT-HEAD DO AMERICA (1996)

The juvenile delinquents wake up one morning to discover their TV stolen. Determined to get it back, they embark on a journey across America.

9 THE FUGITIVE (1993)

Harrison Ford is Dr. Richard Kimble, a Chicago surgeon wrongly convicted of his wife's murder. When the transporter taking him to prison crashes, he seizes the opportunity to escape and track down the real killer.

8 COWBOY BEBOP: THE MOVIE (2001)

In 2071 a deadly virus is released on Mars as part of a wave of terrorist attacks and the bounty hunter crew of the spaceship Bebop are dispatched to catch the culprits.

7 THE NAKED GUN (1988)

Lieutenant Frank Drebin of Police Squad must foil an attempt to kill Queen Elizabeth II on American soil.

6 THREE OUTLAW SAMURAI (1964)

Shiba (Tetsuo Tamba), a wandering ronin, falls in with a pair of samurai charged with recovering the kidnapped daughter of an important magistrate. But as he starts to understand the plight of the downtrodden peasants holding the girl, his opinions begin to shift.

5 STAR TREK (2009)

Fans have decried the variable quality of *Star Trek* movies for over 30 years, so it was a pleasant surprise when wunderkind J.J. Abrams' reboot proved so popular. Setting a film at the midway point of an extensive mythology limits the options, so Abrams intriguingly dispenses with the canon by creating a new timeline, thanks to some mind-bending time travel paradoxes.

4 JACKASS: THE MOVIE (2002)

You know by now whether you love or hate the Jackass boys. And you probably know by now whether you love or hate the *Jackass* movie. But if you haven't seen it, your answer to the first question will give you the answer to the second.

3 SERENITY (2005)

The crew of the Serenity close ranks to protect one of their own when a genetically engineered assassin is sent after her.

2 IN THE LOOP (2009)

The British satirical TV series *The Thick of It* is reworked into a feature film that sort of bridges the gap between the original show and it's U.S. incarnation *Veep*. The characters are all familiar (though often recast) and the situations just as terribly believable.

1 TRAFFIC (2000)

Traffic is determined to show the audience every link in the chain of the cocaine trade. From the Mexican growers and smugglers to the American dealers and users, to the officials fighting the war, the whole process is laid bare. The movie is based on an equally successful British TV series, *Traffik*, which focused on a similar system in Europe and Pakistan.

		MOVIE	DIRECTOR	TV SHOW
	10	*Beavis and Butt-Head Do America (1996)*	Mike Judge	*Beavis and Butthead (1993)*
	9	*The Fugitive (1993)*	Andrew Davis	*The Fugitive (1963)*
	8	*Cowboy Bebop: The Movie (2001)*	Shinichir Watanabe	*Cowboy Bebop (1998)*
	7	*The Naked Gun (1988)*	David Zucker	*Police Squad (1982)*
	6	*Three Outlaw Samurai (1964)*	Hideo Gosha	*Three Outlaw Samurai (1963)*
	5	*Star Trek (2009)*	J.J. Abrams	*Star Trek (1966)*
	4	*Jackass: The Movie (2002)*	Jeff Tremaine	*Jackass (2000)*
	3	*Serenity (2005)*	Joss Whedon	*Firefly (2002)*
	2	*In the Loop (2009)*	Armando Ianucci	*The Thick of It (2005)*
	1	*Traffic (2000)*	Steven Soderbergh	*Traffik (1989)*

TOP 10

This vague term loosely groups together a generation of iconoclastic filmmakers who brought a then unique immediacy to the medium. They often addressed the political and social issues of the day and pioneered a style making extensive use of real locations, natural light, radical editing techniques, naturalistic acting and other tropes more common in documentary than dramatic film.

FRENCH NEW WAVE FILMS

10 LE BOUCHER (1970)
A small French community is gripped by a series of violent murders of young women. At the same time Hélène (Stéphane Audran), a school teacher, and Popaul (Jean Yanne), a butcher, begin an unlikely relationship.

9 THE FIRE WITHIN (1963)
Depressed and desperate, Alain (Maurice Ronet) leaves the Versailles clinic at which he's been treated for alcoholism. With nothing left to live for, he intends to track down his old friends and enjoy one final night of revelry before ending his life.

8 MY LIFE TO LIVE (1962)
The story of Nana (Anna Karina), a beautiful young woman who abandons her husband and child in order to become a famous actress. Unsurprisingly things don't

end well. After failing to make it she becomes a prostitute, and is eventually killed in the crossfire as two pimps fight over her.

7 THE UMBRELLAS OF CHERBOURG (1964)
To sunnier climes, in a way, and this highly atypical film for the new wave movement. Told entirely through song, it's the story of young lovers, separated by war, who eventually find happiness with others.

6 LAST YEAR AT MARIENBAD (1961)
This divisive experimental film toys with time, identity and reality as the hypnotic proceedings play out. None of the characters are named and due to the deliberate lack of information the audience is given it's hard to know whether what we're seeing is real and, if it is, when it happened. Given its eccentricities it's probably needless to say the film isn't for everyone, but many have found great pleasure in tackling the puzzle at its core.

5 PIERROT LE FOU (1965)
Abandoning his family, Ferdinand (Jean-Paul Belmondo) runs away with his baby-sitter Marianne (Anna Karina). Together they drift south on a crime spree but separate when gangsters pursuing Marianne catch up with them. Years later they meet again.

4 JULES AND JIM (1962)
The many shapes of love are investigated in this part frothy, part gloomy classic starring Jeanne Moreau.

3 HIROSHIMA MON AMOUR (1959)
Elle (Emmanuelle Riva), a French actress in Hiroshima, Japan to film an anti-war movie, begins an affair with local architect Lui (Eiji Okada). Together they philosophise, particularly on the subject of war.

2 THE 400 BLOWS (1959)
A misunderstood and neglected young boy slips through the cracks of society to become another victim of an uncaring system.

1 BREATHLESS (1960)
Jean-Paul Belmondo again plays a charismatic criminal on the run with a beautiful woman in tow. And again it doesn't end well for him.

	MOVIE	DIRECTOR	ORIGINAL TITLE
10	Le Boucher (1970)	Claude Chabrol	Le boucher
9	The Fire Within (1963)	Louis Malle	Le feu follet
8	My Life to Live (1962)	Jean-Luc Godard	Vivre sa vie
7	The Umbrellas of Cherbourg (1964)	Jacques Demy	Les parapluie de Cherbourg
6	Last Year at Marienbad (1961)	Alain Resnais	L'Annee derniere a Marienbad
5	Pierrot le Fou (1965)	Jean-Luc Godard	Pierrot le fou
4	Jules and Jim (1962)	François Truffaut	Jules et Jim
3	Hiroshima Mon Amour (1959)	Alain Resnais	Hiroshima, mon amour
2	The 400 Blows (1959)	François Truffaut	Les quatre cents coups
1	Breathless (1960)	Jean-Luc Godard	À bout de souffle

TOP 10

What exactly is a slasher movie? Generally speaking it must feature a psychopath who systematically kills a sequence of victims in particularly gruesome fashion. They are almost always American movies and the killer will generally be a masked male who uses some sort of bladed weapon, usually on promiscuous teenagers.

SLASHER MOVIES

10 WHEN A STRANGER CALLS (1979)
High School student Jill Johnson (Carol Kane) is babysitting for neighbours when she starts receiving intimidating phone calls asking if she's checked the children lately. When she phones the police she learns the calls are coming from... inside the house!

9 THE BURNING (1981)
The caretaker of an upstate New York summer camp is terribly burned when spoilt kids play a prank on him. Years later he's released from an institution and, armed with a pair of hedge cutters, sets off straight to the summer camp.

8 TOURIST TRAP (1979)
A group of teen friends wind up in what seems like a creepy museum full of mannequins. The owner, who has telekinetic powers, is a recluse who treats the mannequins as friends and can control them telepathically.

7 THE PROWLER (1981)
35 years after a man in full WWII combat gear brutally murdered a young couple at a dance, the same sinister killer seems to be back.

6 SLEEPAWAY CAMP (1983)
After her family is killed in an accident, a young girl sees summer camp as a way to start to get over the trauma. Bad idea.

5 MY BLOODY VALENTINE (1981)
The first Valentine's Day Dance in 20 years is due to take place in Valentine Bluffs, a small American mining community. The reason for the hiatus is soon revealed when we learn an accident left five miners dead on the night of the dance two decades before. Could the masked killer suddenly causing havoc be connected to the tragedy?

4 FRIDAY THE 13TH (1980)
American summer camps seem to be the most perilous environment in the world. Their reputation takes another battering in this popular classic.

3 BLACK CHRISTMAS (1974)
Generally considered the first slasher movie, the simple premise of *Black Christmas* sees a crazed killer picking off the girls of a sorority house one by one.

2 THE TEXAS CHAIN SAW MASSACRE (1974)
Although it's on the edge of what qualifies as a slasher, this is just such a well executed and horrible little movie that it deserves mention.

HALLOWEEN (1978)

Black Christmas may be the first slasher, but it was the phenomenal success of *Halloween* that brought the genre to mainstream audiences. Set largely over the course of one day and evening, dangerous psychopath Michael Myers has escaped the institution holding him. In his home town of Haddonfield, Illinois, a group of teenage friends are terrorised by a masked killer – surely no coincidence? Costing just $325,000 to produce, *Halloween*'s box office return of $70 million makes it one of the most profitable indy movies ever made.

	MOVIE	DIRECTOR
10	When A Stranger Calls (1979)	Fred Walton
9	The Burning (1981)	Tony Maylam
8	Tourist Trap (1979)	David Schmoeller
7	The Prowler (1981)	Joseph Zito
6	Sleepaway Camp (1983)	Robert Hiltzik
5	My Bloody Valentine (1981)	George Mihalka
4	Friday the 13th (1980)	Sean S. Cunningham
3	Black Christmas (1974)	Bob Clark
2	The Texas Chain Saw Massacre (1974)	Tobe Hooper
1	Halloween (1978)	John Carpenter

TOP 10

A list of female characters who perform a role more generally associated with men, and do so better than those men might usually manage. They don't need to be tomboys, just good at what they do.

WOMEN IN A MAN'S WORLD

10 PRINCESS MERIDA
Princess Merida of the clan Dunbroch is to be betrothed to the son of one of her father's allies against her will. When none of the potential suitors can match her in an archery contest it sets off a chain reaction that could destroy the kingdom.

9 PAT PEMBERTON
One of nine collaborations between Katharine Hepburn and Spencer Tracy, Pat and Mike is the lighthearted story of a gifted sportswoman struggling to be taken seriously by her domineering fiancé.

8 MAYA LAMBERT
This fictionalised account of the hunt for Osama Bin Laden sees C.I.A. operative Maya Lambert thrown into the deep end of the murky waters that mark the crossover point between interrogation and torture.

7 NAUSICAÄ
Set in the distant future after 'Seven Days of Fire' has left much of the world a toxic wasteland, Nausicaä is an ecologically minded fable following the eponymous hero's attempt to bring peace to her dying planet.

6 HILDY JOHNSON
The buzz of testosterone-charged newspaper offices lure former reporter Hildy back into the mire in this superb Howard Hawks screwball comedy. The fast-paced dialogue she exchanges with her editor and sort-of husband Walter (Cary Grant) is some of the best this venerable genre ever produced.

5 PAI (PAIKEA APIRANA)
The Whangara of New Zealand are a staunchly traditional people who believe the spirit of their mythical ancestor Paikea is present in each of their subsequent chiefs, who have always been first born males. Pai, an 11 year old girl, knows Paikea's spirit is within her, but faces an uphill challenge to convince her grandfather, whose responsibility it is to nominate the next chief.

4 VIENNA
On the outskirts of a miserable old west town, the vivid Vienna juggles the disparate groups of outlaws, cattle men and assorted lowlifes who frequent her saloon. Widely recognised today as an allegory of the McCarthy-era Communist witch hunts, the movie has an ambiguity and intelligence beyond that of most of its contemporaries.

3 ELLEN RIPLEY
Ripley's determination and resourcefulness make her one of the most iconic of tough female characters.

2 CLARICE STARLING

Like the serial killer she is sent to interview, Starling is both capable and perceptive. Unlike him she is also vulnerable and principled, attributes which make her his perfect foil.

1 MARGE GUNDERSON

Unassuming, heavily pregnant police chief Marge Gunderson must be one of the most popular of movie characters. Methodically picking away at the tall tale spun by hopelessly out of his depth kidnap orchestrator Jerry Lundegaard (William H. Macy), the bedrock of the movie's appeal is the level of humanity she brings to it.

	CHARACTER(S)	MOVIE	ACTOR(S)
10	Princess Merida	*Brave (2012)*	Kelly Macdonald
9	Pat Pemberton	*Pat and Mike (1952)*	Katherine Hepburn
8	Maya Lambert	*Zero Dark Thirty (2012)*	Jessica Chastain
7	Nausicaä	*Nausicaä of the Valley of the Wind (1984)*	Sumi Shimamoto and Alison Lohman
6	Hildy Johnson	*His Girl Friday (1940)*	Rosalind Russell
5	Pai (Paikea Apirana)	*Whale Rider (2002)*	Keish Castle-Hughes
4	Vienna	*Johnny Guitar (1954)*	Joan Crawford
3	Ellen Ripley	*Alien (1979)*	Sigourney Weaver
2	Clarice Starling	*Silence of the Lambs (1991)*	Jodie Foster
1	Marge Gunderson	*Fargo (1996)*	Frances McDormand

TOP
10

The ultimate movie in-joke has to be the cameo. Sometimes it's such an in-joke fans don't even know it has happened, as with Cate Blancett's uncredited turn as a fully masked forensic pathologist in 2007's *Hot Fuzz*.

CAMEOS

10 FRANK SINATRA Not the most impressive movie for Frank Sinatra to end his career with, but at least he's funny in it.

9 GARY BUSEY One of many stars to request a part in this adaptation of the Hunter S. Thompson book, Busey was actually friendly with the author. The spin he gives the character, adding an unscripted request for a kiss from Johnny Depp's Raoul Duke, makes the scene.

8 BRUCE SPRINGSTEEN Rob Gordon (John Cusack) is obsessed with two things: music, and his ex-girlfriend Laura. His inability to relate to women leads to Springsteen's cameo, an imagined conversation in which Rob presses him for advice.

7 HUGH JACKMAN A montage showing us the origins of the X-Men features Charles Xavier (James McAvoy) and Eric Lensherr (Michael Fassbender) recruiting mutants from all over the world. In a nondescript bar they find fan favourite Wolverine (Jackman), but are unable to even make their offer before being rudely dismissed.

6 ORSON WELLES After battling their way to Hollywood in search of movie stardom, the Muppets finally gain an audience with studio boss Lew Lord, a brilliantly cast Orson Welles. He only has one line of dialogue, but it's delivered with profound sincerity.

5 CHUCK NORRIS A group of malingering friends enter a dodgeball tournament hoping to raise funds to prevent their gym being taken over by a ruthless fitness fanatic. When they forfeit the all-important match it's down to the judges to vote on whether they can continue.

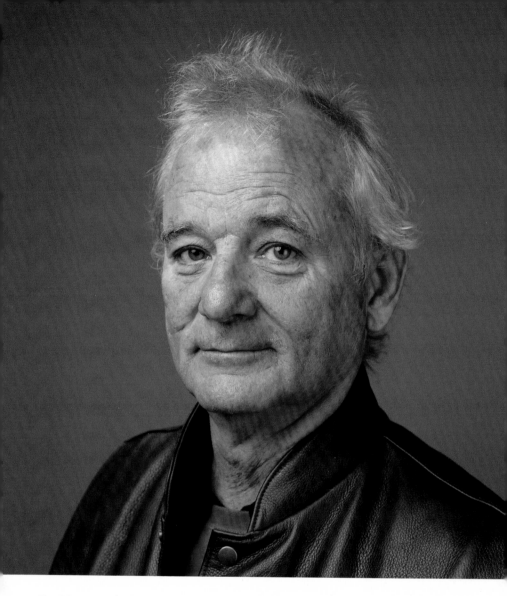

Thankfully, the casting vote belongs to you-know-who.

4 MARCEL MARCEAU
A silent movie about Hollywood producers trying to make a silent movie. When the director telephones to offer Marcel Marceau a role, the famous mime utters the only word of dialogue, and best joke, in the film: 'non!'

3 BRUCE WILLIS AND JULIA ROBERTS
Early on in *The Player* two screenwriters pitch a script for a legal drama to a Hollywood executive, but are horrified at his suggestion it be given a happy ending and cast with stars. By the end of the movie they've been brought into line and are happy to sell out, as demonstrated when Bruce Willis bursts onto the stage to save the day.

2 BILL MURRAY

It's another pesky zombie apocalypse, and a small band of survivors decide it would be fun to hide out at Bill Murray's house. Only Bill Murray turns out to be one of the survivors too – at least until he pretends to be a zombie as a practical joke.

1 MARSHALL MCLUHAN

In line at a movie theatre, Alvy Singer (Woody Allen) becomes incensed at a pseudo-intellectual who fancies himself an expert on cinema. After the misinterprets the analysis of renowned media philosopher Marshal McLuhan, Alvy interjects by producing the real McLuhan, who issues a withering putdown.

	CAMEO BY	MOVIE
10	Frank Sinatra	*Cannonball Run II (1984)*
9	Gary Busey	*Fear and Loathing in Las Vegas (1998)*
8	Bruce Springsteen	*High Fidelity (2000)*
7	Hugh Jackman	*X-Men: First Class (2011)*
6	Orson Welles	*The Muppet Movie (1979)*
5	Chuck Norris	*Dodgeball (2004)*
4	Marcel Marceau	*Silent Movie (1976)*
3	Bruce Willis and Julia Roberts	*The Player (1992)*
2	Bill Murray	*Zombieland (2009)*
1	Marshall McLuhan	*Annie Hall (1977)*

TOP 10

It's curious how movie assassins often have the most clearly defined morality of any character type. It might not be a morality we share, but it's usually a well developed and rigid system to which they will adhere at any cost. Which is more than you can say for some heroes.

ASSASSINS

10 MARTIN BLANK An assassin in the midst of an existential quandary is an inherently funny thing, particularly if you place that assassin at a school reunion and put a hit out on him. Cusack is brilliant as Martin Blank, a killer who gives in to nostalgia and grows a heart.

9 LONE WOLF AKA OGAMI ITTO This westernised mishmash of the first two *Lone Wolf and Cub* movies (a popular Japanese series following the exploits of a swordsman and his young son) is probably the best introduction to the celebrated samurai killer, Ogami Itto.

8 HANNA Director Joe Wright shifted gears dramatically when he abandoned his trademark heavyweight literary adaptations (*Pride & Prejudice, Atonement*) to make this frenzied action thriller about a 16-year-old girl trained to be the perfect assassin.

7 HAWKINS Comedy about a British assassin who suffers a series of farcical episodes while attempting to knock off a pompous politician.

6 GHOST DOG Cult director Jim Jarmusch offers a meditative take on the killer for hire, his Ghost Dog being philosophically inclined and inspired by bushido, the code of the samurai. The movie clearly takes much inspiration from a classic of the genre, 1967's *Le Samouraï*, with various moments lifted intact and the overall tone skillfully recreated.

5 AH JONG Largely responsible for the explosion in popularity of Hong Kong thrillers in the West, writer/director John Woo's contract-killer-classic is unmissable. Disillusioned with his life and determined to help an innocent bystander he mistakenly blinded, Ah Jong takes on one last big job, but it isn't what it seems.

SILENCE

4 Bounty hunters, outlaws and starving villagers fight it out amongst themselves in the bleak landscape of Utah's Great Blizzard of 1899. Either of the main characters could have made the list, with Silence's ultimate opponent Loco (Klaus Kinski) an equally memorable killer.

NIKITA

3 A teen drugs addict winds up in prison, from where she is reluctantly recruited to be an assassin for a secretive government agency known as The Centre. As Nikita is effectively forced into the role of a paid killer the movie focuses on the psychological damage inherent to such a job.

JEF COSTELLO

2 This melancholic character study oozes French style as the suave Costello goes about his business with meticulous precision.

ANTON CHIGURH

1 The most intimidating, remorseless and determined entry on the list has to take the number one spot. Chigurh is an iconic creation, which instantly elevated Spanish star Javier Bardem to the Hollywood A-list.

	CHARACTER	MOVIE	ACTOR
10	Martin Blank	*Grosse Point Blank (1997)*	John Cusack
9	Lone Wolf aka Ogami Itto	*Shogun Assassin (1980)*	Tomisaburô Wakayama
8	Hanna	*Hanna (2011)*	Saorise Ronan
7	Hawkins	*The Green Man (1956)*	Alastair Sim
6	Ghost Dog	*Ghost Dog: The Way of the Samurai (1999)*	Forest Whitaker
5	Ah Jong	*The Killer (1989)*	Chow Yun-fat
4	Silence	*The Great Silence (1968)*	Jean-Louis Trintignant
3	Nikita	*Nikita (1990)*	Anne Parillaud
2	Jef Costello	*Le Samouraï (1967)*	Alain Delon
1	Anton Chigurh	*No Country for Old Men (2007)*	Javier Bardem

TOP
10

It's well over 100 years since Georges Melies' *A Trip to the Moon* saw a group of enthusiastic astronomers launch their makeshift spaceship. The same sort of rickety models served the 1950's alien invasion craze perfectly well, with more advanced techniques eventually allowing photo-realistic work by the late 1960's. The computer revolution has left imagination the only limiting factor, with incredible CGI creations within reach of even budget productions.

SPACESHIPS

Millennium Falcon goes to Eagle 5, a battered Winnebago RV spaceship.

5 THE VALLEY FORGE
Earth in the future is devoid of all plant life, the only remaining examples kept alive in giant glass domes orbiting Saturn. The Valley Forge is a commercial freighter to which six such domes have been attached, their contents tended by botanist Freeman Lowell (Bruce Dern). But when an order comes from Earth to return the ship to normal service, Lowell refuses to comply.

10 THE HEART OF GOLD
Powered by an Infinite Improbability Drive that connects the logic circuits of a Bambleweeny 57 Sub-Meson Brain to an atomic vector plotter suspended in a Brownian Motion producer (a cup of hot tea). Simple really.

9 NOSTROMO
With its endless dank chambers and dark corridors, the industrial mining ship Nostromo proves to be an unfortunately ideal habitat for the eponymous Alien.

8 SERENITY
The ungainly Firefly class Serenity is home to a ragtag band of renegades attempting to earn a living whilst evading the totalitarian rulers of the future galaxy.

7 KLAATU'S SAUCER
This classic saucer shaped craft causes mass hysteria when it circles the earth and lands in Washington DC.

6 EAGLE 5
In Mel Brooks' *Star Wars* spoof the role of the

4 USS ENTERPRISE NCC-1701
The *Star Trek* mythology has seen about a dozen versions of the Enterprise, most of them eventually destroyed during the course of the crew's 'exploration'. The most recognisable has to be the first, which served Captain Kirk

and co trustily through the TV series and first three movies.

3 DISCOVERY ONE

Every detail of the Discovery is based on actual or theoretical (in 1968) science. The engines are gaseous core nuclear reactors, a propulsion system long hypothesised but not yet realised. The ship's systems are controlled by a central computer that's in constant contact with machines on earth. Crew can be kept in hibernation for long journeys, but when conscious enjoy gravity courtesy of the giant centrifuge. Everything has been thought out, whether explained or not, and it all adds to the effect.

2 THE DARK STAR

Mankind is colonising deep space and it's the job of the Dark Star crew to go on ahead and destroy any unstable planets.

1 THE MILLENNIUM FALCON

Originally a light freighter, the Millennium Falcon has been heavily modified for use as a high-speed smuggler's ship. The distinctive shape was inspired by a hamburger, the cockpit being an olive on a cocktail stick poking out of the side.

	SHIP	MOVIE	CAPTAIN/ COMMANDER
10	The Heart of Gold	*The Hitchhikers Guide to the Galaxy (2005)*	Zaphod Beeblebrox (Sam Rockwell)
9	Nostromo	*Alien (1979)*	Dallas (Tom Skerritt)
8	Serenity	*Serenity (2005)*	Malcolm Reynolds (Nathan Fillion)
7	Klaatu's Saucer	*The Day the Earth Stood Still (1951)*	Klaatu (Michael Rennie)
6	Eagle 5	*Spaceballs (1987)*	Lone Starr (Bill Pullman)
5	The Valley Forge	*Silent Running (1972)*	No Captain
4	USS Enterprise NCC-1701	*Star Trek I-III (1979-1984)*	James T. Kirk (William Shatner)
3	Discovery One	*2001: A Space Odyssey (1968)*	Dr. David Bowman (Keir Dullea)
2	The Dark Star	*Dark Star (1974)*	Commander Powell (Joe Saunders)
1	The Millennium Falcon	*Star Wars IV-VI (1977-ongoing)*	Han Solo (Harrison Ford)

TOP
10

There is no shortage of zero budget exploitation movies that could fit this list. But because there are so many, and because it's more fun to mock a disaster that has no excuse, this list favours movies which had the potential to be better.

SO BAD THEY'RE GOOD

10 MASTERS OF THE UNIVERSE (1987)
Whilst the director of this atrocious He-Man adaptation had the good grace never to helm another movie, the lead actors faired rather better. Dolph Lundgren carved out a career as an action hero and Courtney Cox became a megastar on the hit TV show *Friends*.

9 MAC AND ME (1988)
An *E.T.* rip-off that came too late and forgot to be any good. Of all its deficiencies perhaps the most profound is the quality of acting, even though it features Jennifer Anniston, who went on to become a megastar on the hit TV show... which movie is this again?

8 SHOWGIRLS (1995)
Essentially *All About Eve* with strippers, *Showgirls* is either one of the most hilariously bad movies ever made or a hyper real meta-analysis of modern movie tropes. Either way it's very silly and very funny.

7 DELTA FORCE 2: THE COLOMBIAN CONNECTION (1990)
The Special Forces unit lead by Chuck Norris is responsible for foiling a hijacking in the original *Delta Force*, here it's deployed to South America to rescue DEA agents kidnapped by a drug lord. Written down like this it all sounds vaguely reasonable.

6 BATTLEFIELD EARTH (2000)
Terl, leader of the Psychlos, has enslaved the human race and is stripping the Earth of its resources. What we need is a hero. And a script that makes sense. John Travolta was almost bankrupted by this ode to scientology. The studio that made it wasn't so lucky.

5 GYMKATA (1985)
An action movie about an American champion gymnast called on by his country to win a martial arts tournament for some reason. He uses his gymnastics skills to do lots of heroic things that make little sense.

4 MEGAFORCE (1982)
Commander Ace Hunter (seriously) is the heroic leader

of Megaforce, an elite military unit charged with riding motorcycles and shooting big guns at baddies. *Team America: World Police* without the deliberate comedy, Megaforce is an explosion of 80's naffness. But in a good way.

3 FLASH GORDON (1980)

A unique entry on this list because much of the talent behind the lens of *Flash Gordon* had always intended it to be the gloriously campy tongue in cheek slice of kitsch that it is. Whether or not anybody told the cast or studio isn't clear.

2 TROLL 2 (1990)

No trolls, a dentist non-actor for a leading man and a director who didn't speak English, what could go wrong? Recognised by many as the worst movie ever made, and the subject of its own documentary proclaiming as much: *Best Worst Movie* (2009).

1 THE ROOM (2003)

Described as the Citizen Kane of bad movies, *The Room* is a relative latecomer to the 'so-bad-they're-good' movie landscape. But such a successful assault on the competition needs to be recognized: this is almost certainly the worst movie ever made.

	MOVIE	DIRECTOR
10	Masters of the Universe (1987)	Gary Goddard
9	Mac and Me (1988)	Stewart Raffill
8	Showgirls (1995)	Paul Verhoeven
7	Delta Force 2: The Colombian Connection (1990)	Aaron Norris
6	Battlefield Earth (2000)	Roger Christian
5	Gymkata (1985)	Robert Clouse
4	Megaforce (1982)	Hal Needham
3	Flash Gordon (1980)	Mike Hodges
2	Troll 2 (1990)	Claudio Fragasso
1	The Room (2003)	Tommy Wiseau

TOP 10

Time to put pen to paper and create your own top 10 list of Superhero movies...

10

9

8

7

6

5

4

3

2

1

TOP 10

Historically comic books and movies lived in close quarters but seldom met. TV shows and Saturday serials (TV's cinematic predecessor) dabbled, but Hollywood was slow to cotton on to the potential of adapting comics for the big screen. Things have clearly changed, a glance at the summer release schedule will usually reveal a surfeit of superhero cinema.

SUPERHERO MOVIES

10 SPIDER-MAN (2002)

Sam Raimi was considered an odd choice to helm the highly anticipated *Spider-Man* adaptation, but the hugely popular movie he turned out began a successful franchise and launched Raimi into the director A-list.

9 BLADE (1998)

Half-vampire Blade (Wesley Snipes) works to rid the world of evil bloodsuckers.

8 AVENGERS ASSEMBLE (2012)

The long awaited zenith of superhero medleys finally arrived in 2012, and didn't disappoint fans. Iron Man (Robert Downey Jr.), Thor (Chris Hemsworth), Captain America (Chris Evans), Hulk (Mark Ruffalo) and others unite to stop evil God Loki (Tom Hiddleston) unleashing an alien invasion on earth.

7 IRON MAN (2008)

It's not immediately obvious how a smug, alcoholic, arms-dealing billionaire has become one of the most popular movie characters of the age. It must have something to do with Robert Downey Jr's charisma.

6 SUPERMAN (1978)

The first significant and successful superhero movie, *Superman* set the bar for at least the following decade, and is still revered today as one of the best of its type. Christopher Reeve lends Clark Kent and his alter ego a subtle, vulnerable charm that gives the movie an emotional heart rare amongst its successors.

5 THE CROW (1994)

The movie that made Brandon Lee a star is also, tragically, the last he made. Set in a bleak Detroit, Lee plays Eric Draven, a musician who is killed, along with his girlfriend, by a vicious gang of thugs. Resurrected by a supernatural force represented by a crow, Draven prowls the gloomy city seeking vengeance.

4 BATMAN (1989)

Although 1978's *Superman* had already taken the comic book aesthetic seriously, it still kept one toe in the camp pool with characters like Ned Beatty's bumbling henchman Otis. Batman changed everything, going darker

than anyone could have expected and scoring a huge hit as a result. If *Superman* established superheroes as viable mainstream protagonists, *Batman* proved just how wide their appeal can be.

3 X-MEN (2000)

With Hollywood already having gone through several superhero movie cycles, the age of the modern mega-hit began with *X-Men*. After attracting a highly respected director, Marvel Comics turned their $75 million investment into a $300 million international smash, redefining the way movies like this are made.

2 THE INCREDIBLES (2004)

Pixar's take on the superhero movie is an amusingly revisionist affair that revels in showing us their post retirement lifestyles.

1 THE DARK KNIGHT (2008)

With his audience on the ropes after wowing them with *Batman Begins* in 2005, Christopher Nolan delivered a knockout punch with this sequel. It will be some time before another superhero movie gets a look at the top spot in lists like this.

	MOVIE	DIRECTOR
10	Spider-Man (2002)	Sam Raimi
9	Blade (1998)	Stephen Norrington
8	Avengers Assemble (2012)	Joss Whedon
7	Iron Man (2008)	Jon Favreau
6	Superman (1978)	Richard Donner
5	The Crow (1994)	Alex Proyas
4	Batman (1989)	Tim Burton
3	X-Men (2000)	Bryan Singer
2	The Incredibles (2004)	Brad Bird
1	The Dark Knight (2008)	Christopher Nolan

TOP 10

It's often lamented that these days there's a touch less style up on the screen than there used to be. Whether true or not, we'll give more recent movies a helping hand by ruling out the eternally stylish likes of Humphrey Bogart and Audrey Hepburn.

MOST STYLISHLY DRESSED CHARACTERS

10 PRIEST
The 1970's drug dealing New York pimp look isn't for everyone. But Ron O'Neal can pull it off like a pro.

9 SÈVERINE SERIZY
The stunning Catherine Deneuve spends much of *Belle de Jour* looking like a model who has just stepped off the Paris catwalk. Many of the perfectly cut coats, dresses and lingerie have become synonymous with the character and are still considered the height of fashion.

8 HOWARD HUGHES
One advantage to playing a historical figure is the wardrobe takes care of itself. Many of Hughes' real suits were used for reference in this biopic of the extrovert movie producer, but how many other actors could make them look as good as DiCaprio?

7 LORELEI LEE
Dressed throughout the movie like the showgirl she plays, Marilyn shows off some of the most glamorous costumes imaginable.

6 JULIAN KAYE
This whole film is more concerned with superficial appearance than substance, so it's no surprise the protagonist is one of the best dressed in the movies. The camera has

an almost lecherous habit of tracking slowly across his Armani heavy wardrobe, like a lothario oggling pretty girls.

5 GINGER MCKENNA
Casino hustler Ginger makes a living from looking good, so it's no surprise she has the effortless elegance of

a Grace Kelly. At least that's how she starts the movie.

4 MARIE ANTOINETTE
With the extravagant frocks matched only by the equally excessive hairpieces, Marie Antoinette looks like an extra from an Adam Ant video for much of the movie.

Though the look might be a bit grandiose for some tastes, there's no denying the style on show.

3 GEORGE FALCONER
Colin Firth is a man who looks very much at home in the exquisitely tailored 1960's suits he sports in *A*

Single Man. With perfectly judged horn rimmed spectacles and immaculately coiffured hair, the look is one of understated class.

always looks like he's just stepped out of a fashion shoot.

2 DICKIE GREENLEAF

Clothes have a habit of hanging well on Jude Law, so when he plays a character who has been styled to within an inch of his life the effect is almost overwhelming. Whether blazer, casual wear or swimming trunks, Dickie

1 SU LI-ZHEN

The traditional high collared dresses worn by Su Li-zhen throughout In the Mood for Love are almost a character in their own right. The movie itself is hypnotic, creating an atmosphere rather than telling a narrative story, so the changing dresses serve at least one additional

	CHARACTER	MOVIE	ACTOR
10	Priest	*Super Fly (1972)*	Ron O'Neal
9	Sèverine Serizy	*Belle de Jour (1967)*	Catherine Deneuve
8	Howard Hughes	*The Aviator (2004)*	Leonardo DiCaprio
7	Lorelei Lee	*Gentlemen Prefer Blondes (1953)*	Marilyn Monroe
6	Julian Kaye	*American Gigolo (1980)*	Richard Gere
5	Ginger McKenna	*Casino (1995)*	Sharon Stone
4	Marie Antoinette	*Marie Antoinette (2006)*	Kirsten Dunst
3	George Falconer	*A Single Man (2009)*	Colin Firth
2	Dickie Greenleaf	*The Talented Mr. Ripley (1999)*	Jude Law
1	Su Li-zhen	*In the Mood for Love (2000)*	Maggie Cheung

TOP
10

With humour so subjective and exposure to movies dependent on so many factors, it's hard to meet the demand of this list's title. Some may be familiar or even well-known, but then a list of unobtainable curiosities is no good to anyone.

GREAT COMEDY MOVIES YOU MAY NOT HAVE SEEN

10 THE GOD'S MUST BE CRAZY (1980)

Xi, (N!xau) a Kalahari Bushman who has never had contact with the outside world, finds an empty Coke bottle in the desert. His tribe considers it a great wonder but soon start to bicker over it, leading Xi to set off on a journey to return it to the Gods from whence he believes it came. On the way he crosses paths with a teacher, biologist and revolutionaries, all of whose bizarre customs baffle Xi.

9 WORLD'S GREATEST DAD (2009)

Lance (Robin Williams), a failed writer, finds his obnoxious 15 year old son dead after an autoerotic asphyxiation accident. To avoid the embarrassment of revealing the manner of his son's death, Lance fakes a suicide note and goes on with his life. But when the suicide note goes viral he finds himself in a difficult situation.

8 A NEW LEAF (1971)

This largely forgotten farce sees spoilt Henry Graham (Walter Matthau) wind up penniless after running through an enormous inheritance. He decides to marry money, but will true love (and his meddling family) get in the way?

7 OFFICE SPACE (1999)

Mike Judge, the man behind Beavis & Butthead and King of the Hill, makes his live action feature debut with this satire about office drones getting one over on the boss.

6 O LUCKY MAN (1973)

In this sequel to *If...* (1968), Mick Travis has left school and entered the job market, becoming an enthusiastic travelling coffee salesman. The film satirises capitalism mercilessly, and by delving into the surreal it offers a unique concoction of styles and themes.

5 SMALL CHANGE AKA POCKET MONEY (1976)

The children of a French town learn lessons as they live their lives.

4 WITHNAIL AND I (1987)

This cult British comedy follows two out of work alcoholic actors as they escape London for a few days in a primitive country cottage. Their inability to fend for themselves sees them almost starve to death when attempts to fish for salmon with a shotgun and cook a chicken in a kettle fail miserably.

3 THE DISCREET CHARM OF THE BOURGEOISIE (1972)

Buñuel's great masterpiece is an absurdist assault on the pretension of Europe's chattering classes.

2 JOUR DE FETE (1949)

Tati's directorial debut features himself as a postman in rural France, where residents of his district are being visited by a travelling fair.

1 KIND HEARTS AND CORONETS (1949)

The illegitimate scion of the upper class D'Ascoyne family sets out to bump off the eight relatives that stand between him and a fabulous inheritance. This superb black comedy was produced by an Ealing Studios at the top of its game and features wonderful performances from Alec Guinness (who plays all eight of the doomed D'Ascoynes), Dennis Price as the killer and enigmatic Ealing regular Joan Greenwood.

	MOVIE	DIRECTOR
10	The God's Must Be Crazy (1980)	Jamie Uys
9	World's Greatest Dad (2009)	Bobcat Goldthwait
8	A New Leaf (1971)	Elaine May
7	Office Space (1999)	Mike Judge
6	O Lucky Man (1973)	Lindsay Anderson
5	Small Change aka Pocket Money (1976)	François Truffaut
4	Withnail and I (1987)	Bruce Robinson
3	The Discreet Charm of the Bourgeoisie (1972)	Luis Buñuel
2	Jour de Fete (1949)	Jacques Tati
1	Kind Hearts and Coronets(1949)	Robert Hamer

Documentaries have seen a conflict between the need to be both authentic and entertaining since scenes were first staged for 1921's *Nanook of the North*. Faux documentaries eschew claims to authenticity, but can still inform us though, more usually, they amuse.

FAUX DOCUMENTARIES

10 **F FOR FAKE** (1973)
Superficially, *F for Fake* asks why an original artwork, such as a painting by a great master, should be worth more than an indistinguishable copy. But there's much more going on in Orson Welles' final masterpiece, which is essentially an analysis of the meaning of truth.

9 **INCIDENT AT LOCH NESS** (2004)
Werner Herzog, eminent documentarian, filmmaker and all round cinematic lunatic, plays himself as part of a team side-tracked looking for the Loch Ness monster. It's never quite clear what's real and what isn't, but the effect is a barrel of laughs.

8 **THREADS** (1984)
Bleak, theoretical presentation of the effect of nuclear war on a typical Northern English community.

Among other things, we learn that dying in the initial blast could be preferable to struggling through the savagely dysfunctional radioactive aftermath.

7 MAN BITES DOG (1992)

A thief is approached by a film crew wishing to follow him around and document his life. As his crimes escalate to brutal murder, the crew are drawn into helping and the movie becomes about the documentary maker's struggle for objectivity.

6 THE WAR GAME (1965)

Similar to *Threads*, both deserve a place for their success in relating the reality of nuclear war to an uninformed public. In fact *The War Game* was considered so effective that for 20 years it remained off limits to TV broadcasters for fear it would spread panic.

5 FORGOTTEN SILVER (1995)

Peter Jackson's touching tribute to his long-forgotten cinematic idol is no less entertaining as a result of the man never having existed. This highly inventive movie is played so straight it's likely you'll want to seek out some of McKenzie's work.

4 WAITING FOR GUFFMAN (1996)

With a rumour that Broadway 'talent scout' Mort Guffman will attend opening night of their new play, the amateur dramatics society of Blaine, Missouri get carried away over the potential of their latest production.

3 EXIT THROUGH THE GIFT SHOP (2010)

Anonymous street artist Banksy maintains a mysterious air with his movie debut by focusing on people and events that seem to be a mixture of fact and fiction. By the end we're no closer to knowing which is which, but that's just part of the fun.

2 ZELIG (1983)

An account of Leonard Zelig (Allen), a man with the uncontrollable ability to transform his appearance to match those around him. Though there is ample opportunity to drive home some heavy allegory, it's generally passed over in favour of humour.

1 THIS IS SPINAL TAP (1984)

Whether it's turning it up to 11, smuggling a cucumber through a metal detector or recounting the various demises of a string of former drummers, *This Is Spinal Tap* is full of jokes that will be almost as familiar to those who haven't seen it as those who have.

	MOVIE	DIRECTOR(S)	SUBJECT
10	*F for Fake (1973)*	Orson Welles	Trickery and deception
9	*Incident at Loch Ness (2004)*	Zak Penn	The enigma of Loch Ness
8	*Threads (1984)*	Mick Jackson	Nuclear holocaust
7	*Man Bites Dog (1992)*	Rémy Belvaux and André Bonzel	A ruthless criminal
6	*The War Game (1965)*	Peter Watkins	Nuclear holocaust
5	*Forgotten Silver (1995)*	Peter Jackson	Fictional filmmaker Colin McKenzie
4	*Waiting for Guffman (1996)*	Christopher Guest	An amateur theatre group
3	*Exit Through the Gift Shop (2010)*	Banksy	Leading street artists
2	*Zelig (1983)*	Woody Allen	A human chameleon
1	*This Is Spinal Tap (1984)*	Rob Reiner	An egotistical British rock band

TOP
10

The movies have done much to elevate our view of the larcenist. When necessary they are vilified, but often charm seems to be the only differentiator when it comes to celebrating the daring of a cat burglar or denouncing the dishonesty of a common thief.

THIEVES, PICKPOCKETS & BURGLARS

10 FRANK
Frank has become a successful jewel thief by being extremely careful and methodical about his work. When his intense desire to settle down and start a family encourages him to compromise his rules of engagement, his life starts to unravel.

9 PROFESSOR MARCUS
The sinister ringleader of a gang of criminals who pull off a security van heist, Marcus is better suited to dealing with hardened thugs than he is a little old lady. Guinness based his performance on those of his acting hero, Alastair Sim.

8 BOB MONTAGNÉ
Professional gambler Bob Montagné, a popular charmer, is left penniless and desperate when his luck finally runs out. After learning of a particular casino that's vulnerable to a heist he starts putting a gang together and forms a plan.

7 BILBO BAGGINS
Not an obvious choice but throughout the series Bilbo Baggins is referred to as the 'burglar', his job (due to his size, spirit and, ironically, honesty) is to steal. Whether he'd have much in common with the other entries on this list seems unlikely.

6 THE ARTFUL DODGER
The Artful Dodger (aka Jack Hawkins) is the mythical leader of a gang of pickpocket orphans that terrorise London in this Charles Dickens adaptation. Although the miserly Fagin is the ultimate authority, Dodger has the skill and the heart.

5 JACK FOLEY
After breaking out of prison a bank robber embarks on that infamously elusive last big score. Channelling Cary Grant (not for the first time), George Clooney's Foley has the charisma to simply talk his way into a bank vault if necessary.

4 MICHEL
A young man slides inescapably into criminality when he joins up with a gang of highly coordinated pickpockets. Director Robert Bresson (famous for using non-professional actors) discovered another amateur gem in lead Martin LaSalle.

3 SIR CHARLES LYTTON AKA THE PHANTOM
This first in the Pink Panther series focuses less on the popular Inspector Clouseau (Peter Sellers) than it does his antagonist, The Phantom. Sadly Niven didn't return to the role and later films miss the chemistry between these wonderful adversaries.

2 JOHN ROBIE

The archetypal gentleman thief, John Robie is retired to the French Riviera when a cat burglar imitating his style causes him unwelcome attention from the authorities. He decides to get back in the saddle in an attempt to scupper the imposter.

1 SELINA KYLE AKA CATWOMAN

Batman has always been used to address issues of duality and demonstrate the common traits of apparently opposite characters. To that end Catwoman, although a criminal by trade, is written and presented as a reflection of Batman himself.

	THIEF	ACTOR	MOVIE
10	Frank	James Caan	*Thief (1981)*
9	Professor Marcus	Alec Guinness	*The Ladykillers (1955)*
8	Bob Montagné	Roger Duchesne	*Bob le Flambeur (1956)*
7	Bilbo Baggins	Martin Freeman	*The Hobbit series (2012-2014)*
6	The Artful Dodger	Anthony Newley	*Oliver Twist (1948)*
5	Jack Foley	George Clooney	*Out of Sight (1998)*
4	Michel	Martin LaSalle	*Pickpocket (1959)*
3	Sir Charles Lytton aka The Phantom	David Niven	*The Pink Panther (1963)*
2	John Robie	Cary Grant	*To Catch a Thief (1955)*
1	Selina Kyle aka Catwoman	Anne Hathaway	*The Dark Knight Rises (2012)*

TOP 10

Hollywood studios are said to be prone to copying proven ideas rather than pursuing original ones, but is it that simple? If a good movie fails to find an audience because, for example, it's subtitled, is it really that wrong to remake it and tailor the idea to the audience?

REMAKES BETTER THAN THE ORIGINALS

10 TRUE LIES (1994)
This high concept actioner sees secret agent Harry Tasker (Arnold Schwarzenegger) have to reveal his true profession to wife Helen (Jamie Lee Curtis) when both are kidnapped by terrorists threatening to nuke the U.S.

9 BEN-HUR (1959)
William Wyler's version of the perennial favourite fable of a Jewish prince sold into slavery is the most successful and popular of many.

8 OCEAN'S ELEVEN (2001)
Movies with a great concept but flawed execution are prime candidates for the remake treatment. *Ocean's Eleven* is a good example of this, with the original (starring Frank Sinatra and the rat pack) oozing superficial cool but failing to make us care about proceedings.

7 A STAR IS BORN (1954)
The career trajectories of a bright ingenue and an established actor go in opposite directions in this classic take on the cruel reality of stardom. The 1937 version is also excellent, but Judy Garland does something special with the role of the ambitious young performer in this one.

6 THE MAN WHO KNEW TOO MUCH (1956)
Unsatisfied with his first attempt, Alfred Hitchcock decided to remake his own movie about a complicated assassination plot. Whereas he felt the first film was 'the work of a talented amateur', the second is the work of a professional on fine form.

5 INVASION OF THE BODY SNATCHERS (1978)
There's an intriguing

comparison to be made between these two movies, both of which use the same premise but were made in profoundly different times. The earlier offering reflects the paranoia so prevalent in the 1950s concerning communist infiltration. The idea that personality could be changed through indoctrination was a prominent concern. The later movie demonstrates the feelings of alienation and disillusion that were so rife in the period following the collapse of the hippie ideal. Both are great films, the latter just toys with a more interesting allegory.

4 THE FLY (1986)
Both movies feature a scientist transformed into a fly, but that's about the extent of the similarity. The original's camp fun is replaced with hardcore body horror in the remake.

3 TRUE GRIT (2010)

A young girl seeking revenge for the death of her father hires a cantankerous U.S. Marshal to help her.

2 HEAT (1995)

Michael Mann adapted his own small scale TV movie for the big screen just six years after the original.

1 HIS GIRL FRIDAY (1940)

Howard Hawks' legendary light touch with comedy is demonstrated wonderfully in arguably his greatest work. Both movies have the advantage of being based on a strong stage play, but the fast-paced dialogue, sublime performances and near perfection of the later movie is a particular joy to behold.

	MOVIE	DIRECTOR	ORIGINAL
10	*True Lies (1994)*	James Cameron	*La Totale (1991)*
9	*Ben-Hur (1959)*	William Wyler	*Ben-Hur: A Tale of the Christ (1925)*
8	*Ocean's Eleven (2001)*	Steven Soderbergh	*Ocean's Eleven (1960)*
7	*A Star is Born (1954)*	George Cukor	*A Star is Born (1937)*
6	*The Man Who Knew Too Much (1956)*	Alfred Hitchcock	*The Man Who Knew Too Much (1934)*
5	*Invasion of the Body Snatchers (1978)*	Philip Kaufman	*Invasion of the Body Snatchers (1956)*
4	*The Fly (1986)*	David Cronenberg	*The Fly (1958)*
3	*True Grit (2010)*	Ethan & Joel Coen	*True Grit (1969)*
2	*Heat (1995)*	Michael Mann	*L.A. Takedown (1989)*
1	*His Girl Friday (1940)*	Howard Hawks	*The Front Page (1931)*

TOP
10

If drama is conflict, you can't get much more dramatic than two characters beating each other senseless. Like the wandering ronin of Kurosawa's Yojimbo, this list believes an honourable fight cannot be waged with firearms.

FIGHTS (FIST FIGHTS)

10 JAMES BOND VS. RED GRANT

With Dr. No, Bond's big screen bow, failing to deliver a character with the physical presence to threaten 007, producers ensured the followup would feature a villain who shared Sean Connery's imposing stature. Robert Shaw was certainly that man.

9 DRAGON VS. COLT

Though friendly off screen, this is the only time the two most popular and skilled martial arts movie stars appeared together on it. Who would have won if the contest were real is still hotly debated by fans and experts. The quality of the fight is not.

8 JOHN J MACREEDY VS. COLEY TRIMBLE

No additional reason should be necessary to seek out Bad Day at Black Rock, an expertly played, supremely taut thriller of the first order. But if some

icing on the cake is required, remember it features a one-armed Spencer Tracy doing karate.

7 BORAT VS. AZAMAT

It might be closer to wrestling than fist fighting, but one day this scrap will define the aesthetic of early 21st century cinematic fight scenes. Or not. If Ken Russell and John Waters collaborated on a fight scene, this is what it would look like.

6 THE NARRATOR VS. HIMSELF

As its revealed one lead character is just an invention of the other's fractured mind, we see scenes play out as they really happened, not as we initially saw them. The Narrator fighting himself is a potent allegory, as well as being quite funny.

5 WONG FEI-HUNG VS. JOHN

Although Jackie Chan's post 1980s career has failed to enthuse some fans of his earlier successes, this attempt to revisit one of them proved a surprise hit. The fight is crucial to the movie's appeal and demonstrates Chan's extraordinary athleticism.

4 HAPPY GILMORE VS. BOB BARKER

Although Bob Barker (here playing himself) is a kindly legend of U.S. TV, he proves to be one of the most badass entries on this list. Gilmore doesn't stand a chance in this scuffle, which is the result of Barker criticising his golf game.

3 SEAN THORNTON VS. WILL DANAHER

Tension over an unpaid dowry erupts into seemingly endless old school fisticuffs. Whilst marauding through an Irish village the combatants somehow find time to stop for a pint, and inevitably they end up friends.

2 PHILO BEDDOE VS. JACK WILSON
As with *The Quiet Man* these two brawlers are clearly destined to be pals, as a result the fight is punctuated by spontaneous outbreaks of friendliness. The massive bare knuckles, huge swings and loud cracks still make you wince.

1 NADA VS. FRANK
Nada wants Frank to put on special glasses that reveal the world as it really is. Frank doesn't want to put the glasses on. A legendarily excessive brawl ensues and the movie's point is rammed home: we don't like to open our eyes to unpleasant truths.

	COMBATANTS	WINNER	MOVIE
10	James Bond vs. Red Grant	Bond, of course	*From Russia With Love (1963)*
9	Dragon vs. Colt	Dragon	*Way of the Dragon (1972)*
8	John J Macreedy vs. Coley Trimble	Macreedy	*Bad Day At Black Rock (1955)*
7	Borat vs. Azamat	They both lose, frankly	*Borat: Cultural Learnings of America for Make Benefit Glorious Nation of Kazakhstan (2006)*
6	The Narrator vs. Himself	Hard to say	*Fight Club (1999)*
5	Wong Fei-hung vs. John	Wong Fei-hung	*The Legend of Drunken Master (1994)*
4	Happy Gilmore vs. Bob Barker	Bob Barker	*Happy Gilmore (1996)*
3	Sean Thornton vs. Will Danaher	Both of them	*The Quiet Man (1952)*
2	Philo Beddoe vs. Jack Wilson	Philo Beddoe	*Any Which Way You Can (1980)*
1	Nada vs. Frank	Nada	*They Live (1988)*

TOP 10

With the relaxation of censorship allowing more graphic content, the 1970s saw a revolution in exploitation cinema, a hitherto fairly benign genre. Parents who had fretted over the previous era's toothless monster movies were suddenly faced with something far more depraved.

70'S EXPLOITATION MOVIES

10 THE LAST HOUSE ON THE LEFT (1972)

Incredibly, this nasty little movie is based on Ingmar Bergman's *Virgin Spring*, though that didn't help with the controversy it attracted on release. The killers of a teenage girl seek refuge with her parents, who soon cotton on to what's happened and extract their revenge.

9 HANZO THE RAZOR (1972)

This surprisingly intricately plotted period samurai movie (or Chambara) is the first of a series featuring Hanzo (Shintaro Katsu), a uniquely honest law enforcer. Here he slashes and threatens his way through the corruption of the ruling elite.

8 FACES OF DEATH (1978)

Footage of unpleasantness masquerading as a documentary, *Faces of Death* draws few mainstream

defenders. But its infamy and status amongst the movie fan subculture means it warrants a place on this list.

7 THEY CALL HER ONE EYE (1973)

Sweden wasn't exactly a powerhouse behind the wave of exploitation movies that swept through the 70's. But it did produce this archetypal revenge thriller, a favourite of Quentin Tarantino and one of the many overt influences on his *Kill Bill* films.

6 FOXY BROWN (1974)

Foxy Brown (Pam Grier) seeks revenge for the death of her boyfriend. Grier was the queen of Blaxploitation, a subgenre designed to show African American characters with control over their own fate and identity.

5 ILSA: SHE-WOLF OF THE SS (1974)

One of the more curious exploitation subgenres mixes

softcore nudity with cartoonish Nazi authority figures. It may sound like an attempt to offend as many people as possible, but tongue is planted firmly in cheek.

4 MASTER OF THE FLYING GUILLOTINE (1976)

Martial arts master Wang is pursued by an evil assassin seeking revenge for incidents in this movie's predecessor, *One Armed Boxer* (1971). It's one of few exploitation movies

Foxy's in lov
so gather 'rou
watch a real st
'Cause she's
and that ai
She don't b
bring 'em bac

FOXY BROWN

PAM GRIER_{AS}
FOXY BROWN

Also starring
PETER BROWN · TERRY CARTER as Michael · Co-starring KATHRYN LODER · HARRY HOLCOMBE
Produced by BUZZ FEITSHANS · Written and Directed by JACK HILL · COLOR by Movielab · An AMERICAN INTERN

to be well respected at the more discerning end of the movie fan spectrum.

3 DEATH RACE 2000 (1975)

Thirty years in the future the sport of the moment is a cross country road race offering extra points for running people down. The significant kitsch appeal lead to a 2008 remake, but it's this wonkily charming original that's worth seeing.

2 DEEP THROAT (1972)

One of the most notorious movies ever made, *Deep Throat* took full advantage of newly relaxed rules on what could be shown on screen. Its popularity amongst the middle class mainstream was unexpected and lead to a wave of so called 'porno chic' movies.

SHAFT (1975)

Shaft's success saved the MGM studio from bankruptcy, kickstarted the blaxploitation phenomenon and changed the way theme music was used forever. It's no surprise the movie has been deemed worthy of preservation by the U.S. Congress.

	MOVIE	DIRECTOR	SUBGENRE
10	The Last House on the Left (1972)	Wes Craven	Shocksploitation
9	Hanzo the Razor (1972)	Kenji Misumi	Chambara
8	Faces of Death (1978)	John Alan Shwartz	Mondo
7	They Call Her One Eye (1973)	Bo Arne Vibenius	Rape-revenge
6	Foxy Brown (1974)	Jack Hill	Blaxploitation
5	Ilsa: She-Wolf of the SS (1974)	Don Edmonds	Nazisploitation
4	Master of the Flying Guillotine (1976)	Yu Wang	Chopsocky
3	Death Race 2000 (1975)	Russ Meyer	Carsploitation
2	Deep Throat (1972)	Gerard Damiano	Sexploitation
1	Shaft (1975)	Gordon Parks	Blaxploitation

What can make TV movies interesting is the creativity stemming from the limitations the medium imposes on them. Rules dictate the language, violence and sexual content that can be used, and they must adhere to a structure providing for regular commercial breaks and a specific running time.

MADE FOR TV MOVIES

10 DON'T BE AFRAID OF THE DARK (1973)

One of those simple horror movies that stuck in the mind of all who saw it at the time. It has since been remade as a disappointing big budget theatrical movie by horror and fantasy aficionado Guillermo del Toro.

9 AN EARLY FROST (1985)

This powerful tearjerker was one of the first movies to address the burgeoning AIDS crisis. Homosexual lawyer Michael (Aidan Quinn) discovers he has AIDS and encounters all manner of uninformed prejudice as he attempts to deal with it.

8 THE WOMAN IN BLACK (1989)

Based on Susan Hill's gothic novella, this British TV adaptation precedes a more recent version starring Daniel Radcliffe. It's a chilling ghost story about a young solicitor sent to a remote corner of England to tie up a client's affairs.

7 SPECIAL BULLETIN (1983)

In many ways way ahead of its time, *Special Bulletin* uses the then unusual device of presenting the narrative as a series of news reports. The crisis being covered is a terrorist threat to bomb the U.S. unless it's nuclear arsenal is disabled.

6 THE NIGHT STALKER (1972)

Although it lead to its own series, *The Night Stalker* is perhaps best known now as the inspiration for *The X-Files*.

Intriguingly, it follows a fairly standard TV mystery formula, but has more imagination as well as a supernatural antagonist.

5 THE DAY AFTER (1983)
Part of a wave of nuclear apocalypse movies that swept through cinemas and living rooms in the 70's and 80's. By focusing on a

typical Kansas community it spoke to a huge audience, with 100 million Americans seeing its first airing.

4 WHISTLE AND I'LL COME TO YOU (1968)
Professor Parkin (Michael Hordern) holidays in a near deserted, windswept coastal village. After finding a bone whistle he's terrorised by

surreal sounds and visions that gradually increase in intensity until he, and we, can stand it no longer.

3 DUEL (1971)
Amongst the most well known TV movies thanks to being Steven Spielberg's sort-of debut, *Duel* is more than a curiosity for completists. Its story of a motorist terrorised

by a trucker produces more tension than such a simple setup sounds capable of.

2 FATAL VISION (1984)

The true story of U.S. Army Captain Jeffrey MacDonald (Gary Cole) and the murder of his wife and child. MacDonald claims the tragedy was perpetrated by a gang, but suspicion he himself was the killer led to a series of contradictory trials.

1 BRIAN'S SONG (1971)

Another true story that uses terminal illness to highlight positive aspects of humanity. Brian Piccolo (James Caan), a football player stricken with cancer, is ceaselessly supported by teammate Gale Sayers (Billy Dee Williams), before the inevitable tragedy.

e tender true story
Gale Sayers and Brian Piccolo.

lumbia Pictures Presents

AMES | BILLY DEE
AAN / WILLIAMS in

BRIAN'S SONG

ck Warden · Shelley Fabares · Judy Pace
ced by Paul Junger Witt · Directed by Buzz Kulik · Screenplay by William Blinn

	MOVIE	DIRECTOR
10	Don't be Afraid of the Dark (1973)	John Newland
9	An Early Frost (1985)	John Erman
8	The Woman in Black (1989)	Herbert Wise
7	Special Bulletin (1983)	Ed Zwick
6	The Night Stalker (1972)	John Llewellyn Moxey
5	The Day After (1983)	Nicholas Meyer
4	Whistle and I'll Come to You (1968)	Jonathan Miller
3	Duel (1971)	Steven Spielberg
2	Fatal Vision (1984)	David Greene
1	Brian's Song (1971)	Buzz Kulik

TOP
10

It's impossible to know how many browbeaten parents have been cajoled into pet ownership after their children watched one of these movies. If you fear such a fate, avoid anything with cute dogs and convince the kids to see more dinosaur movies. Tribute to *Lassie*.

PETS

10 WANDA (FISH)
Career criminal and devout animal lover Ken Pile adores his collection of exotic fish, in particular the elegant Wanda. In fact, he loves her so much he's prepared to give up the proceeds of a jewel heist to prevent her being eaten!

9 HEDWIG (OWL)
Harry Potter's faithful feathered friend, a female Snowy owl, is integral to the mythology of the series as well as a handy means to avoid buying stamps. Her death in the Second Wizarding War is a huge blow to both Harry and the audience.

8 ELSA (LION)
When three tiger cubs are orphaned, naturalist Joy Adamson rears them as best she can, eventually sending the biggest to zoos. But she forms a strong bond with the smallest, Elsa, and decides to try and rehabilitate her into the wild.

7 FLIPPER (DOLPHIN)
Although the TV series is now legendary, some may not remember the movie that preceded it. Here we're introduced to Flipper who, after being rescued by young Sandy Ricks (Luke Halpin), chooses to remain with him and his Ranger father.

6 ASTA (DOG)
This wire fox terrier was one of the first movie pets to grab the imagination of audiences. Played by Skippy (who enjoyed a long and successful Hollywood career), his fame and appeal lead to an explosion in the breed's popularity.

5 CHEETA (CHIMP)
Although played by many chimps (and even a few humans), one ape in particular found great success as Tarzan's comic relief. After

retiring from the movies, Jiggs IV (aka Cheeta), had a successful career as an artist and even wrote his memoirs.

4 REMY (RAT)
Rodent gourmet Remy (voiced by Patton Oswalt) has charm, culinary talent and a burning desire to cook. For obvious reasons that desire remains unfulfilled, at least until he meets Linguini, a talentless chef who's up for some convoluted chicanery.

3 GIZMO (MOGWAI)
Just in case one were needed, here's another good reason not to give pets as Christmas presents. It's a shame though, because Gizmo is the most unfeasibly cute critter imaginable...as long as you don't feed him after midnight.

2 WILLY (WHALE)
It might be a bit of a push to call Willy a pet, but due to the strength of the bond between he and 12-year-old Jesse he makes the list. Both characters exhibit unruly behaviour due to a troubled past and effectively administer lifesaving therapy to one another.

1 JACK (DOG)

So popular was Jack the dog (played by Uggie the dog) that there were petitions to award him an honorary Academy Award alongside the *The Artist*, which had been crowned best film.

	PET	MOVIE	OWNER
10	Wanda (Fish)	*A Fish Called Wanda (1988)*	Ken Pile (Michael Palin)
9	Hedwig (Owl)	*Harry Potter series (2001-2011)*	Harry Potter (Daniel Radcliffe)
8	Elsa (Lion)	*Born Free (1966)*	Joy Adamson (Virginia McKenna)
7	Flipper (Dolphin)	*Flipper (1963)*	Sandy Ricks (Luke Halpin)
6	Asta (Dog)	*The series (1934-1947)*	Nick and Norah Charles (William Powell and Myrna Loy)
5	Cheeta (Chimp)	*Tarzan series (from 1932)*	Tarzan (various)
4	Remy (Rat)	*Ratatouille (2007)*	Alfredo Linguini (Iou Romano)
3	Gizmo (Mogwai)	*Gremlins (1984)*	Billy Peltzer (Zach Galligan)
2	Willy (Whale)	*Free Willy (1993)*	Jesse Greenwood (Jason James Richter)
1	Jack (Dog)	*The Artist (2011)*	Valentin (Jean Dujardin)

TOP
10

There are plenty of bizarre movies out there but delving into the surreal can be more irritating than rewarding. These entries cover the full spectrum of crazy; the only common feature is that they're well outside the mainstream, but well worth seeing.

STRANGEST MOVIES (THAT ARE WORTH SEEING)

10 PITFALL (1962)
Theoretically a story about a man looking for a job, *Pitfall* descends into hypnotic surreality as unexplainable encounters and events engulf the lead character. Almost dialogue free and utterly impenetrable, *Pitfall* is like nothing else.

9 FORBIDDEN ZONE (1982)
Through a secret door in her basement (and, subsequently, a large intestinal tract) a young girl finds herself in the sixth dimension. There the king falls in love with her and the queen tries to kill her. Deliberately offensive in numerous ways.

8 LOST HIGHWAY (1997)
There's very little one can say about *Lost Highway*. There is a murder... probably. Someone did it... probably. It features Fred Madison (Bill Pullman... sometimes), a jazz

saxophonist. Beyond that it's all down to interpretation.

7 TETSUO (1989)
After running down a metal fetishist in his car, a Japanese everyman starts turning into metal. Black and white photography and a uniquely frenetic filming and editing style contribute to making Tetsuo an extremely memorable experience.

6 VISITOR Q (2001)
A mysterious stranger moves in with a dysfunctional Japanese family. It's shot on videotape and comes from the highly prolific modern master of weird, Takashi Miike. No other details are suitable for a book aimed at the whole family!

5 PAPRIKA (2006)
Although there is a plot (concerning the theft of a machine that allows the user to enter people's minds), *Paprika* is really an exercise in style, with its beautiful animation soaked in vibrant colour.

4 THE IDIOTS (1998)
A group of people pretend to be mentally retarded and cause mayhem everywhere they go. Only

superficially is *The Idiots* a strange movie. Underneath the peculiar surface is an attack on mindless conformity and an aimless society.

3 THE PHANTOM OF LIBERTY (1974)

Even by Buñuel's standards *The Phantom of Liberty* is a surreal experience. We jump about in time and place, starting with a statue kicking a soldier and ending on a close up of an ostrich. In the intervening 100 minutes it all gets a bit odd.

2 MEET THE FEEBLES (1989)

This puppet based (very adult) behind the scenes look at a TV variety show has been described as 'violently surreal' and 'The Muppets on acid'. When a walrus cheats on his hippo girlfriend you know you're watching niche cinema.

1 THE HOLY MOUNTAIN (1973)

Although Jodorowsky was a collaborator and friend of Buñuel, his type of surreal cinema feels far less grounded. The form is almost impossible to make sense of, but the critique of greed and materialism that underpins it is perfectly clear.

	MOVIE	DIRECTOR
10	Pitfall (1962)	Hiroshi Teshigahara
9	Forbidden Zone (1982)	Richard Elfman
8	Lost Highway (1997)	David Lynch
7	Tetsuo (1989)	Shin'ya Tsukamoto
6	Visitor Q (2001)	Takashi Miike
5	Paprika (2006)	Satoshi Kon
4	The Idiots (1998)	Lars von Trier
3	The Phantom of Liberty (1974)	Luis Buñuel
2	Meet the Feebles (1989)	Peter Jackson
1	The Holy Mountain (1973)	Alexandro Jodorowsky

TOP
10

ACKNOWLEDGEMENTS

Picture Credits

Alamy AF Archive 12, 33, 50, 52, 69 left, 73 right, 94, 115, 159, 259; Archives du 7e Art 161; Fine Art Images 41; Moviestore Collection 30; Pictorial Press Ltd. 14, 102, 162. **Getty Images** 63, 69 right, 90, 230, 234, 264, 285; 20th Century-Fox 1; ABC Photo Archives 279, 280; Andrew Cooper 121; Apic 267; Archive Photos 9, 11, 16, 17 left, 18, 23 right, 25 left, 25 right, 26, 27, 28, 38, 40 left, 57, 59, 75 left, 78, 81, 85, 89, 97, 100, 104, 106, 113, 116, 125 left, 136, 143, 148 left, 164, 181, 190, 193, 196, 197, 200, 205, 206, 209, 216, 218, 223, 236, 243 right, 245, 246, 247, 254, 258, 262, 271 right, 273, 277, 282; Bryan Bedder 149; Buyenlarge 8, 239; Chip Hires 51; Clarence Sinclair Bull 145; Columbia TriStar 15 left, 36; Dirck Halstead 42, 179; Donaldson Collection 46, 80 right, 150; Evening Standard 99 left; Fotos International 243 left; Frederic Lewis 211; Gianni Ferrari 67 left; Gjon Mili 186; Gordon Anthony 92; Gregg DeGuire 157 left; Gus Stewart 189; Hulton Archive 54, 62 right, 99 right, 135, 173, 176, 195, 202, 227, 233, 241, 268; J. P. Aussenard 154; James Devaney 174; Jason LaVeris 284; Jean Ayissi 171; John D. Kisch/Separate Cinema Archive 126, 250, 276, 281; John Kobal Foundation 6, 60, 235; Karine Weinberger 141; Kevin Winter 175; Keystone Features 13; Keystone-France 134, 170; Matt Carr 248; MGM Studios 23 left, 45, 119, 183; Michael Ochs Archives 10, 44, 48, 58, 61, 80 left, 84, 96, 107, 108, 111, 130, 133, 138, 144, 177, 229, 231, 261, 263, 265, 275, 278, 287; Mondadori 37, 56, 212, 220, 253, 271 left; Mondadori Portfolio via Getty Images 215; Murray Close 91, 122, 266; Orion Pictures 73 left; Paramount Pictures 15 right, 40 right, 77; Peter Mountain 283; Philippe Le Tellier 153; Photoshot 203; Pictorial Parade 120; Pool Benainous/Duclos 128; Popperfoto 158; Print Collector 169; Reporters Associes 240; RKO Pictures 75 right; Ron Galella 129, 182; Sean Gallup 140; Serge Benhamou 101; Silver Screen Collection 21, 35, 39, 62 left, 64, 65, 67 right, 71, 79, 82, 87, 88, 103, 105, 109, 117, 125 right, 139, 147, 148 right, 157 right, 163, 166, 178, 184, 187, 198, 208, 217, 221, 224, 237, 255, 257; Stanley Bielecki Movie Collection 228, 249, 286; The Graham Stark Photographic Library 219; Theo Westenberger 29; Toby Canham 260; United Artists 17 right;
Universal Pictures 252; Walter Daran 127; Warner Bros. 191, 225.
Thinkstock kyoshino/iStock 32, 70, 114, 172, 214, 256.